RACIAL THINGS, RACIAL FORMS

Contemporary North American Poetry Series

SERIES EDITORS
Alan Golding,
Lynn Keller, and
Adalaide Morris

RACIAL THINGS, RACIAL FORMS

Objecthood in Avant-Garde Asian American Poetry

Joseph Jonghyun Jeon

UNIVERSITY OF IOWA PRESS

IOWA CITY

University of Iowa Press, Iowa City 52242

www.uiowapress.org
Printed in the United States of America

Design by April Leidig-Higgins

The University of Iowa Press is a member of Green Press Initiative and is committed to preserving natural resources.

Printed on acid-free paper

Library of Congress Cataloging-in-Publication Data
Jeon, Joseph Jonghyun, 1971–
Racial things, racial forms: objecthood in avant-garde Asian American poetry / Joseph Jonghyun Jeon.
p. cm. — (Contemporary North American poetry series)
Includes bibliographical references and index.
ISBN-13: 978-1-60938-086-1 (pbk)
ISBN-10: 1-60938-086-X (pbk)
1. American poetry — Asian American authors — History and criticism. 2. Race in literature. 3. Object (Philosophy) in literature. 4. Experimental poetry, American — History and criticism. 5. Avant-garde (Aesthetics) — United States. I. Title.
PS153.A84J46 2012
811'.5409895 — dc23 2011035856

For my parents,

Sang Joong Jeon and Chung Ja Jeon

CONTENTS

ACKNOWLEDGMENTS

It has been confirmed to me at every turn in the writing of this book that academic labor is not only solitary toil but also participation in a series of intellectual conversations, exchanges, and communities, without which the endeavor would be unsatisfying. I have benefited enormously from generosity that has not only improved this book in quality but also energized me when the work seemed too daunting. During my graduate studies at Berkeley, it was my great fortune to meet Dorothy Hale, whose mentorship, goodwill, and guidance I have enjoyed well past my years there. I am indebted to Charles Altieri for his abiding support and friendship and for teaching me how to read poetry. I thank Sam Otter, in whose graduate seminar, Representing Race, the idea for this book was first hatched.

I shudder to think about what this book might look like without the following people, who graciously shared their time and intelligence. I thank Charles Tung, Josephine Park, Hsuan Hsu, Abe Stoll, Florence Dore, Timothy Yu, and Juliana Chang for reading drafts of the manuscript, providing invaluable suggestions, and serving as sounding boards for my ideas. Special thanks are in order to Mei-mei Berssenbrugge, Myung Mi Kim, John Yau, and Shin Yu Pai, who were generous in offering permissions and in reading my accounts of their work at crucial points in the revision process. I am grateful to my colleagues and students at the University of San Diego (USD)—especially Peter Kanelos, Gail Perez, Atreyee Phukan, David Cantrell, Joe McGowan, Eren Branch, Mary Quinn, Cynthia Caywood, Mary Hotz, Doug Payne, Fred Robinson, Stefan Vander Elst, Jericho Brown, Can Bilsel, Juliana Maxim, Sally Yard, Alberto Pulido, Michelle Jacob, Esteban del Rio, and May Fu—for providing me with a rich atmosphere in which to work. I have benefited enormously from a broad network of scholars and friends, including Warren Liu,

Dan Grausam, Jeannie Chiu, Mayumi Takada, Xiaojing Zhou, Stephen Burt, Eric Hayot, Viet Nguyen, Jim Lee, Min Hyoung Song, Christopher Bush, Steve Yao, Shi Pu Wang, Omri Moses, Aaron Jaffe, Kyung Hyun Kim, Stephen Sohn, Sunyoung Lee, Kim Magowan, and Amanpal Garcha. I owe a particular debt of gratitude to Benjamin Widiss, who has read nearly everything that I have written since we met at Berkeley and has always been the person I turn to in those early moments of formulation when ideas are most inchoate.

Support was provided by faculty research grants from the University of San Diego and Pomona College. A well-timed grant from USD's Center for Diversity and Inclusion, headed ably by Carlton Floyd, defrayed the cost of permissions and reproductions. An early version of chapter 2 appeared in *Studies in the Literary Imagination*. I thank Stephaine Cannizzo and Genevieve Cottraux from the Berkeley Art Museum for their help with the Cha archives and permissions. I am particularly grateful to Stephanie for taking the time to sit with me while I perused the Cha material and for the fortuitous incident that turned me to the subject matter of this book's coda. I thank the staff at the Milton S. Eisenhower Library at Johns Hopkins University, especially Amy Kimball and Paul Espinosa, and the people at the Woodson Research Center at Rice University, particularly Dara Flinn, for their kind assistance. Alison Smith from the Visual Artists and Galleries Association was incredibly kind and helpful. I thank Jasper Johns, along with his assistant Lynn Kearcher, for permissions to reproduce the image that he so generously provided. I am grateful to Kiki Smith, and her assistant Heather Monahan, for permissions. Katherine Sullivan was wonderful in providing some timely photographic help. I am indebted to the anonymous reviewers, whose suggestions greatly improved the manuscript. Thanks are due to the editors of the Contemporary North American Poetry Series—Alan Golding, Dee Morris, and Lynn Keller—for their support through the publication process, and in particular Lynn for first showing interest in my project. I thank my editors, Joe Parsons and Charlotte Wright, at the University of Iowa Press, my copy editor Jamie Greene, and my indexer David Prout, for shepherding my manuscript to the end.

I am fortunate to have the support of a wonderful family. My sister, Christina Cha, has been a lifelong friend. I thank my parents, Sang Joong Jeon and Chung Ja Jeon for their love and devotion. This book is dedicated to them. Their granddaughter, and my daughter, Isobel, was born just as I was finishing this book. And though she may have slowed the final steps, this was a small price to pay for all the joy and cheer she brings me daily. In addition, I am grateful to Jun-Seok Choe and Soon-Nyu Choe for their kindness and hospitality during our summer visits to Korea. Finally, this book would not be possible without Youngmin Choe, who has been my companion since we met at Berkeley many years ago. She has read every word of every draft of this manuscript, and she experienced firsthand my every high and low in writing them. I thank her not only for her caring interlocution throughout but also, more importantly, for our shared life together—one that is always lively and free from the various states of torpor to which I am prone when left to my own devices.

Permissions

Acknowledgment is given for the generous permission to reprint selections from the following works: From *Under Flag*, by Myung Mi Kim, copyright © 1991 by Myung Mi Kim, reprinted by permission of the author and Kelsey St. Press, whose website, www.kelseyst.com, contains a podcast of the poet reading from and talking about the book. From *Dura*, by Myung Mi Kim, copyright © 1998 by Myung Mi Kim, reprinted by permission of the author. From *The Bounty*, by Myung Mi Kim, copyright © 1996 by Myung Mi Kim, reprinted by permission of the author. From *Commons*, by Myung Mi Kim, copyright © 2002 by the Regents of the University of California, reprinted by permission of the University of California Press. From *Hiddenness*, by Mei-mei Berssenbrugge and Richard Tuttle, text copyright © 1987 by Mei-mei Berssenbrugge, edition copyright © 1987 by Whitney Museum of American Art, reprinted by permission of the Whitney Museum of American Art and the author. From *Endocrinology*, by Mei-mei Berssenbrugge, copyright © 1997 by Mei-mei Berssenbrugge, Kiki Smith, and Universal Limited Art Editions, Inc., reprinted by permission of ULAE, Inc., Kelsey St. Press (www.kelseyst.com), and the author. From *The Heat Bird*, by Mei-mei Berssenbrugge, copyright © 1983 by Mei-mei Berssenbrugge, reprinted by permission of Burning Deck Press and the author. From *Picture Bride*, by Cathy Song, copyright © 1983 by Cathy Song, reprinted by permission of Yale University Press. From

Borrowed Love Poems, by John Yau, copyright © 2002 by John Yau, reprinted by permission of Penguin Books and the author. From *My Symptoms*, by John Yau, copyright © 1998 by John Yau, reprinted by permission of the author. From *Works on Paper*, by Shin Yu Pai copyright © 2007, reprinted by permission of the author.

INTRODUCTION

SEEING RACE IN THINGS

Among the objects displayed in the Berkeley Art Museum's 2001 retrospective on Theresa Hak Kyung Cha were a pair of enigmatic pieces, both entitled *Surplus Novel* (1980) (fig. 1 and 2).[1] Resembling cups of paper noodles, each of the matching pair of small bowls contains the fragments of two poems on thin strips of paper. Occasioned by a stranger derisively calling out to Cha, "Hey Yoko," as she was walking down the street, the text takes the form of "Beatles-type" song lyrics that read as a defiant rejoinder to this unwelcome imposition of racialized identity: "they calling me / they calling after me / hey yoko / hey yoko ono . . . i ain't your / i ain't no i ain't / your yoko ono."[2] Though its avant-garde context seems worlds away, *Surplus Novel* subtly rehearses a dark trope in American history, in which racializing objectification erases subjectivity, and the piece responds by defying the stranger's implicit claim of ownership. The stranger literally hailed Cha as an Asian type, and the artwork rejects this call in order to reclaim selfhood. Most powerfully demonstrated in slavery, which transformed personhood into property, racialization and dehumanizing objectification have long exposed the limits of American democratic ideals. Because these powerful forces silence the racialized figure, the most prevalent gesture of resistance in literature has been to voice one's own marginalized story, often in autobiographical form. Narratives of freed slaves, racial Bildungsroman, immigrant memoirs, and activist lyrical poetry thus share in common this reclamation logic: The telling of one's own story in one's own words defiantly claims individual autonomy in the face of oppression.

FIGURE 1. Theresa Hak Kyung Cha: *Surplus Novel*, 1980; porcelain with thread and typewritten text on paper; 1-3/4 × 2-1/2 in. diameter; private collection of James H. Cha. Photo: Benjamin Blackwell. Courtesy of University of California, Berkeley Art Museum and Pacific Film Archive.

A striking feature of *Surplus Novel*, however, is that one cannot read for this mode of resistance because one can scarcely read it at all. The largely illegible text sits, disordered and shredded into pieces, in a pair of bowls. Although one might appreciate *Surplus Novel* for its formal unruliness—its blurred generic categories (combining prose fiction, pop songs, and poetry) and transgressions of media (mixing writing, sculpture, and ready-made art)—the original social context of the piece retreats into the background. Far from defiant, the insubordinate sass of words seems inert in the bowls that contain them, both literally and figuratively. So if the racist slur that occasioned the piece threatened to objectify the subject by misrecognizing her as a generic type, then what does it mean to present the rejoinder itself as an inscrutable object? Does *surplus* here refer less to a dangerous supplement and more to leftover waste?

FIGURE 2. Theresa Hak Kyung Cha: *Surplus Novel*, 1980; porcelain with thread and typewritten text on paper; 1-3/4 × 2-1/2 in. diameter; private collection of Bernadette Hak Eun Cha Silveus. Courtesy of University of California, Berkeley Art Museum and Pacific Film Archive.

The questions then turn fundamental; can we regard this piece as politically engaged if it remains largely illegible? Does the language here signify? Perhaps, if further exasperated, we may ask: What is this *thing*?

Not uncoincidentally, this last question is shared by uninitiated spectators and detractors when encountering a good deal of abstract avant-garde art. The word *thing* here would serve as a placeholder for something unnamable (this, this . . . *thing!*), registering a failure or refusal to identify or recognize that which is difficult to categorize and falls outside our normative experience of objects—aesthetic or otherwise. The tone of the question might range from confused to frustrated to derisive, but it invariably expresses the distance one experiences from the object, an inchoate yet irrepressible sense of otherness. As such, an art object such as *Surplus Novel* promotes a provisional disidentification on the part of its viewer, an emerging sense of otherness and differentiation that ironically doubles the racialization effected by the stranger's comment. An act of calculated estrangement, *Surplus Novel* indeed obfuscates its own legibility, but it does so in a manner that parallels and thus illustrates the very operation of racialization that occasioned it.

In this vein, *Surplus Novel* might be read as a subtle critique and interrogation of racialization—the process through which a person becomes racially differentiated. The alienated viewer who experiences distance from an "othered" art object becomes oddly complicit with the stranger who interpellated Cha in racial terms. For both the viewer/reader and the stranger, the rejoinder printed on those shredded strips of paper, more inert objects than signifying words, falls on deaf ears. The viewer is of course not assumed to be a callous racist. Rather, aided by the contextualizing museum placard, he or she is instead invited to coordinate his or her experience of the foreign art object self-consciously in relationship to the racializing encounter that occasioned the artwork in the first place. Though the viewer doubles the position and function of the stranger, he or she is also offered a critical distance. Unlike the stranger, the viewer is invited to overcome the initial disorienting experience of the art object as an inscrutable thing by gradually contextualizing the object within a discursive frame. *Surplus Novel*, in short, functions as a kind of literal object lesson.

The stranger's use of Yoko Ono as a slur turns out to be appropriate in another manner. In the late 1970s and early 1980s (which was the context for *Surplus Novel*), Yoko Ono registered in two distinct but related ways, particularly for the sort of person who would use her name as a standalone insult. First, she was vilified in often racial terms as the scheming "dragon lady" responsible for the breakup of the Beatles; second, she was known for her bizarre (according to popular opinion) avant-garde art, which gained more notoriety than most of its kind because of her public profile and for her highly visible musical endeavors, which many regarded as abrasive. Since Ono herself was regarded as such an eccentric, mysterious figure, her art became a site on which to read not only aesthetic ethos but also personal neuroses. The characterization of Ono's artistic practice as symptomatic of a personal psychosis, as evidenced by Julia Goldman's 1971 article, "The Two Women Who Broke Up the Beatles," was not uncommon:

> Since childhood there had been Yoko's art, a nihilistic art rooted in Dada, but with a lovely imaginative intelligence. Its themes were voids hiding (Concert Piece: "When the curtain rises, go and hide and wait till everybody leaves you. Come out and play."). Masks, dismemberment, sleep, and escape. Her art was arrogant. Like a character out of R. D. Laing's *Knots*, Yoko was perverse—once hurt she lashed out to shock and be hurt and rejected again.[3]

What begins here as a semi-complimentary assessment of Ono's artist aesthetic turns quickly into pop-psychological account of her pathologies.[4] As I argue in this book's coda, the two dominant manifestations of Ono in American popular culture—dragon lady destroyer and avant-garde wing nut—became nearly indistinguishable from each other, and it is precisely this recoding of artistic aesthetic as the stuff of abnormal psychology that authorizes such a collapse. The slur "Hey Yoko" was thus not only a kind of racial insult but also one in which the figure of the inscrutable Asian as distrustful foreigner, an abiding trope in American culture since the nineteenth century, becomes deeply intertwined with the inscrutable nature of avant-garde art. The name *Yoko Ono* thus came to signify simultaneously a specifically Asian form of insidious instrumentality, at a time when rapid Japanese capitalist development seemed increasingly threatening to the United States, as well as an avant-garde impenetrability that dovetailed with Asian inscrutability. In this context, *Surplus Novel* takes up not only the question of the racial-other-as-object through the idiom of avant-garde artistic practice but also, more specifically, the extent to which the perceived strangeness of the avant-garde art object might function as a mode of interrogating the way in which Asianness gets racially coded and visualized in contemporary American discourse.

Focusing on the work of Theresa Hak Kyung Cha, Myung Mi Kim, Mei-mei Berssenbrugge, and John Yau, this book argues that one important overlooked site in which the two seemingly disparate discourses of minority politics and avant-garde aesthetics converge is their shared interest in objecthood as the site of intersection between aesthetic and political concerns. Like *Surplus Novel*, this work characteristically discomforts the reader/viewer so he or she will ask, "What is this thing?" This discomfort is provoked in various ways: by manipulating artistic media and the interpretive practices and expectations that usually come with them; by integrating foreign languages that question possibilities of expression; by translating prosaic phenomena into unfamiliar forms; and by closely scrutinizing iconic images whose strangeness has become overcome by familiarity. To conclude that the texts examined in this book, like *Surplus Novel*, resist categorization is to announce what is by now a critical commonplace that leaves underexamined the widely variant, multiple strategies through which such shape-shifting might be accomplished. My title term, *racial things*, encompasses then not just a series of objects that exemplify these strategies but also a nexus of thought through which we understand the complexities of contemporary racial forms—their physical, material, and visual manifestations. To be clear, I am not arguing that all avant-garde art objects are somehow categorically about race; rather, the artists I examine exploit this point of overlap as a means of interrogating the various ways in which racial form has been constructed, in a similar manner as the defamiliarizing oddness of a piece such as *Surplus Novel*, which invites the viewer to think about how racial stereotypes can objectify otherwise individualized subjects. For these artists, the peculiarity of the art object offers a concrete formal figuration through which one might query the equally strange operations of racial objectification.

Defined in opposition to the subject, the *thing* in American literature and culture has stood for nothing short of dehumanization. In nineteenth-century racial discourse, a thing is an epithet for the racialized body, as in Harriet Beecher Stowe's original subtitle for *Uncle Tom's Cabin*: "*The Man Who Was a Thing*." In transmuting an enslaved human being into crude objecthood, this forceful pejorative denies subjectivity to the slave who becomes regarded as a mere commodity. Jump-cutting forward and across contexts, things seem to improve in twentieth-century, avant-garde, and philosophical usages. William Carlos Williams's famous dictum "No ideas but in things" celebrates the thing as an avenue to an intense perceptual intimacy and echoes Edmund Husserl's valorization of seeing that yields "the things themselves."[5] However, even here, the primacy of the thing remains secondary to an implied universal subject whose phenomenological vision invigorates it. This usage thus parallels in subtler terms its earlier status as a denigrated object because the viewed thing remains subordinate to the viewer. Both discursive traditions elide the thing by collapsing it into the role of the object whose meaning or value is guaranteed only by the subject who observes and attributes meaning to it, thereby reducing its inherent complexity to a perceived value.

Fast-forwarding further still, recent major exhibits—including the 1996 exhibition at the Museum of Contemporary Art, Los Angeles, entitled "Reconsidering the Object of Art, 1965–1975," and the 2007 show at the New Museum of Contemporary Art in New York, entitled "Unmonumental: The Object in the 21st Century"—have explored the particular vigor that is located in objects when they are removed from everyday routines and reifications, the kind of removal that gallery and museum space is especially adept at accomplishing. Exhibits such as these consider the legacy of early twentieth-century interest in objects, like that of Duchamp as well as that of mid-century minimalist experimentation. Though some of this art poses itself as invested in what Lucy Lippard has called the "dematerialization of the art object," this conceptual art does not so much do away with the art object as much as it makes claims on behalf of more prosaic, inexpensive, and banal objects (paper, video, snapshots), in contrast to modernist monumental forms. Although this avant-garde thing-art generally strives to make the physicality and visuality of things more dynamic than objectification might lead us to believe, it has tended to disarticulate itself from a specifically racial context and politicized its aesthetics instead along the lines of Frankfurt School critiques of mass culture.[6] Offering a partial explanation, Lippard suggests that conceptual artists "looked and sounded like radicals" in a milieu "that still idolized Clement Greenberg," despite the fact that the art itself mostly "seems supremely apolitical."[7]

In modern theory, the most dominant account of the thing is the Marxian commodity, which implies the alienated subject's rapidly deteriorating intimacy with the material world. In Lukács's development of Marx's concept of reification (literally *thing-ification* in German), relationships among people take on the character of things because commodities transform human relationships into relations among the products of their labor; so, as the products of labor become gradually understood as commodities, human beings become more and more alienated from material objects.[8] The commodity thus supplants the material thing itself, which in turn becomes increasingly remote in a trajectory of increasing alienation. In recent analyses of material culture, such as many of the essays collected in Appadurai's influential collection *The*

Social Life of Things (1986), the thing itself tends to dissipate within critical examinations of consumerism, circulation, and exchange networks.[9] It is of course impossible and unnecessary in one swift paragraph to challenge the descriptive accuracy of these lines of thought, whose insights are undeniably valuable for understanding contemporary consciousness and culture. The point, rather, is simply to suggest how they tend to perpetuate the very dynamic they critique—that is, the loss of intimacy with things. Although it would be too much to call this criticism a self-fulfilling prophecy, the very success of these materialist accounts of commoditization comes at the expense perhaps of thinking of the thing as anything other than a commodity.

Attempting to fill this critical gap, Bill Brown suggests that these examinations of the way in which "people code, recode, and satisfy their material wants and needs" have "left things behind" by "never quite asking how they become recognizable, representable, and exchangeable to begin with."[10] As a corrective, Brown argues that *things* should be disarticulated from *objects*, which are usually characterized by utility. Playing off Marxian accounts of valuation, Brown locates in things a *misuse value*, which we glimpse when, for example, a knife is used improperly as a screwdriver. In these irregular moments of decontextualization, the strangeness of the thing flashes its "secret life"—a previously unseen complexity that offers intimate access to what might otherwise seem a reified commodity—and thus privileges a metacritical form of vision that invites us to reevaluate what we thought we knew all along. Brown also suggests that these characteristics are exemplified in avant-garde art, such as Duchamp's Dada or camp, which appropriates, reanimates, and recodes everyday objects. In such work, one becomes aware of "both the object defamiliarized (as physical thing) as well as the codes and cathexes by which it has long been trapped (the history *in* the thing)."[11] In avant-garde art's deployment of misuse value and irregularity, the thing signals its own physicality and makes its own inappropriateness manifest. In so doing, the thing renders everyday life momentarily uncanny and draws attention to the normalizing codes that otherwise escape notice.

For Brown, the stake of these uncanny, unconscious intrusions into familiar discursive contexts is often historical. Attention to the secret lives of things accesses the history trapped in those things, which frequently complicates, in literary examples, the cartography of a text's more explicit attempts at historical mapping. Among the numerous articles Brown has written on things, two focus on race and ethnicity as a subset issue. In both cases, the texts that Brown investigates—Shawn Wong's *Homebase* (1979) and Spike Lee's *Bamboozled* (2000)—serve not as focal points of analysis but, rather, as entry points to robust historical, discursive networks in which issues of materiality, ethnic identity, and racial form provocatively intersect. Significantly, these texts function in Brown's argument as locations in which what Brown describes as an uncanny material unconscious emerges *despite* the texts' more explicit concerns, and thus these texts become exemplary not for the possibilities they open, but for the limits they expose. It is also at these moments, however, that Brown's otherwise virtuosic critical displays are themselves limited, because the historiography here is dedicated to pointing out uncanny instances of sameness within what seem to be pronouncements of difference.

In "How to Do Things with Things (A Toy Story)" (1998), one of the essays that articulates much of this argument, Brown dabbles in Asian American Studies and correlates thing theory and racial politics in Wong's *Homebase* and, to a lesser degree, Frank Chin's *Donald Duk* (1991). He argues that *Homebase,* by recoding the Charlie McCarthy puppet as Chinese, misses its own unconscious identification with another (Irish) minoritized immigrant subject and thus represses an unforeseen complication in its desire to negotiate Asian and American identities; the McCarthy puppet thus provides "access to something other than" the protagonist Rainsford's desire for an American identity.[12] The secret life of the thing, in this case that of the puppet, functions independently of its metaphoric function within the literary text, complicating what is otherwise a narrative of cultural negotiation between native and immigrant subject positions by introducing a figure that is more similar to the subject position Rainsford wishes to dispense with rather than become. The history of Irish minority subjectivity, however,—the history *in* this particular thing—is more complex than Brown describes; one could argue that the McCarthy puppet represents not just a minority subject position but also the process through which one abandons this position to become American and deracialized. As David Roediger suggests, throughout the course of the nineteenth century, Irish workers were gradually understood as both American and white by disarticulating themselves from blacks with whom they were closely associated (in both racial and nativist terms) in antebellum America.[13] It is thus possible to read Rainsford's identification with the McCarthy puppet not as an unwitting embrace of a minority subject position but as a connection to a formerly minority subjectivity that has succeeded in accomplishing precisely the same transformation that he himself desires. My point here is not simply to quibble with Brown's historical reading of the McCarthy puppet; rather, it is to suggest what is at stake when the figure can be easily read in alternative terms. In other words, it becomes difficult to choose the more appropriate alternative because what arbitrates between these readings is not one's reading of the text but one's reading of the object in increasingly infinite discursive space.

In a later essay entitled "Reification, Reanimation, and the American Uncanny" (2006), Brown develops the link between reification and racialization in American racial politics, which Christopher Bush describes "as historically related modalities of the relationship between abstraction and concretion."[14] According to Bush's logic, both racialization and reification produce a sense of otherness and distance—be it an experience of racial difference or an alienation from the material world. Brown makes a similar claim, using the black memorabilia in *Bamboozled* as exemplary figures, arguing that the history of racial objectification uncannily reappears in the personification of these racially charged objects throughout the course of the film. For Brown, this is the American uncanny, the possibility of unfamiliarity within the familiar: "the history of ontological ambiguity—human or thing" that "remains repressed within U.S. culture."[15] In Brown's account, Lee's film does not so much explicitly express this anxious site in American history so much as things themselves in the film reveal their "material unconscious."[16] The persistence of racialization is thus the silent secret buried deep within reification, of which we see glimpses in *Bamboozled*. Furthermore, the film simply confirms the persistence of this consistent form: "Lee works to produce a different kind of uncanniness: not ontological ambiguity but historical ambiguity, the incapacity to differentiate the present from the past, despite history, because, despite change over time, there's been no change."[17] Although it is certainly true that Lee's film acknowledges the repetition of racialized forms in American culture over time, so much of the film's critical effort seems also to track the different, specific manifestations that these forms take in contemporary culture and throughout history, often through the character of Sloan (Jada Pinkett-Smith). As demonstrated by a pair of montage sequences near the end of the film—the documentary of pop culture images of African Americans that Sloan compiles for Delacroix (Damon Wayans) and the images of race memorabilia that play over the closing credits—it becomes clear that archiving the historical progression of images and objects, along with their historical similarities and differences, is central to the film's historiographic task. In addition, the film is ruthless in its exacting portrayals of contemporary manifestations of race—racially targeted marketing, liberal white guilt, cross-racial identification, unintentionally parodic forms of racial militancy, white appropriations of racialized speech, and so on. Indeed, one explanation that film implicitly offers for the lasting power of such racist forms is its adaptability to emergent contexts. Though racism persists over time, Lee's film suggests that it changes in form.

Brown's emphasis on the uncanny implies that the aspect of the texts he examines is outside of its control: Agency is displaced onto the things themselves (the operations of their secret lives), and the material unconscious emerges often in conflict with what seem to be the text's more explicit aims. However, as the uncanny becomes increasingly legible, more conscious forms become less so. So, although the defamiliarizing function of the thing for Brown can be surprisingly illuminating in its ability to open alternative contexts of intelligibility and to creatively engage broader discursive frames, as a critical methodology, it also threatens contextual specificity. Therefore, the danger with Brown's materialism is that it authorizes, in the name of history, an ahistorical compulsion, in which the expansion of the historiographic frame threatens to render specific historical contexts illegible and in which historical materialism becomes a kind of hermeneutics, interested in sheer interpretive possibility, in seeing what scripts a given object can bear. More specifically, the difficulty emerges in weighing the relative value of the material unconscious in relation to the text's more explicit maneuvers.

Like Brown, *Racial Things, Racial Forms* is interested in the alternative interpretive possibilities that the defamiliarizing function of the thing accesses. Thinking things in avant-garde Asian American poetry allows for discursive connections among otherwise disparate contexts. Whereas Brown focuses on texts in which this material unconscious emerges, often despite the text's more explicit aims, *Racial Things, Racial Forms* examines texts that, though they no doubt have their own unconscious identifications, are much more self-conscious about this particular connection between racial and physical things, and for which this connection is an open concern. *Racial Things, Racial Forms* thus considers the link between reification and racialization—between race and things—in avant-garde attempts to seek out material forms for uncanny phenomena, through which one can engage unconscious matter in more self-conscious terms. Like Brown, I am interested in the way in which things access alternative histories and contexts of intelligibility, but I am more interested in the way avant-garde texts authorize rather than elide them.

Surplus Novel, for example, responds simultaneously to both reification and racialization by foregrounding a sense of thingness that mimics (with a difference) stereotypical typologies that circumscribe Asian as foreign. It both invokes and frustrates categories that might make the piece coherent and legible, be they material (food, art object, text) or generic (poetry, song, ready-made art). It invites the viewer to experience its misuse value, which emerges in its failure to reproduce the recognizable codes for a given category, and it blurs the line between the Kantian aesthetic object that is without purpose (though purposive) and the ordinary, everyday object that is defined by its purpose (such as bowls and food). *Surplus Novel* thus imbricates the feeling of distance from a material object that reification describes and the experience of racial otherness; it is a radically foreign thing in its insistence on perpetuating rather than ameliorating its own foreignness. As such, the piece is not so much an allegorical or metaphoric embodiment of an Asian American subject—not an anthropomorphic thing[18]—as it is an abstract figure of *perpetual foreignness*. This is Tina Chen's description of a fundamental characteristic of Asian American public identity throughout the last two centuries. Imposture and fraudulence, Chen suggests, have come to be seen as defining Asian American traits.[19] Asian Americans have thus come to seem more capable of assimilative impersonation than other minorities, of adapting to normalizing codes in order to escape notice.

A subtle incarnation of this imposture in fact emerges in Brown's account of Buzz Lightyear in *Toy Story* (1995) who, in the moment he discovers his Asian origins ("Made in Taiwan"), discovers he is merely a toy.[20] Though he serves as a figuration of a quintessentially American bravado (a robust astronaut hero with the requisite U.S. flaglike insignia on the wing of his spaceship), Buzz Lightyear, it turns out, is also marked, however faintly, by racial traces, and his surprise before this realization quietly rehearses the anxiety about the invisibly foreign nature of Asianness that Chen develops. Furthermore, the moment that Buzz discovers his Asian origin is precisely the moment that confirms he is not in fact a heroic astronaut but merely a toy; it is the moment that verifies he is not a subjective agent but, rather, an instrumental object. As such, he becomes melancholic and emasculated, listlessly playing the role of Mrs. Nesbit at a young girl's tea party. Nevertheless, Buzz Lightyear is not quite a racial thing. As in *Surplus Novel*, this moment in *Toy Story* repeats an exercise in seeing things and in seeing race in things; it is, however, only temporarily destabilizing. By contrast, *Surplus Novel* gains a critical distance from racialization—from its objectifying tendencies—and calls attention to the operations through which race is visualized and coded.

Avant-Garde Asian American Poetry in Context

Surplus Novel marks a critical and theoretical lacuna that has only recently been addressed in Asian American Studies—namely the widely regarded incompatibility between avant-garde artistic forms and racial politics. Asian American Studies was born out of the Asian American movement of the late 1960s and 1970s, which was influenced by the civil rights and war protests of the period. The decidedly egalitarian ethos that drove this movement tended to foreground literature that represented the empirical realities of social injustice, and works that were more aesthetically oriented were typically regarded as either assimilationist or elitist because of their resistance to clearer communicative modes. Avant-garde poetic forms thus mark a very specific fault line in this discourse. As opposed to novels and memoirs, which have been more prominent in Asian American literature, and to the activist poetry most fully realized in the 1960s and 1970s,[21] avant-garde Asian American poetry was sometimes regarded as overly obtuse and failing to address the realities of the lived world. Often difficult and unfamiliar, avant-garde poetry seemed anathema to the populist ethos of Asian American Studies and ambivalent to the history that occasioned the social movement in the first place. Josephine Nock-Hee Park argues that such dichotomies are at least in part the result of a vexed modernist legacy in which formal experimentalism is burdened by a history of Orientalism. According to Park, Asian American poets face "a uniquely perplexing legacy: they were the heirs to an avant-garde shot through with Orientalism. Though they could and did forcibly decry fantasies of the Orient, their avant-garde poetics were themselves a part of an American revolutionary lineage."[22] This predicament leaves a difficult choice between the ethnic nationalist's call to racial and cultural authenticity that risks reproducing racist essentialism on one hand and the avant-gardist's celebration of indeterminacy that threatens to forget history while unwittingly perpetuating an Orientalist heritage on the other.

As writing authored by racial and ethnic minorities gained a wider audience in the 1990s, when Asian American poets began to experience a degree of mainstream success within an emerging ethos of multiculturalism, this condition became exacerbated by market forces. As Harryette Mullen suggests in a slightly broader context, "Although both the 'avant-garde poet' and the 'minority poet' may be perceived as the other of the 'mainstream' (regardless of the distance and the different concerns that might separate them from each other), it would seem that the mainstream has far more to gain by appropriating minority poets who work in recognizable and accessible forms and who can thus be marketed to the broadest possible audience of readers."[23] A poet who breaks down such dichotomies, Mullen explains why these categories have become so deeply entrenched and why denigrations of experimental form as somehow incompatible with political demands have abided. Avant-garde form becomes tantamount to bad marketing—a form uninterested in communicating clearly with its audience. The ensuing fear is that it is also bad politics.

Realizing this unease, Jinqi Ling argues that the subversive potential of avant-garde texts that valorize complexity, such as Theresa Hak Kyung Cha's *DICTEE*, is "often a theoretical construct" and that an overemphasis on such a construct can "work falsely to justify ahistorical tendencies toward avant-garde celebrations of difference." Thus, the application of "relativism" and "Nietzschean perspectivism" to Asian American issues that such texts presumably encourage threatens the ability of "the socially disenfranchised . . . from talking meaningfully about their social betterment."[24] Instead, Ling favors a return to realist narratives for their commitment to history. Although Ling's argument appropriately responds to the blanket deployment of poststructuralist models in recent Asian American criticism,[25] which hazard misreading in their rush to rehearse prefabricated models of political form, his denigrations of complexity risk limiting the possibilities of avant-garde art in precisely the same way that he argues contemporary critics have circumscribed realist literature.[26] There is no need, however, to think of avant-garde and realist modes as locked in a zero-sum struggle, and Ling's critique appears more applicable to programmatic poststructuralist criticism in general than to avant-garde form in particular. Criticism indeed loses specificity and historical relevance when indeterminacy and difference become the only point, but formal complexity in the avant-garde poetry examined in this book is never complexity for its own sake. Rather, it is merely the price of admission for a more thorough critique and reformulation; more than just a generic intransigence, it interrupts complacencies and instead clamors for reexamination in order to clear the way for more viable modes of political engagement. Such a distinction is important because the prevalence of programmatic poststructuralist criticism in Asian American Studies has elided the paucity of critical attention paid to avant-garde Asian American writing. Even today, roughly three decades after the publication of *DICTEE*, a focal point for Ling, and nearly two decades after it became a canonical text in Asian American Studies, there remains a scarcity of criticism focused on the rest of Cha's body of work and even on the second half of the *DICTEE* itself. The fact that such a canonical writer could be so narrowly read should signal the need for more—not less—attention to avant-garde Asian American writing.

Although it has only gained significant critical attention fairly recently, avant-garde poetry is not exactly a new development in Asian American literary history. One could argue for this classification for the earliest Asian American poets, such as Sadakichi Hartmann and Yone Noguchi, who experimented with Japanese literary forms in English during the late nineteenth and early twentieth centuries, or for José Garcia Villa, who published poetry that toyed with rhyme and punctuation during the 1940s and 1950s. Asian American poetry as such, however, was a product of the Asian American movement of the late 1960s and 1970s, when the term *Asian American* first gained popular usage, and the genre developed rapidly from the late 1960s to the mid 1990s. Critics have described this period in genealogical terms, beginning with early activist poetry in the 1960s and 1970s (by poets such as Janice Mirikitani, Lawson Fusao Inada, Francis Naohiko Oka, and Merle Woo) and moving toward a more mainstream, postactivist, antiessentialist phase in the

1980s and early 1990s, which was dominated by poets (such as Cathy Song, Li-Young Lee, Garrett Hongo, and David Mura) who were trained in American M.F.A. programs and whose work tended to foreground the complexities of identity construction.[27] Although it is tempting to place avant-garde Asian American poets, usually Theresa Hak Kyung Cha and John Yau, as the next period in this genealogy, the resulting progression as a whole elides the greater complexity of the history it attempts to explain. Sunn Shelley Wong, for example, points out that the robust Asian American poetic production of the 1970s consisted not only of activist modes but also "a range of poetic styles and themes that resist conflation."[28] In addition, both John Yau's first collection, *Crossing Canal Street* (1976), and Cha's *DICTEE* (1982) were published before landmark antiessentialist texts, such as Cathy Song's *Picture Bride* (1983), David Mura's *After We Lost Our Way* (1989), and Li-Young Lee's *The City in Which I Love You* (1990). Furthermore, the periodizing of these poets tends to ignore their development in careers that outlast the small window of time with which they are associated. Thus, rather than treating this rapid gestation period of Asian American poetry as a series of quick epistemic changes from activist to antiessentialist to avant-garde periods, I prefer to think of the first two not as discrete stages but as polarities engaged in a dialectical relationship. I understand the third term—avant-garde—as a recurring and prominent mode of negotiating between and imaginatively synthesizing the first two, often in a manner that self-consciously foregrounds its own highly theoretical, abstract approach.[29] This conceptual shift allows not only for different kinds of poets to coexist at various moments but also for the blending of both polarities within the work of individual poets.

Such a reconfiguration dovetails in spirit with Timothy Yu's compelling assertion that the activist poets of the 1960s and 1970s were avant-garde. Though he maintains a genealogical structure, Yu recharacterizes the individual stages, suggesting that this initial activist period fits both Renato Poggioli's definition of the avant-garde, which foregrounds sociological characteristics in addition to aesthetic practices, and Peter Bürger's foundational treatise on the subject. Yu argues that Asian American poets of that earlier period represented both "an attempt to create community by aesthetic means" and an effort to formulate a distinctively Asian American sensibility in both formal and sociopolitical terms.[30] The consequence for this shift in genealogical understanding is profound. Not only does it debunk the myth that avant-garde Asian American poetry is a new phenomenon, it also serves to devalue the Asian American poets who have achieved the most mainstream success and who become recognized less as part of a second reactionary phase that responded to perceived problems in the activist tradition and more as "an anomaly within the development of an Asian American poetry whose allegiances are much more appropriately placed within the avant-garde."[31] Yu is convincing on sociological grounds, but the range of aesthetic maneuvers with which he characterizes this avant-garde moment is relatively limited; he is chiefly concerned with the articulation of anxieties regarding individual or cultural self-definition—a characteristic often attributed, ironically, to the antiessentialist mode of Asian American poetry. Furthermore, focusing on Mirikitani, Inada, and Oka, Yu leaves out writing of the period that would fit more comfortably and conventionally under the rubric of avant-garde, such as that of Jessica Hagedorn or the earlier works of Cha and Yau, perhaps because these examples adhere less to the sociological model he proposes.

Although Yu demonstrates an avant-garde strain within the activist polarity, its flexibility and vigor remain circumscribed. This is most visible in his accounts of more contemporary avant-garde examples—Cha and Yau in their later works—who function in Yu's genealogy primarily as figures of incommensurability between Asian American and experimental modes rather than of new and imaginative syntheses. Cha demonstrates "a way of keeping these two paradigms in productive tension, always visible but never resolved"[32]; whereas Yau's poetry "shows us not so much a means of bridging Asian American and experimental modes as a map of the continuing conflicts between the two."[33] Indeed, as Yu powerfully demonstrates, avant-garde Asian American poetry is not free from the inheritance it receives from its predecessors in the 1960s and 1970s, whether we term them *activist* or *avant-garde*, but it is not so circumscribed, I would argue, by this inheritance either. Part of what distinguishes the newer avant-garde poetry from earlier modes is precisely the burden of a multifaceted legacy—of political activism, identity poetics, and liberal multiculturalism—that must be digested and resynthesized. The task for this avant-garde Asian American poetry, then, is to reconfigure and realign inherited fault lines according to the exigencies and contingencies of contexts—emergent and inherited—and to seek alternative modes of articulation, not mere reprisals of previously effective forms. More specifically, whereas in the activist mode, self-definition becomes a resistant gesture aimed at wresting away representational power from hegemonic forces that determine stereotypes, avant-garde poetry tends to place a greater degree of emphasis on metacritical examinations of the formation of representational power itself. Steven Yao has termed the ethos of this later group of poets as "ethic abstraction," describing it as a rejection of individual voice and lyric testimonial modes in favor of "'experimental,' nonrepresentational strategies," which then serve to expand "both the formal and thematic concerns of Asian American poetry, oftentimes in order to interrogate the very condition of ethnicity itself precisely as a social and discursive formation."[34]

Racial Form and Visuality

One significant interpretive concern of the poetry examined in *Racial Things, Racial Forms* is its emphasis on racial form and, thus, an understanding of race in formal terms. In foregrounding race as a set of formal questions, this poetry has taken up many of the theoretical questions that Colleen Lye prescribes as a new direction for Asian American Studies and ethnic studies in general. Proceeding from the materialist approach to form of Raymond Williams, Lye argues that "the problem of race might instead be reformulated as a question of the relationship between language . . . and other material processes—between race understood as representation and race as an agency of literary and other social formations."[35] In Michael Omi and Howard Winant's famous definition, racial signification is an imprecise, often arbitrary, social and historical process. Race is thus neither biological fact nor artificial myth, neither an essence nor an illusory ideological construct, but rather "a concept which signifies and symbolizes social conflicts and interests by referring to different types of human bodies."[36] The lasting power of this definition has to do with its acknowledgment of symbolic signification in relation to material bodies, all within the context of ideological discourse that changes over time. However, as Lye suggests, though Omi and Winant demonstrate how "race is an active social relation rather than a transhistorical abstraction,"[37] they also emphasize "the foundational status of racism to U.S. society at the expense of describing its historical variability."[38] In relation to historically contingent forces, *Racial Things, Racial Forms* follows Lye and begins with the assumption that racial form is continually revisualized and materialized in order to smooth over and elide ideological ambiguities and ambivalences. The objectified body thus becomes reified as a racialized object, covering over imprecision and arbitrariness in order to produce the effect of essence. Although the most prominent modes of resistance to these objectifying impositions in Asian American Studies have been attempts to reclaim subjectivity and identity, critics such as Susan Koshy and Viet Nguyen point out that this identity politics can often unwittingly become complicit in the very operations of reification and racialization that it purports to oppose.[39] Thus, rather than focusing on the subject—on interiority and individual experience—*Racial Things, Racial Forms* instead uses the calculated strangeness of avant-garde art as an occasion to emphasize the physical and visual oddness of racial constructs, as a series of ever-changing, contemporary phenomena that is in conversation with, but not entirely determined by, its historical legacy.

One prominent mode of racial form in American history has been the visual. In the wake of the civil rights movement, axiomatic in contemporary American racial politics was the belief that greater visibility yielded greater political power. Although this belief persists as a dominant trope in the rhetoric of racial identity, visibility itself remains underinterrogated within the realm of racial discourse. As Anne Anlin Cheng argues, "the rhetoric of 'becoming visible' that has energized so much of progressive racial politics often elides the contradictions underpinning social visibility and remains ineffective in the face of phenomenological, social, and psychic paradoxes inhering in what it means to *be* visible."[40] One of the challenges to contemporary racial politics then is an attention to the visual complexities of racial visibility itself.[41] No longer regarded as *a priori*, the visibility of race itself instead must be understood as a visuality that complicates how race might be recognized at all; the *visible*, which denotes the fact of being seen, must be distinguished from the *visual*, which connotes the broader possibilities of seeing. By visuality, I refer therefore not only to the wide range of visual characteristics that one associates with both race and avant-garde language art but also to the conflict between icon and logos—between image and word—that W. J. T. Mitchell makes the object of study in his account of critical iconology. Operating on the assumption that "all media are mixed media, and all representations are heterogeneous; there are no 'purely visual or verbal arts,'"[42] Mitchell argues for the utility of an iconological theory of images that would "resign hope in a scientific theory that might master the image" and instead historicize the constant struggle between words and images in order "to see what interests and powers it serves."[43] In foregrounding the visuality of race beyond mere visibility, *Racial Things, Racial Forms* moves toward a kind of racial iconology that focuses on the ongoing contestations that comprise contemporary visions of race. The writers I examine add fuel to this fire by mobilizing the unwieldiness of things as an occasion to explore the contemporaneity of racial visuality and as a means of participating in its ongoing construction project. The groundwork for such an investigation has been laid in recent critiques of identity politics. Although identity politics continues to wield a good deal of power in contemporary life, remaining a fairly effective mode of mobilizing and empowering minority groups, it has never been more embattled in the academy.[44] Calls for the increased visibility of a racial identity seem to tread too closely to historical racist visualizations of racialized bodies as a means of enforcing exclusionary structures of power.

Peggy Phelan critiques the alignment of visibility with political power by challenging the notion "that 'selves' can be adequately represented within the visual or linguistic field." Ignoring "the 'hole in the signifier,' 'the Real-impossible' which is unsayable, unseeable, and therefore resistant to representation," identity politics fails to see these representations as repetitive *re-presentations*.[45] For Phelan, what is visible about identity is not the Real itself, but a set of uninterrogated signs that repeatedly masquerade as authentic. Signs taken for wonders, the visible marks of racial or other identity forms elide their own artificiality. Racial visibility becomes accepted as a given, and vision is reduced to the recognition of given codes. Because these codes remain uncontested, as in Phelan's account, the mark of race on the body escapes the kind of scrutiny that contemporary thought places on other kinds of signifying marks, as if racial visibility were not constructed but merely recognized. Elided is the way in which visible racial signifiers themselves operate as representations within a larger visual field. A fundamental and underexamined aspect of racism is the mode of seeing that racialization uncritically employs in order to understand race in visual terms, which is unwittingly reproduced even in resistant discourses.

Robyn Wiegman argues that this blindness to the complexity of racial visuality is so deeply embedded in American culture that any form of self-conception in current discourse "outside of the regimes of corporeal visibility is not only at some level unthinkable but also intolerable to our own conceptions of who and what we 'are.'"[46] Accordingly, Wiegman shows how a fundamental epistemological concern for visibility underlies modern conceptions of race. Adapting Foucault's account of modernity to fit Western racial discourse, she argues that "the production of the African subject as non- or subhuman, as an object and property, arises not simply through the economic necessities of the slave trade, but according to the epistemologies attending vision and their logics of corporeal inscription: making the African 'black' reduces the racial meanings attached to flesh to a binary structure of vision, and it is this structure that precedes the disciplinary emergence of the humanities and its methodological pursuits of knowledge and truth."[47] Racism requires a reductive stabilization of visual racial codes, which in turn are bound to larger structures of knowing. Because the assumptions that inform modern conceptions of race are deeply tied to fundamental epistemological structures, they have far-reaching political effects: "Modern citizenship functions as a disproportionate system in which the universalism ascribed to certain bodies (white, male, propertied) is protected and subtended by the infinite particularity assigned to others (black, female, unpropertied)."[48] For Wiegman, corporeal inscription is so potent because it becomes naturalized through the polymorphic operations of power that inform our fundamental structures of knowledge.

In light of these analyses, we begin to see the problem of viewing race in the United States strictly as an inheritance. Though it would be myopic, irresponsible, and indeed dangerous to think of race as entirely independent of its historical legacy, the emphasis on inheritance can often occlude the emergent ideological demands, to which race must be continually remade and refashioned to fit. Race as the product of racialization, in other words, threatens to become reified. We already think we know what it is because it has been so central to American history, and our discussions about what to do about racial problems can often crowd out more fundamental questions about what form race takes in the present. The breakdown of the coalitional racial politics of the 1960s and 1970s, for example, poses new challenges to understanding racial formation that, as Susan Koshy points out, can no longer be conceived in simple binaries, such as insider and outsider, native and alien.[49] The study of contemporary racialization thus requires a constant vigilance to the new forms racialization might produce, balancing phenomenological investigations that privilege seeing as if for the first time with historical contextualization.

This book explores the problematic of visuality in Asian American racialization, which Lye articulates with respect to American literary naturalism as a problem of invisibility: "The visuality of Asiatic racial form has a distinctive character insofar as the sense of its deceitfulness or mystery always points to the presence of something not shown. To put it another way, we recognize the Asiatic as a figure for the unrepresentable. Yet how is the unrepresentable to be visualized? Does it have a human body? If not, what shape, as a whole or in part, does it take?"[50] Lye describes racialization in the context of American industrial modernity on an international scale instead of as merely an antebellum legacy, and she reads Asian racialization as something distinct from a belated recycling of older models. Rather than understanding it simply as a mechanism through which white supremacy reproduces itself, she argues that racialization develops because of its ability to suit the often contradictory political and economic necessities of a rapidly expanding nation with imperialist aspirations.[51] For Lye, then, the racial visualization of the Asiatic becomes an expediency shaped by the force of ideological pressures, which she recounts in a historical genealogy that forms a continuum from older notions of yellow peril to more contemporary iterations of the model minority.

Though less interested in continuing this genealogy up through the present, *Racial Things, Racial Forms,* in exploring contemporary modes of racialization, complements Lye's historicization of racial visuality by articulating possibilities of meaningfully engaging the legacy of the ideological forces Lye elucidates and by tracing what happens to Asian American racial form in contemporary American culture. Indeed, my attraction to avant-garde Asian American poetics is for its treatment of ideological questions as formal problems without reducing the former to the latter. Lye's study follows in the wake of David Palumbo-Liu's work, which argues that any contemporary notion of *Asian American* arises not out of a "teleologically predetermined and irreversible phenomenon," but instead as the result of continual and multidirectional rearticulations of the relationship between *Asian* and *American*.[52]

Like Lye, who downplays the legacy of racial discourse in order to emphasize its relationship to industrial modernity, Palumbo-Liu foregrounds the contemporaneity of race—how race is continually remade in the present according to newly emerging ideological forces and conditions. Both of these formulations pose a new problem for racial politics, which has been largely geared toward resisting the hegemony of a dominant normative model against which race is defined. If race itself becomes a function of larger ideological forces on an international scale, for which the exclusionary logic of white normativity is just another symptom, then what form should contemporary racial politics take? *Racial Things, Racial Forms* considers how one might then think about visualizing race in this new context and applies critical pressure on the physical and visual itself in avant-garde poetic art, whose abstract and experimental inclinations are particularly suited for interrogating contemporary racial form and visuality.

Post-Identity Racial Poetics

Because of their commitment to avant-garde modes, the writers and artist examined in *Racial Things, Racial Forms* share a somewhat ambiguous status in Asian American art. Cha's work, for example, was largely ignored until the publication of *Writing Self, Writing Nation* in 1994. Berssenbrugge participated in the Asian American political movement of the 1970s; she was friends with, among others, Frank Chin, Shawn Wong, and Lawson Inada, and her earlier work was included in various anthologies of Asian American writing. However, as it became increasingly abstract, her poetry received less attention from Asian American scholars. Others, such as Myung Mi Kim and John Yau, attracted the attention of those interested in contemporary experimental poetry, but they only recently became more important in Asian American literary criticism. Yau's credentials as a minority poet, in fact, were the subject of an angry debate in 1994 with Eliot Weinberger, whose anthology of American poetry Yau reviewed negatively.[53] In most of these cases, it is aesthetic experimentalism that somehow counteracts any claim that these writers might have to an Asian American identity.

Although much of the writing examined here may appear ambivalent to racial politics, *Racial Things, Racial Forms* suggests that it is instead ambivalent toward the idiom in which this politics has traditionally been expressed. Perhaps because of this characteristic, one of the early criticisms of this project was that it relies too much on analogy and, concomitantly, that some of the texts I discuss only seem to engage the topic of race when put next to other texts by the same author that are more explicit on the topic. Indeed, the avant-garde thing effect described in *Racial Things, Racial Forms,* whether manifested in a literal object such as *Surplus Novel* or rendered within poetic language, involves the production of an analogous form that brings together disparate contexts in a mutually elaborating engagement. Analogies themselves, however, are assertions of similarity across relationships of difference, and, as such, some analogies disclose more significance than others, depending on whether they rely on incidental similarities or on more fundamental coherences. When I describe analogous figures and formulations in this book, I am suggesting the latter relationship and not the former—what might be reducible to mere analogy.[54] Many of the texts I treat in this study, I argue, address racial issues, but they do not do so conventionally, and a great deal of their imaginative energy is expended in formulating new modes of engaging current iterations of old problems. What might seem to be avoidance of social issues is actually the avoidance of their more conventional forms in hopes of gaining significant interpretive advantages by adopting more oblique approaches. Indeed, not only do the avant-garde forms discussed in *Racial Things, Racial Forms* demand to be read in broader discursive contexts—whether in relation to works by other authors, theoretical traditions, or indeed works by the same author—but, in addition, this recontextualizing effort is often fundamental to the artistic practice. That is, the defamiliarizing effect produced by the thing authorizes viewing it in alternative contexts. On the broadest level, the avant-garde things I examine contribute to racial discourse and call attention to the discursive contours of human interactions: how we engage that which is regarded as normative (Cha); how language affects these interactions (Kim); how we view and conceive our own bodies relative to other bodies (Berssenbrugge); and how we look at visual depictions of race (Yau).

Eschewing many of the conventions of minority writing, these poets investigate the nexus of issues that I have grouped under the rubric of *things*, instead of rehearsing the traditional claims of resistant subjectivity that characterizes more recent iterations of identity politics, which tend to challenge political marginalization without contesting a priori assumptions about how race is fundamentally visualized. Because it privileges political recognition and visibility, identity politics must either implicitly accept racist visions of the body, in which race is habitually identified as a series of unproblematic marks, or it must reject the visual entirely as unreliable. Critics such as Lisa Lowe, Viet Nguyen, and Kandice Chuh argue that the claims of racial identity that were so important to Asian American politics emerging out of the civil rights movement have not only proved unstable or vulnerable to critiques of essentialism but also become commoditized and thus transformed into unintentional repetitions of ideological power.[55] In the context of a long history of anxieties about representing race throughout American history that is epitomized by the vagaries of the "one-drop rule," my turn to avant-garde interrogations of racial form affords a new perspective from which to consider the ongoing complex dynamics of contemporary racial discourse. More than simply redefining *things* in positive terms that might redress their traditional denigration, *Racial Things, Racial Forms* approaches *things* as the site of a new problematic, one which avoids the false choice of identity politics by treating the physicality, materiality, and visuality of race as implicated in a highly contested, historically specific system of racial signification. By refashioning avant-garde queries of the thing into abstract questions about how American discourse manifests race in physical or visual forms or even about how human beings interact in contemporary life, the work of the examined poets implicitly seeks alternatives to the unreflective stances of current dominant ideological models, which identity politics sometimes reproduces.

As the introductory reading of *Surplus Novel* demonstrates, racial objectification is a metaphoric kind of containment that Cha's piece renders literally as a physical container. Appropriately then, *Racial Things, Racial Forms* proceeds to examine a series of literal and metaphoric containers. It begins with the most prominent figure in the history of Asian American avant-garde art, Theresa Hak Kyung Cha. Picking up where critics such as Lisa Lowe and Viet Nguyen leave off in positioning Cha at the end point of studies that call attention to the limits of subjective identity politics, I situate her as foundational in Asian American literary investigations of what it means to be a *thing*. Rather than focus on *DICTEE* (1982), however, one of the few canonical avant-garde texts in Asian American literary studies, I choose to focus on the abundant and underexamined mixed-media language art in her oeuvre. Much of Cha's work calls attention to containers by focusing on the physical properties of different artistic media. By blending and confusing poetry, film, video, sculpture, and photography, Cha calls attention to the befuddling thingness of her often difficult, alienating pieces in order, I argue, to represent in physical form the foreignness often ascribed to Asian American immigrants as well as the ideological apparatuses that enforce this status. In so doing, Cha's work implicitly brings together disparate uses of the word *objecthood* in two very different canonical pieces of criticism: Frantz Fanon's *Black Skin, White Masks* (1952) and Michael Fried's "Art and Objecthood" (1967). Foregrounding the dynamic objecthood of the medium itself, as well as the complex whiteness of the page or the film screen, Cha undercuts the fictions of blankness and innocence associated with white privilege and calls attention to the cultural machinery embedded in surfaces otherwise regarded as blank. Cha thus mobilizes various kinds of containers in order to stage the encounter with otherness as an encounter with both physical and ideological apparatuses.

The second chapter focuses on containers of a more metaphoric kind—specifically on mouths as physical containers of language—in Myung Mi Kim's poetry. The defamiliarizing gesture in much of her work calls attention to the physicality of the often tongue-tied mouths of nonnative speakers who struggle with English not just to communicate with foreign idioms but, more fundamentally, to orchestrate their lips, throat, and breath to make the necessary sounds. Occasioned by the fact that letterforms in *Han'gŭl*, the written Korean language, are based on the shape of the mouth when producing the corresponding sounds, Kim figures these foreign mouths struggling to pronounce English words as unassimilated things. More than simply a meditation on the sound of a foreign accent, Kim's poetry considers the physical properties of mouths that mark racial difference and need to be retrained in order to meet normative demands. This attention to the physicality of mouths, occasioned by these linguistic difficulties, comes implicitly in conversation with de Manian accounts of materiality, in which the signifier fails to function when one acknowledges its thingness—its *shape*.[56] Taken as an object instead of a sign, the signifier becomes a kind of thing, an inert, nonsignifying mark, unintelligible and discrete from any system of signification that would render it coherent. In a similar logic, Kim attempts to transcribe into English the physical sensibility implicit in Han'gŭl, thus reimagining the materiality of the signifier in language as the physicality of the mouths that struggle to speak it. Particularly in *Under Flag* (1991), however, Kim also attempts to invest the mouth's thingness with a dynamic energy. In the space opened by this disruption of normative speech, Kim redresses the abjection of these mouths not by reasserting a capable representative voice that might simply declaim resistance but instead by dramatizing how poetry might misuse (in Brown's sense) the mispronounced words of foreign mouths as notes in poetic flights of sound. These marginal mouths thus become central to her poetics, which, in emphasizing transliteration, comes to resemble Walter Benjamin's idealized vision of translation, seeking, beyond transcription, a mutually transformative encounter between languages. Instead of functioning as a kind of racial mark or as failed containers of language, foreign mouths thus shed their unassimilated awkwardness by embracing their thingness.

The third chapter explores Mei-mei Berssenbrugge's use of two different kinds of containers—books and bodies—which she treats as analogous forms. More specifically, her handmade collaborative art books, *Hiddenness* (1987) with Richard Tuttle and *Endocrinology* (1997) with Kiki Smith, imagine the book as a kind of physical body. Although these texts are more abstract and philosophical than some of her other work, which is easier to coordinate with the interests of Asian American Studies, Berssenbrugge's exploration of positioned phenomenology keenly stages a central problematic in visualizing race in contemporary American life. On one hand, phenomenology provides an attractive critical avenue for examining the kind of primordial, prediscursive perception involved in the construction of contemporary racial form and thus of refusing the reifications that make it seem impossible to view anew, without importing the baggage of the past. On the other hand, phenomenology seems in danger of denying specific social positionality and historical particularity in its attempt to formulate abstract universalist accounts of human perception. Berssenbrugge engages implicitly both the phenomenology of Maurice Merleau-Ponty, who calls attention to the role of the body in perception, and the kind of critiques raised by Judith Butler, who argues that the subject of Merleau-Ponty's phenomenology is concrete and masculine despite its universal pose. Berssenbrugge's implicit paradoxical formulation, positioned phenomenology, is ultimately an attempt to articulate a mutually corrective balance among opposing, problematic alternatives, circumscribing the difficulties that contemporary racial politics must confront.

In the fourth chapter, containers modulate into their most metaphoric register as iconic baggage, the legacy of images carried forward throughout history in various iterations. Focusing on poet and art critic John Yau, whose work is particularly attuned to the power of images in both high art and mass culture in relation to racial politics, this chapter examines Yau's representation of racial visibility as a kind of iconicity—that is, as a matrix of images and affective associations that circulate around a highly visible figure, be it an iconic painting by Jasper Johns, a Golden-age Hollywood actor such as Peter Lorre, or a racialized minority such as Asian Americans. What connects these disparate interests for Yau is the subgenre ekphrasis, which entails the verbal representation of visual representation. Perhaps most famously exemplified by Keats's "Ode on a Grecian Urn," ekphrasis stages both the compatibility and incompatibility of visual and verbal modes of artistic expression, and, thus, otherness is a fundamental condition of the form. Yau uses this formal condition to interrogate the social construction of racial difference. Contrasting Yau's distinctive mode of ekphrasis in his poetic treatments of various forms of visual art against that of Cathy Song, I suggest that Yau's work responds to the often stereotypical, ideological impositions of objecthood on the racialized body by prescribing a racial iconology that constantly contests and recontextualizes the coding of visual representations of race in an effort to articulate what is contemporary about it. Guided by the belief that racial objectification loses its power when understood not as a priori and naturalized but in the ideological context that produced it, Yau's racial iconology as exemplified in his ekphrastic practices demands a metacritical examination of the otherwise powerful ideological compulsions toward stasis and reductive simplifications that have historically dominated how race is visualized. In contrast to readings of Yau's work that call attention to how his poetics foreground the falsity and constructedness of racial identity, my emphasis on racial iconology preserves an attention to the power of these visual constructs, which remains despite their falsity.

Foregrounding the figure of a virus as a kind of invisible container, the coda returns to *Surplus Novel* to examine a rarely discussed figure in Asian American Studies: Yoko Ono. This is a move backward in time to an older artist in order to explore the future political stakes and racial implications of avant-garde modes of artistic expression, specifically by examining the two kinds of antipathy that coalesce in the figure of Yoko Ono: yellow peril and hatred of the avant-garde. As a meeting point for these two strong sentiments, Ono functions as a contested site for the visualization of Asianness in the context of emergent cultural and economic globalization. Her denigration—both by those who cast her as a parasitic infection that destroyed The Beatles and by those who are put off by her inscrutable, avant-garde art—figures the reductive, objectifying tendencies, I suggest, typical of a new emergent form of yellow peril, in which what is feared and loathed from Asia is imagined not in bodily forms but in less-visible, viral forms.

Racial Things, Racial Forms interrogates both the racist convention of reductively visualizing race as stigma and the avant-garde tradition that privileges things as a way to push art toward new discoveries and departures. This project began with the observation that the lexicon of the avant-garde has always shadowed racial discourse, that the characterization of avant-garde innovation as freedom of expression and escape from the oppression and subjugation of earlier dominant aesthetic forms has always doubled the same sentiments in a decidedly less figurative arena. Whereas racial theorists and avant-garde critics always seem to use the same words, they rarely seem to be talking to one another. In the work of these avant-garde Asian American poets, such a gap collapses. By integrating into the study of poetry a visual cultures approach that attends to the relationship between vision and knowledge, *Racial Things, Racial Forms* complements more traditional histories of racial stigmatization by magnifying the operations implicit in racialization as they adapt to new ideological demands and contemporary pressures. That one of the most prominent racial marks of Asianness, the slanted eye (as the 2008 Spanish Olympic basketball team so inelegantly reminded us), is also the organ of vision is significant. Narrow and nearly closed, slanted eyes become racial things, reduced to racial marks by an Orientalist viewer who, like the stranger that occasioned *Surplus Novel*, is unaware that they look back.

RACIAL THINGS, RACIAL FORMS

CHAPTER ONE

BLACK THINGS, WHITE THINGS

Objecthood in Theresa Hak Kyung Cha's Language Art

Frantz Fanon and Michael Fried are not likely to be mentioned in the same breath, and the juxtaposition that follows would hardly be mistaken as a conversation. Though published only fifteen years apart, *Black Skin, White Masks* (1952) and "Art and Objecthood" (1967), both seminal works in their respective critical fields, speak to disparate concerns.

> "Look, a Negro!"
>
> I came into the world imbued with the will to find a meaning in things, my spirit filled with the desire to attain the source of the world, and then I found that I was an object in the midst of other objects.
>
> Sealed into that crushing objecthood, I turned beseechingly to others. Their attention was a liberation, running over my body suddenly abraded into nonbeing, endowing me once more with an agility that I had thought lost, and by taking me out of the world, restoring me to it. But just as I reached the other side, I stumbled, and the movements, the attitudes, the glances of the other fixed me there, in the sense in which a chemical solution is fixed by a dye. I was indignant; I demanded an explanation. Nothing happened. I burst apart. Now the fragments have been put together again by another self.[1]

> I remarked earlier that objecthood has become an issue for modernist painting only within the past several years. This, however, is not to say that before the present situation came into being, paintings, or sculptures for

that matter, simply *were objects*. It would, I think, be closer to the truth to say that they *simply* were not. The risk, even the possibility, of seeing works of art as nothing more than objects did not exist.[2]

Despite their clear differences, one notices that the lexicon of each conspicuously shares a central term—not only the simple noun *object* but also the more abstract condition *objecthood*. At the beginning of the famous chapter entitled "The Fact of Blackness," Fanon discusses the denial of subjectivity to black people, a denial that becomes tragically absorbed and internalized such that the will, spirit, and desire that occasion optimism early in the passage above gradually fade, ceding agency to unseen hands. The fact of blackness is, in short, objecthood itself.[3] Though the term describes a postslavery mental condition, it echoes an older objectification and commoditization of the enslaved black body. For Michael Fried, however, objecthood is a key feature of an aesthetic embodied by minimalist art, and it is one that he vehemently opposes. It refers specifically to the conceit of art objects that do not function as representations or compositions but rather exist as things in and of themselves. That is, they do not *depict* things, even abstractly; they *are* things. As such, minimalist art emphasizes what Fried elsewhere terms *theatricality*, which foregrounds the spectator's relationship to the work in the moment of viewing as fundamental to the logic of the piece.[4] Despite the different contexts, both Fanon and Fried regard the condition of objecthood as stultifying and burdensome. Counterposed against autonomous subjectivity in Fanon and successful art in Fried, objecthood is a debased condition. For both, to be an object is to be static, inert, and abject.

By bringing together this otherwise disparate set of concerns, the language art of Theresa Hak Kyung Cha considers objecthood at precisely this juncture of racial and aesthetic theory. I choose the broader rubric of language art, as opposed to poetry, in order to reflect Cha's concern for mixing and challenging the boundaries of genre and media. For Cha, I suggest, the often befuddling objecthood of avant-garde art objects—be they books, films, or sculptures—becomes a means of investigating the foreignness of racialized bodies, which have become objectified in the way that Fanon describes. Although critics appreciate the refusals in her aesthetics and offer poststructuralist accounts of how the fact of breached aesthetic boundaries implicitly challenge social boundaries (the gesture that Jinqi Ling finds so empty), they tend to ignore Cha's more synthetic treatments of racialization—her subtle cross-pollination of different modes of objecthood. Because it focuses on the physical apparatus of various artistic media, her avant-garde approach may seem to address Fried's concerns more than it does Fanon's. Cha's work, however, ultimately turns to the sociopolitical bearings of Fanon's vision, precisely by embracing the aesthetics that Fried critiques, and abject objecthood becomes, for Cha, both a social and aesthetic condition.

The term *objecthood* becomes a somewhat inappropriate descriptor because Cha's combinatory ethos functions to revitalize the formerly static object. Cha's art pieces are more things than objects in the sense that Bill Brown articulates:

> As they circulate through our lives, we look *through* objects (to see what they disclose about history, society, nature, or culture—above all, what they disclose about *us*), but we only catch a glimpse of things. We look through objects because there are codes by which our interpretive attention makes them meaningful, because there is a discourse of objectivity that allows us to use them as facts. A *thing*, in contrast, can hardly function as a window. We begin to confront the thingness of objects when they stop working for us: when the drill breaks, when the car stalls, when the window gets filthy, when their flow within the circuits of production and distribution, consumption and exhibition, has been arrested, however momentarily.[5]

The thing is that which is recognizable but difficult to name or, as Brown puts it, "the thing baldly encountered" but "some thing not quite apprehended."[6] The object is like a tool, closely associated with a specific instrumentality (such as drilling holes or hammering nails), whereas the thing marks the point of interruption where action and thought are arrested. Objects have a clear utility, whereas things, by contrast, are momentarily bewildering. The potential virtue of the thing is its ability to awaken us from complacency in the arrested moment when the object becomes something other, some strange thing unmoored from its normative context. Unlike the thing in Brown's account, though, which surprisingly and ephemerally emerges in unexpected moments of disruption, Cha's art attempts very explicitly to produce these moments of disorientation as a calculated effect.

Particularly by emphasizing the physical properties of artistic media, Cha's language art constantly reconjures the moment in which one encounters a not-quite-apprehended thing. Immediately defamiliarizing, it typically blurs distinctions among literature, film, poetry, sculpture, and even mail, producing discomfort specifically with the viewer's ability to recognize whatever form, medium, or genre the art happens to employ. Furthermore, Cha relocates the Duchampian tradition of destabilizing attitudes toward ordinary objects in a more positioned social context by continuously dilating not upon racialized bodies themselves but, rather, the terms in which these bodies have traditionally been racialized. The not-quite-apprehended avant-garde thing comes to feel alien, an entity that frustrates coherence in order to force the audience to reconsider how it regards and engages alternative othered embodiments. Finally, by registering as figures of inscrutability, Cha's things become locatable within the discursive tradition of specifically Asian racialization, in which the racial form of the perpetual foreigner registers as a problem of legibility.[7]

Invoking the bowls in *Surplus Novel*, this chapter foregrounds two containers of language in Cha's work: the book and the film. These containers do not function directly as symbols of racialized bodies. Cha's work has little to do with the literal corporeal inscription of race and does not so much figure racialized bodies anthropomorphically as it represents the abstract categories that characterize these bodies, and the focus on the thingness of these media engages with questions of racial form. This chapter focuses, ultimately, on Cha's poetic art book *Earth* (1976) and her film-based installation *Exilée* (1980), both of which carefully attend to the materiality of the medium and fixate on the whiteness of both the page and screen. In these pieces, Cha provocatively stages the unlikely conversation between Fanon and Fried with which this chapter began, by binding the foreignness of the avant-garde object to the trope of the Asian as perpetual foreigner while also interrogating the fictions of whiteness (blankness, immateriality) against which race becomes understood as objecthood.

Abject Objecthood, Privileged Whiteness

If we were to broaden our scope to include Fried's literary criticism, which includes a brief foray into postcolonial discourse via Joseph Conrad, we might be surprised to find that Fanon and Fried share more in common that we originally thought, particularly in their treatments of white privilege, which both critics position in opposition to the attenuated agency of objecthood. For both, this privilege becomes increasingly powerful the more whiteness becomes immaterial and blank. In fact, in their discussions of this dynamic, Fanon and Fried seem to cross over momentarily into each other's discursive realms. Fanon makes this border crossing in appropriating W.E.B. Du Bois's famous notion of double consciousness, modulating his predecessor's ocular emphasis ("this sense of always looking at one's self through the eyes of others"[8]) into an interest in embodied phenomenological perception. Whereas Du Bois maintains a kind of reserved distance from the experience, calling it a "peculiar sensation," Fanon offers a phenomenology of objecthood by narrating the affective experience from an immersed and embodied point of view that emphasizes moment-to-moment perceptual developments and fluctuations:

> And then the occasion arose when I had to meet the white man's eyes. An unfamiliar weight burdened me. The real world challenged my claims. In the white world the man of color encounters difficulties in the development of his bodily schema. Consciousness of the body is solely a negating activity. It is a third-person consciousness. The body is surrounded by an atmosphere of certain uncertainty. I know that if I want to smoke, I shall have to reach out my right arm and take the pack of cigarettes lying at the other end of the table. The matches, however, are in the drawer on the left, and I shall have to lean back slightly. And all these movements are made not out of habit but out of implicit knowledge. A slow composition of my *self* as a body in the middle of a spatial and temporal world—such seems to be the schema. It does not impose itself on me; it is rather, a definitive structuring of the self and of the world—definitive because it creates a real dialectic between my body and the world.[9]

Fanon's phenomenological approach to the experience of race within a postcolonial context is oddly coherent here with the language of the avant-garde, even embodying a version of Friedian theatricality. A familiar, commonplace action (smoking a cigarette) is slowed and protracted into an extended experience, and familiar objects become transformed into things. The slowness of the account accesses a heightened, defamiliarized perspicacity—

an awareness of the body in relation to the spatial-temporal world that one would otherwise take for granted—and it allows for a critical distance from an activity (smoking) that is usually characterized by automated compulsion. Fanon's description of smoking here is in fact similar in effect to Yoko Ono's performative piece, *Smoke Painting* (1961)—to invoke a more typically avant-garde example—in which viewers were invited to ignite canvases with their cigarettes. In this case, cigarettes are deployed to upset familiar conventions involved in the viewing of art, and the removal of the familiar activity from the realm of ordinary habit gives rise to something like a third-person consciousness that resonates with Fanon's experience of himself in triplicate, a fleeting outer-body experience that encourages an alternative perspective on one's relationship to the object world. Like Fanon's emphasis on phenomenology, Ono's defamiliarizing treatment of the familiar magnifies the operations of perception.

Fanon thus expresses racial experience in contrast to this phenomenological experience, asserting that the establishment of bodily schema, one's physical sense of self in space and time, is thwarted for a man of color in a white world because whiteness itself transcends objecthood and rises to the status of idealized standard bearer. Instead of the black subject defining himself with respect to the world, "he must be black in relation to the white man."[10] Race therefore determines the phenomenological, and the colonial situation suffuses the fundamental questions of perception and experience that are the traditional concerns of phenomenology. Bodily schema is then ultimately determined by the "eyes of the white man," in which the "black man has no ontological resistance."[11] Without minimizing the more overt forms of colonial power, Fanon calls attention to the more subtle ontological and metaphysical consequences of these impositions on the black subject. Accordingly, whiteness in Fanon becomes increasingly abstract and takes on a symbolic power. As Homi Bhabha argues, whiteness in Fanon functions as a kind of ideality: "The black child turns away from himself, his race, in his total identification with the positivity of whiteness which is at once colour and no colour. In the act of disavowal and fixation the colonial subject is returned to the narcissism of the Imaginary and its identification of an ideal ego that is white and whole."[12] Fanon thus uses phenomenology—specifically, the extent to which a person of color is denied the universal phenomenological subject position—as a way to consider how the relationship between historical colonial subjugation and the colonial subject's complicity with that subjugation complicates questions of subjective eligibility in relation to this white, ideal ego. For Fanon, the crushing objecthood of the black subject is both imposed from without and guaranteed from within by the identification with an ideal whiteness on the part of the black subject.

Furthermore, as blackness becomes more material and increasingly associated with objecthood, whiteness seems to dematerialize and move toward the abstract realms of the symbolic and ideal. Material objecthood comes to oppose not only subjecthood but also whiteness. Fanon's choice of the adjective *crushing* to modify *objecthood* is appropriate in its inference of forceful, overwhelming weight. The dynamic subject that thinks and feels becomes reduced to an inert thing, the heavy burden of which is a final subjective and political ineligibility that is both imposed and imbibed. By contrast, the power of whiteness seems bound to its ascendance to immaterial abstraction, as if it were a form of weightlessness. As Sara Ahmed argues in phenomenological terms, "White bodies do not have to face their whiteness. . . . By not having to encounter being white as an obstacle, given that whiteness is 'in line' with what is already given, bodies that pass as white move easily, and this motility is extended by what they move toward."[13]

Fried's interest in whiteness begins in characteristically aesthetic terms, as an interest in the blank page, but elsewhere in his work, this interest expands into an exploration of imperialist consciousness. As in Fanon, objecthood in Fried is an impediment to agency. "Art and Objecthood" positions minimalism, as James Meyer points out, "as modernism's principal antagonist" and by extension as anathema to art in general because it understands art precisely as the activity of transcending objecthood.[14] In order to count as art, it needs to be *not* an object. As in his earlier *Realism, Writing, Disfiguration: On Thomas Eakins and Stephen Crane* (1987), Fried's 1990 article, "Almayer's Face: On 'Impressionism' in Conrad, Crane, and Norris," extends the logic of "Art and Objecthood" to the written word. In this article, Fried recapitulates his earlier argument about Crane in order to establish the parameters of his analysis. For Crane, Fried writes, "the materiality of writing [is] simultaneously elicited and repressed: elicited because, under ordinary circumstances, the materiality precisely doesn't call attention to itself . . . in the intimately connected acts of writing and reading; and repressed because, were that materiality allowed unimpededly to the surface, not only would the very possibility of narrative continuity be lost, the writing in question would cease to *be* writing and would become mere mark."[15] In other words, once the written word's materiality becomes recognized as such, it ceases to count as a word and instead can only be regarded as a kind of object, an inert mark incapable of signification. Just as art needs to refuse objecthood to count as art, the legibility of the word thus depends on the repression of its material characteristics. Similarly, Fried compares a barren desolate landscape in Frank Norris's *A Man's Woman* (1899) to a white page: "as one more image of an overwhelming materiality that defeats the possibility of writing."[16] Materiality functions as a threat that operates in the starkest of terms; it not only impedes the clarity of writing, but, more radically, it cancels the very possibility of clarity. Posed as the enemy to fundamental characteristics of the artistic form, materiality functions as it did in "Art and Objecthood," threatening nothing less than legibility itself.

Fried's argument then moves to Conrad and unexpectedly back toward the realm of Fanon by linking the whiteness of the page to the logic of imperialism. In contrast to Crane, in whose work the materiality of writing functions to cancel the possibility of writing entirely, Conrad, in Fried's account, employs these thematics toward other ends. He calls attention to Conrad's characteristic "problematic of erasure," which "first makes the paper black, then makes it blank, not just once but repeatedly."[17] He then moves to connect the blankness of the white page and the consciousness of the white European youth venturing off to foreign lands, seeking experiences over fortune. Using *Heart of Darkness* as an example, Fried emphasizes

> the analogy between the blank page as . . . a field of boundless possibility for the writer seated before it and the white space on the map as a comparable field of imaginative self-realization for the young male European (that is, white) bourgeois subject in the late nineteenth and early twentieth centuries. Understood in this light, maps of the world with their unmarked spaces, color codings, and exotic place-names play a vital role in the technology of imperialism not so much because they give objective expression to the struggle for geopolitical domination as because they help mobilize the youthful energies of an entire class of persons in a seemingly individual-

> ist but in fact largely collective undertaking whose economic and political consequences, when not actually occulted, at any rate need never be recognized as such.[18]

Accordingly, the blank, white page comes to figure the consciousness of the white European youth, deeply affected by "one of imperialism's fundamental mobilizing strategies." That is, the compulsion "to imagine, for all their prior formation in European society and the actual economic work they were carrying out, that they were engaged in a strictly personal enterprise of self-realization that cast them in the passive role of blank surfaces on which their experiences of the East (or Africa, or South America) would inscribe the first identity-defining marks."[19] Not only a figure for a map of the world imagined as an unmarked space—a "field of boundless possibility" upon which the white European youth would inscribe his mark—the blank page also becomes the youth himself, on whom experiences of foreign worlds are written. The white page becomes blank, uninhabited, and associated with possibility.

As in Fanon, the power of whiteness in Fried lies in its ability to dematerialize and enforce its own blankness. Blackness must be erased from the page in order to experience it as white blankness in the same way that the indigenous people of foreign lands require erasure in order to understand the world as an open field of possibility. Indeed, the page itself must be understood not only as blank but also, more radically, as an immaterial absence. Furthermore, participation in this imperialist fantasy requires that the white European subject understand himself not as a part of some large-scale act of aggression but rather as part of a smaller, personal journey in which he is the passive receptor of experience. What authorizes the aggression and violence of imperialism is the belief that it is not imperialism at all but rather a young man's personal journey in search of his own identity. If there is a privilege accorded to whiteness, it is the ability to act in self-interest (and in the interests of imperialism) while seeming to be doing nothing at all—an aggression reimagined as passive. In Fanon, the power of whiteness is in its ability to function as an ideality. Sealed within a crushing objecthood, the black subject becomes increasingly material, and the movement toward thing status underwrites the political ineligibility that colonialism imposes. In Fried, the power of whiteness is similarly abstract: to impose power yet seem entirely immaterial. That the blank page becomes the site of power depends on a disappearing act, a fiction of blankness. Though the whiteness of the page in Fried's logic is indeed attributable to the white male, it does not directly figure white skin or otherwise reference bodily characteristics. Rather, it is the notion that youth offers a blank, white page that can be marked up with experiences of the foreign and that the world itself, despite being well populated with competing interests, becomes itself a blank page waiting to be marked. White privilege then is the blankness itself, of oneself and of the world.

Although their concerns are radically different, both Fanon and Fried share a belief that the recognition of materiality—the turn toward objecthood—has tragic effects by threatening to reduce that which is complex and dynamic to an inert thing. In Fanon, the recognition of a black subject's objecthood underwrites political ineligibilty, in which political exclusion is doubled and enforced by an implicit existential exclusion. In Fried, treating the word as an object renders it illegible. These twin conceptions of objecthood in turn yield related notions of whiteness. Both ultimately associate the privilege of whiteness with its ability to dematerialize while maintaining a potent presence—what Richard Dyer describes in his plainly titled book *White* (1996) as the "non-located and disembodied position of knowledge."[20]

White Page, White Screen

White is prevalent in Cha's body of work, and not just because white is a fundamental characteristic in her choice of media, including the book and black-and-white film. Though she never specifically engages Fanon or Fried, Cha's language art addresses precisely the overlap of their critical concerns, and it engages their respective discursive traditions by complicating the category of objecthood and by upsetting the fictions of blankness associated with whiteness. In Cha's work, whiteness functions in two distinct but related registers; it operates generally as an ideological figure that calls attention to the physical medium itself (in order to interrogate ideologically human interactions), and it serves, more specifically, as a figure for the disappearance of particular marginalized, objectified others within such interactions. The development of this collective ethos for Cha was greatly inspired by her engagements with the film theory of the period.

One characteristic gesture in her work is the confusion of one medium for another. As critics such as Trinh T. Minh-Ha have argued, for example, the whiteness of the page in Cha's work often doubles the whiteness of the cinematic screen.[21] This slippage is immediately visible in *Commentaire*, Cha's contribution to the book she edited on cinema, *APPARATUS* (1980). The title of the book refers to film apparatus theory, which was prominent in the 1970s, many examples of which are contained in Cha's collection. A central premise of this theory is that the ideological nature of film is a function of its physical and mechanical apparatus, which encompasses everything from film techniques (such as cutting and camera work) to its literal machinery (which apparatus theorists tend to associate with a more ideological instrumentality) to the characteristics of the viewing environment (such as a darkened room and light projection). In her brief preface to the volume, Cha describes the ideological work that her volume, and apparatus theory in general, proposes to accomplish: "to turn backwards and call upon the machinery that creates the impression of reality whose function, inherent in its very medium, is to conceal from its spectator the relationship of the viewer/subject to the work being viewed."[22] The epigraph for the preface cites Jean-Luc Godard, who makes a similar point with respect to the Marxist concern for the "nature of the relationships between things."[23] The point of this brand of filmmaking and theory is to restore the viewer's lost intimacy with things—in this case, the machinery of cinema—in order to interrupt the hegemony of cinematic illusion. The ideological valences of Cha's experimentalism are legible within this context.

Greatly influenced by film apparatus theory, Cha manipulates artistic media in order to interrogate its ideological content, and one of her primary strategies is to imagine transformations of one medium into another. *Commentaire* attempts to blur the boundary between the pages of a book and the surface of a film screen by juxtaposing white and black pages, some blank and others with words printed on them; photographs by Richard Barnes of film screens, one flanked by palm trees at a drive-in and another at an indoor theater with patrons shown sleeping in the foreground; close-up images of solid brick walls; and a pair of stills that frame the piece from Carl Theodor Dreyer's *Vampyr* (1932). Unlike Dreyer's *La Passion de Jeanne d'Arc* (1928), stills from which Cha uses in *DICTEE*, *Vampyr* employs the new sound technology of the period, but because of the difficulties involved with having to film in

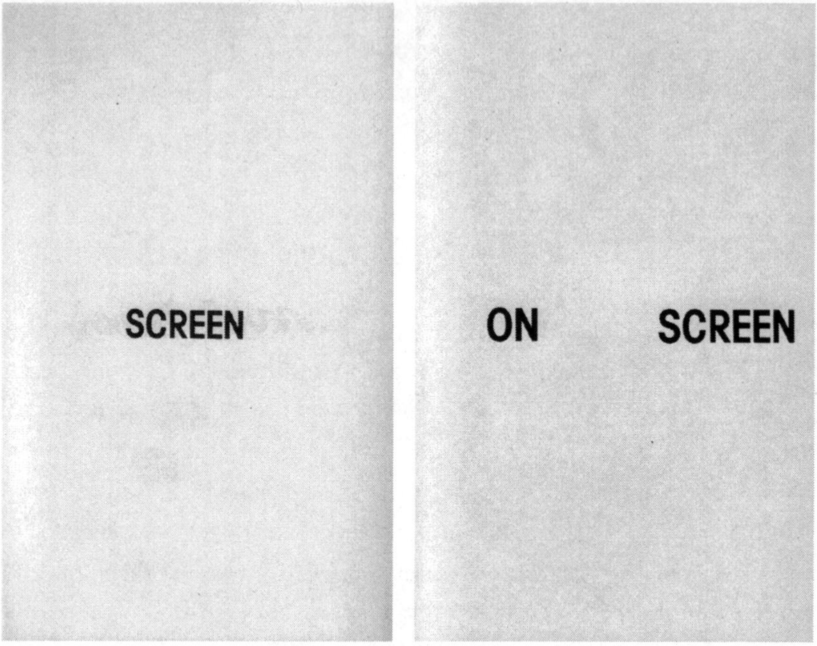

FIGURE 3. Theresa Hak Kyung Cha: *Commentaire*, from *APPARATUS—Cinematographic Apparatus: Selected Writings*, edited by Theresa Hak Kyung Cha (New York: Tanam Press, 1980). Photos: Richard Barnes. Courtesy of University of California, Berkeley Art Museum and Pacific Film Archive.

three different languages, Dreyer still used traditional silent-era intertitles. The printed words that appear throughout *Commentaire* thus call attention not only to the surface of the page as a markable linguistic space but also to a very particular filmic device. This confluence is realized most forcefully in the piece where the words *SCREEN* and *ON SCREEN* are printed across the binding's gutter from each other, dividing a pair of otherwise blank, white pages; they are subsequently followed by the photographs of white cinema screens (figs. 3 and 4).[24] Read in the context of apparatus theory, the point here seems to invite the viewer's appreciation of the material elements of two different artistic media in order to interrupt the passivity of viewers who, like the sleeping figures in one of the photographs, encounter art without actively engaging with it.

The whiteness of both the book's page and the cinema screens in the pho-

FIGURE 4. Theresa Hak Kyung Cha: *Commentaire*, from *APPARATUS—Cinematographic Apparatus: Selected Writings*, edited by Theresa Hak Kyung Cha (New York: Tanam Press, 1980). Photos: Richard Barnes. Courtesy of University of California, Berkeley Art Museum and Pacific Film Archive.

tographs is thus paradoxically abyssal and excessive; the screens in the photographs are blank not because of the absence of projection but because they are flooded and overexposed with light. Although the piece is politically engaged in the manner of apparatus theory, the whiteness, or the blackness for that matter, of the aesthetic medium in *Commentaire*, however, is never understood explicitly in relation to bodily markers of race.[25] Though comparably expansive and alienating, it does not function quite like the uncanny whiteness of the stranger's skin at the end of Edgar Allan Poe's *The Narrative of Arthur Gordon Pym of Nantucket* (1838), a whiteness that Toni Morrison describes as "impenetrable" and as an "antidote" to the "dark and abiding presence" of racial blackness in American literature.[26] Neither is it is exactly like the whiteness of the whale in Herman Melville's *Moby Dick* (1851), which Samuel Otter argues "allures then disappoints" as a racial signifier, only to give way to other bodily (phrenological) markers of race.[27] In both of these nineteenth-century American examples, whiteness simultaneously invokes phenotype (if only to deflect attention from it thereafter) as well as its political resonance in that particular historical context. Whiteness is ultimately abstracted in both cases, but the abstraction initially emanates from a bodily whiteness.

Cha would have been aware, however, of the 1971 film *Vladimir et Rosa*, by the *Groupe Dziga Vertov* (organized by filmmakers Jean-Luc Godard and Jean-Pierre Gorin), some of whose written work is included in *APPARATUS*, and its use of a blank, black screen to represent "the absence/presence of the Black man at the trial."[28] Cha's whiteness is similar to the *Groupe*'s abstract usage, but even this example ventures further into allegorical registers than her work does. White figures in Cha do not figure white people, though this possibility would not have been lost on her; rather, they figure the false sense of blankness that viewers perceive in their interactions with various physical and material others—often bodies. Part of a calculated attempt to avoid subjective representation and anthropomorphic forms, both of which would detract attention from ideological apparatus by focusing excessively on interiority, her abstract engagements with whiteness transfer the apparatus theorist's interest in the relationship between the audience and the ideological operations of filmic machinery to human interactions. If apparatus theory proposes to undo film's concealments by laying bare the invisible, structural ideological conditions of film viewing in order to awaken the viewer to the material conditions of a medium that otherwise lulls her into a dreamlike ambivalence, then Cha's treatment of whiteness, inspired by this theory, aspires to expose the hidden ideological content involved in any human encounter, especially when the viewer imagines himself or herself to be looking at the surface of an object that would otherwise be regarded as blank.

In this context, it is notable that in her performance pieces (when the object of the viewer's gaze was her own body), Cha would often don entirely white clothing, as she did in *Aveugle Voix* (1975), in which Cha wore white pants, a long-sleeve white T-shirt, and white strips of fabric over her eyes and mouth printed with the words *VOIX* and *AVEUGLE*. Perhaps more suggestively, in *A Ble Wail* (1975), not only did she wear a floor-length white nightgown and headband, but the audience also viewed her through a white cheesecloth.

Whiteness thus characterizes the object of the gaze as well as the filter through which it is viewed. Cha wrote that she intended this piece "to be the dream of the audience."[29] This comment is striking for the way in which it appropriates from apparatus theory an interest in the unacknowledged complicity of the audience's unconscious participation in what might seem a passive activity. Looking at (and through) whiteness becomes a way of probing the visuality of human interactions, a way of revealing what is inherent but unacknowledged in them.

Looking at white surfaces in Cha thus subtends looking at bodies, not socially positioned bodies in most cases but rather abstract figures that call attention to the ideological nature of the viewer's active participation in spectatorship. Her art book, *Markings* (1976), for example, imagines the book as a kind of literal body in these terms. A mail art book that Cha actually mailed to various recipients, *Markings* consists of a cover fashioned out of a letter-sized envelope and is marked by an actual postmark. Inside, the clean white pages are marred only by small rubber-stamped words that seem nearly to disappear. The words are in order: *BLACK AND BLUE*, *bruise*, *blacks and blues*, and *heartache*. Together, they seem to thematize bodily and emotional injury. The word *bruise* is rubbed over and smudged, creating the effect of a small cloud surrounding the word, similar in appearance to a bruise on human skin (fig. 5). Although a connection between the white page and the surface of a human body is clearly implied, it lacks any kind of historical or discursive particularity.[30] The book does not, for example, seem a gendered body, nor does it indicate any broader context in which to understand the bruise—whether the bruise results from abuse or accident—and the only sense of context comes from the postmark, the fact that it was mailed. Rather, whiteness here, as in Cha's larger oeuvre, takes precedence as a figuration of the medium itself, in which the medium of transmission, whether we understand it as the page of a book or a human body, subsumes its explicit content. As in the case of *Commentaire*, whiteness is not an absent blankness but rather a robust presence. Furthermore, transmission and communication are emphasized by the material history of the object—that it has been literally sent through the mail—but this focus on its communicative function is balanced against its relative illegibility. In other words, *Markings* represents a

FIGURE 5. Theresa Hak Kyung Cha: *Markings* (detail), 1976; artist's book; ink on paper, with string; 11-1/2 × 9 in.; courtesy of University of California, Berkeley Art Museum and Pacific Film Archive; gift of the Peter Norton Family. 1993.29.1.

body that foregrounds its communicative function but that is literally difficult to read. Something is lost in transmission, and the medium both invites and precludes identification.

During the mid-1970s, Cha regularly experimented with mail art as a means of probing the relationships among identification, communication, and medium. Her 1976 piece entitled *Faire-Part* (or "announcement"), for example, consists of fifteen envelopes with black frames printed at their edges on either side, as if to emphasize the containing function of this literal container of language. Language in envelopes travels through space and time both literally, as in the case of posted letter, and figuratively, as in the act of translation. (The various words and phrases are printed in French on most of the envelopes.) Her 1978 mail-art piece, *Audience Distant Relative*, similarly consists of six empty, unsealed envelopes with words printed on one side or the other. In order, they are: *audience distant relative*, *letter sendereceiver*, *messenger*, *echo*, *object/subject*, and *between delivery*. The piece, like Cha's mail art in general, articulates the hope of communicative transmission through the physical materials it inhabits. As the word play in the title of *Audience Distant Relative* implies, this hope becomes an aspiration for a kind of kinship, as if the viewer were a distant relative. The medium itself, as in the case of both filmic apparatus and language, allows one to think about literal and figurative relations of proximity. Envelopes, words, and film all function as material carriers that occupy the in-between time and space of transmission.

In *Markings*, the whiteness of the page similarly figures the medium of transmission that occupies the space in between artist and audience, one that aspires toward a communication that it fails to achieve. This in-between space has been articulated in racial and ethnic terms, most notably by Elaine Kim and specifically with respect to *DICTEE*, as the space of the immigrant caught between languages and cultures. The space in-between is the site of double alienation, and the formal in-betweenness of the text mirrors the vexed social position of the racialized and gendered immigrant. "Cha creates and celebrates a kind of third space, an exile space that becomes a source of individual vision and power. Indeed, far from dropping a specific identity in favor of endless difference, she predicts the breakdown of binaries that are part of the logic of domination. She foregrounds a highly specific cultural context, inserting Korean, Korean women, and Korean Americans into the discourse, thereby opening the space for an individual search for selfhood as well as a non-reified, non-essentialized collectivity."[31] Although the work I have focused on thus far does not assert the specific context that Kim attributes to *DICTEE*, it does position the whiteness of the medium (in various forms) as a kind of in-between exile space. Rather than figuring the social position of, say, Korean American women, I would argue that, in calling attention to thwarted acts of transmission and identification in artistic media that propose to overcome such communicative barriers, the whiteness of these media in Cha's work not only represents the unseen ideological contours of all human interactions but also foregrounds the way in which such interactions result in the kind of failed identifications that characterize racialization. If *Surplus Novel* mimics the way in which racialization transforms a person into thing, whiteness in Cha's work represents the breakdown of identification and thus functions as an abstract figure of illegibility and difference.

Kim's essay, as well as the work of her co-contributors in the influential 1994 collection on *DICTEE*, *Writing Self, Writing Nation*, foregrounds the interest in the processes of identity formation that prevail in the first half of the text in order to validate its coherence with the concerns of minority politics. This line of analysis helps clarify the text's interest in dictation exercises, exiled figures, gender, and assimilation. By linking the formal unruliness of the first half of *DICTEE* to a generally rebellious political disposition that resists various logics of domination, these critics read Cha's attempts to mix genre and media as part of a larger unwillingness to conform to hegemonic ideological structures. In locating what is resistant about the avant-garde, this line of thought tends to limit avant-garde experimentation such that it becomes only legible in terms of resistance,[32] and this overemphasis leaves the account of how avant-garde experimentation functions underdeveloped.

For example, Mayumi Takada points out that this emphasis leaves large parts of *DICTEE* unattended, particularly its second half, which critics have virtually ignored.[33] Focusing on its filmic appropriations in the Erato section of *DICTEE* and on whiteness as a trope, Takada outlines a way to attend to these avant-garde sections without abandoning the interests of Asian American Studies, arguing that whiteness functions as the site of audience identification and failure: "Whiteness simultaneously promises the potential for boundarilessness even as the emergence of the screen redefines the difference between the film and the viewer."[34] From this dual position, "the text solicits and repels the reader into desiring, but never succeeding in identifying or identifying with the accounts presented."[35] The payoff is that the text allows one to bear witness to "the specific experiences and memories of others" without reducing and absorbing them into the drama of the narcissistic subject.[36] Takada's analysis counteracts the tendency to oppose avant-garde art and racial politics. Even though racial identity slips into the background as an explicit question in the Erato section of *DICTEE*, the politics of racialization remain in the text's concern for how the subject responsibly engages others. My claim about Cha's use of whiteness parallels Takada's reading of the sections of *DICTEE* that have been largely ignored in Asian American Studies. In focusing on the in-between quality of the aesthetic medium, Cha places an emphasis on the strange materiality of the art object. This thingness becomes an occasion, in Cha's language art, to critique the dynamics involved in human interactions, to interrupt the fictions of blankness that allow us to understand social interactions as undetermined individual encounters (rather than as part of an unseen ideological machinery), and to present in physical form the abstract terms through which bodies have been historically understood in racial terms.

Earthen Media, Exiled Things

In "Paths," part of her 1978 M.F.A. thesis, Cha describes her artistic practice, and particularly her experiments with the physicality of media, as a kind of alchemy: "The artist's path is close to that of an alchemist in that his/her path is that of a medium. His/her vision belongs to an altering, of material, and of perception. Through this attempt, the perception of being altered, of being presented a constant change, Re volution."[37] Punning on the word *medium* to imply both an artistic mode and a quasi-supernatural ability, Cha conflates the transformation of the literal objects in alchemy with the transformation of perception, and, subsequently, the mediating function of art seems to turn political. Alchemy becomes a form of "Re volution" and (to allow for the pun) "volition," and its value is measured less by the object rendered (such as gold from lead) and more by the extent to which such transformations alter our views about how we see. What one perceives when one views art, in the other words, is the transformation of the very operations of perception.

Cha's 1976 art book, *Earth*, might be read as an attempt at this kind of alchemy. There are many sections that reference the same materials that she mentions in "Paths."[38] However, the larger transformation that the text seeks occurs not through the combination of these elements within the text but through how one regards the text itself as a material thing. A collection of arranged words and visual poems, *Earth* operates in the mode of Stéphane Mallarmé, whose work Cha read with interest as a student. Informed by Mallarmé's typographic experiments, which Johanna Drucker describes as more presentational than representational and focused on the dynamics of "visual and verbal relations,"[39] Cha's own typographic experimentation grants a similar priority to its visual orientation and to the relationships between words and images. Although there are certainly conventional poetic tropes repeated throughout the volume—associations of the earth to motherhood and fertility—these symbolic aspects of the text seem to be points of departure for a recalibration of the viewer's field of vision—away from a field of symbolic images and toward the physicality of the text itself.

Though visually oriented, *Earth* at least resembles poetry, perhaps more so than any of the language-based work in Cha's oeuvre. Throughout the first half, the text adheres more or less to traditional structures of lineation, especially when compared to the second half of the book. There are, however, a number of typographic irregularities, such as the lines of the volume's opening poem, for example, which waver as they move across the page, mimicking the undulating movements of the tide and wind that the words describe. Additionally, font style, size, spacing, and capitalization fluctuate from page to page, and occasionally an ostensibly omitted letter will appear as a superscript or above a word entirely, as if to imply an insertion, but none of these irregularities are as radical as those of the second half of the volume.

In the first half, the thematic concerns of *Earth* broadly echo those of Romantic lyric poetry, in which natural phenomena occasion subjective interrogation and open onto more abstract questions about, for example, language and history. The early poems in the volume also establish a series of tropes that link images of natural elements such as water and wind to figures of vision, voice, and estrangement. Furthermore, among these are the poems that most directly address recognizable Asian American topoi. The brief opening poem, for example, broaches a familiar immigrant problem, the feeling of exile: "broken shell / the third piece / carried in / high tide / be silent / it has not but a moment's remember / as the unfound voices in the wind." By moving from the image of a broken shell carried by water to the invocation of silence and unfound voices, the poem alludes, however obliquely, to the difficulty of constituting a subjectivity and of finding one's voice when faced with displacement and alienation; it thus shares some of the concerns that critics such as Kim discuss in the first half of *DICTEE*. Although the first person occasionally enters the poems throughout the volume, *Earth* generally departs from this fundamental feature of the Romantic lyric and seems uninterested in using lyric energy to repair the broken shell or to redress the subjective damage caused by dislocation.

Rather than focusing on subject formation, *Earth* foregrounds the challenges to this process, most explicitly in the untitled poem on the 27th page of the volume. Here, the bodies of Asian American laborers seem sealed into precisely the kind of racial objecthood that Fanon associates with colonial power:

SOUTHERN PACIFIC RAILROAD
RUNS THROUGH   WEST
MASSES CHINA   MEN
CONCEIVED
MANIFEST DESTINY

EACH THRUST OF
HAMMER TEARING AT
BLACK GREASED HANDS   BODY
BACKS TURNED TO THE
MUTE UNIVERSE

STRENGTH LUST OF THE STARS
STRIPES LIE
WITHIN THE BLOOD
LIFELESS AS SPRING   BREEZE

RED AGAINST THE UNENDING
METAL   TIME
OTHERS ARE MOUNTAIN SHADOWS
THEIR BRAIDS
CORDS ARE CUT

Attending to the Chinese laborers that helped build the Southern Pacific Railroad in weighty capital letters that parallel the sense of heavy burden that pervades it, the poem documents the objectification of these workers, whom the poem names in a detached, anthropological voice ("MASSES CHINA MEN"). Their bodies in turn seem devoid of subjectivity, seeming to evacuate even spring of its optimism: "WITHIN THE BLOOD / LIFELESS AS SPRING BREEZE." Their objecthood is confirmed by the ambivalence of an unconcerned "MUTE UNIVERSE" and a nation whose monstrous appetite for growth, fueled by its sense of manifest destiny, leaves it apathetic about the labor that facilitates it. A line break divides "STARS" from "STRIPES," and, hence, patriotic associations of the American flag are displaced by immoral acts, lust, and lies. As reiterated in the description of "BLACK GREASED HANDS BODY," the alienated labor of these Chinese railroad workers seems to define their foreign bodies, which here become, to adopt Fanon, objects in the midst of other objects, divested of identity and value, as in the poem's closing metonymic invocation of the stereotypical coolie and the image of severed locks of hair: "THEIR BRAIDS / CORDS ARE CUT."

This objectification of inassimilable racialized bodies in the first half of *Earth*, I suggest, establishes a context in which to recognize and understand the increasingly foreign quality of the text itself as a material thing in the second half. This is done by sounding one of the most resonant notes in Asian American history, the hardships of the Chinese railroad worker. These workers are not simply described as objects; the poem also seems to reify this description rather than combat it. Beginning about halfway through the book and continuing through the end, however, *Earth* abruptly changes course. The use of a relatively conventional poetic form ceases, the font changes to resemble that of a typewriter, and the smaller words on the page seem to recede into increasingly blank white pages. In a more conceptual register, the reader's relationship to the previously mentioned objectified, racialized bodies modulates into a physical awareness of the medium itself, and the literal object, the book, emerges as an abstract manifestation of the previously articulated social phenomenon. Because of the smaller typeface and because the center of the page is often left blank, the whiteness of the page becomes more prominent. In contrast to the first half, where the poetic structures printed in large fonts draw the eye, the whiteness of the page in the second half becomes visually dominant. When words do occupy their typical place at the center of the page, they are either nearly illegible because of compressed line spacing or they float chaotically about in a kind of visual entropy. Whereas the first half of the book seemed governed visually (if only loosely) by the rules of poetic lineation, the second half abandons any semblance of traditional poetic structure. The final ten pages have scarcely any words on them at all.

In staging an alchemic transformation of the artistic medium to further emphasize its manipulations of the physical medium, the movement from first to second half of *Earth*, I argue, reimagines the reading of poetry as if it were the viewing of film, confusing and rearticulating the relationship between two overlapping experiences of text—that of reading and that of seeing. Similar to *Commentaire*, *Earth* transforms the whiteness of the page into the whiteness of the cinematic screen. In the second half, which was not included in the original 1973 version but added in 1976 when Cha began to take an interest in filmmaking, the page operates according to the logic of projected images that appear randomly in a visual field, free of the proverbial tyranny of the poetic line. The white page as screen, flooded with light, becomes a field of possibility. This material transformation of media occurs, however, within a context established by the materiality of objectified, racialized bodies, and the possibilities afforded by this transformation seem to redress the limits of these prior figures. In contrast to the objectified bodies of anonymous Chinese laborers earlier in the text—depersonalized as "MASSES," a yellow-peril term that reimagines Chinese immigration as burdensome materiality—words here seem to float about uninhibited by the strictures of lineation. A handwritten dedication in a copy of the 1976 version archived at the Berkeley Art Museum reveals Cha's hope that her words are "not in vain but carry a weight," and she continues with this wish: "May we not be burnt washed out this outrageous place of surprises every corner of our eyes."[40] Where is this place? Though she ostensibly seems to refer to the titular earth, the actual rendering of earth in the volume does little to validate the optimism of the dedication, and Cha's rendering of the earth seems hardly worthy of her description. The dedication makes more sense, I would suggest, when read less as a kind of neoromantic appreciation of nature and more as a statement of faith in the possibility inherent in artistic media. This place becomes the medium itself as a transformative, indeed alchemic, site.

Decreasingly girded by the grammatical, poetic, thematic, metaphoric, and historical structures that make the early part of the text more intelligible and recognizable within established forms and genres, words toward the end of *Earth* seem to aspire toward a Friedian materiality that suppresses their signifying function. Rather than thwart further interpretive activity, this material turn invites alternative modes of textual engagement. The viewer is left to scan the field of whiteness, sometimes out of the corners of his or her eyes, in order to see words whose physical location on the page competes for importance with their increasingly oblique semantic content. This is not to say that the viewer does not eventually read and make sense of the words as words, but it is significant that before reading them, the viewer must often first find them, since they are sometimes hidden at the corners and margins of the page in tiny typeface (fig. 6). In imaging itself as a film as well as a book, *Earth* does not so much bend genre as it does media. In this alchemic transformation, the previously articulated racial objecthood of the Asian American body becomes subsumed into the thingness of the artistic apparatus.

Explicitly returning to a consideration of whiteness, the third visual poem in the section is self-referential about its own artistic medium. With the word *Nirvana* perched toward the upper left-hand corner of the page, the rest of the piece occupies the center, unlike the first two visual poems in the section, which leave the center blank. The poem proceeds to consider what it means to occupy the middle:

> this white sheet
> empty within
> being middle balance
> become is
> the color word fold
> paper,
> seed and transmitter
> without one but all

Absent from this passage is any concern for something like a soul or subject, yet it does reflect on a mode of existence or being that might remain despite and perhaps even as a result of emptiness. Printed at the center of a white page, this passage might be imagined as an expression of the medium itself. Nirvana in the Buddhist/Hindu sense implies the freeing of the soul from bodily or material concerns, but the movement here seems to accomplish an inverse kind of freedom, unmooring material from context in which its physical thingness is not primary. Small letters printed on a large white page, the poem seems an effort to bespeak its own materiality, its emptiness, its position in the middle, and thus its communicative function. The second half of the poem fragment proceeds as something of a list ("the color word fold / paper, / seed and transmitter"), which enumerates a quiet abundance that complicates the sense that this white sheet is empty. In so doing, this visual poem, characteristically for Cha, invites the viewer to confront the materiality of artistic

this moment's smell
scent
orange peels
sound
long gone

still

FIGURE 6. Theresa Hak Kyung Cha: *Earth* (detail), 1976; artist's book; 11 × 8-1/2 in.; courtesy of University of California, Berkeley Art Museum and Pacific Film Archive; gift of the Theresa Hak Kyung Cha Memorial Foundation. 1992.4.137.45, 61.

media and to divest its whiteness of associations with blankness. Emptiness is not its actual condition but rather the result of precisely the false perception that the poem attempts to correct.

In "Blinking, Flickering, and Flashing of the Black-and-White Film," one of the essays Cha chose to include in *APPARATUS*, Marc Vernet considers a similar emptiness in the apparatus of an artistic medium, specifically "a spot of brilliant light" on the film screen in the course of what he calls "*film de scintillement*," or the "flicker film."[41] This bright light, particularly in a genre defined by darkness, comes to signify "an unreadable and unmarked area where representation is abolished to reveal the stubborn nudity of the medium."[42] It shatters the diegetic, narrative frame of the film and exposes the apparatus. In its most extreme form, the audience itself becomes the object of spectatorship: "The white light invades the theatre audience completely. The shadows of the spectators are then outlined on the walls, which have turned white; and it is as if they are projected into a two dimensional space."[43] Vernet locates within the filmic apparatus the capacity to objectify the audience, which Vernet suggests menaces them with the threat of castration. Suddenly, sitting in a dark room, the tables are turned on the spectator, who becomes the object of the gaze.

For Vernet, the threat of the filmic apparatus depends on a reversal in which the artifice of the artistic medium is dramatically revealed: "The screen becomes a projector," and the audience becomes disoriented by being yanked out of the cinematic illusion.[44] Cha's alchemic confusion of book and film similarly provokes through disorientation. Through its media-bending experiments, *Earth* transforms itself into a foreign thing, departing from the comforts of a more familiar sense of form, genre, and medium. In Vernet, the cinematic audience is reminded of the disappointing material world that immediately surrounds it—one that hardly compares to the seductive world cast onto the screen—and it breaks free of the illusion. Similarly, in *Earth*, Cha jars the reader/viewer out of complacency toward the text by calling attention to its fundamental strangeness. Beyond Vernet, though, Cha's increasingly foreign text also mimics the imposition of racial objecthood, which in turn comes to be understood not as a nefarious willed act but as something passively accomplished. Contextualized by its earlier representation of socially positioned Asian American objectified bodies, this is art that ultimately encourages in its viewer an awareness of one's relationship to objects as an abstracted form of one's relationship to other human beings. This insight ironically reveals the limits of one's vision, and, despite the emphasis on the visual, eyes in *Earth* typically function as the objects rather than the organs of vision ("RAIN IN / BLUE LEAVES IRIS," "YOUR EYES WATER," "IN YOUR SOFT, DISTANT EYES"), or they are compromised in their ability to see ("eyes closed closed," "a film over eye's," "eyelids falling / through the floor"). Indeed, as the text becomes more visually oriented as a material thing, the possibility of seeing becomes ironically denigrated within it, as if the act of looking at a film causes a film to form over one's eyes. Seeing, it seems, becomes the capacity to appreciate the limits of one's own vision. Insight becomes an awareness of one's blindness.

By examining the associations of a concrete material thing to the often illusory associations that cling to it, Cha's *Earth* explores the oppositional terms between which Omi and Winant locate their conceptualization of race: "There is a continuous temptation to think of race as an *essence*, as something fixed, concrete, and objective. And there is also an opposite temptation: to imagine race as a mere *illusion*, a purely ideological construct which some ideal non-racist social order would eliminate." Omi and Winant find it necessary to challenge both positions to think of race as "an element of social structure rather than as an irregularity within it."[45] Cha's work shares with Omi and Winant's project an effort to think out the dynamics of racial formation; though their terms do not map exactly out on one another, they share an interest in how essences and illusions conflict and conspire in the production of racialized constructs. Cha's entry point into this discourse is certainly indirect. As the two halves of *DICTEE* suggest—one embraced by Asian American critics; the other largely ignored—Cha seems to alternate between the apparently widely disparate concerns of race on one hand and artistic media on the other. What I have tried to suggest here is how the latter operates as a version of the former, how the avant-garde conceptual dimensions of her work circle around to address the very kinds of questions posed by critics such as Fanon, Omi, and Winant.

Significantly, in "Paths," Cha's M.F.A. thesis, she writes about the audience for her work, which is both active and estranged.

> Each viewer is an integral part of the artist's work . . . in that S/He is the receptor as well as the activator of the pieces. It is through the presence of the "Other," any form of communication is established, completed.[46]

The category of the "Other" is oddly reserved here for the audience. In Berkeley, California (particularly in 1978), this was already a racially charged term, as Cha's scare quotes around the word seem to acknowledge. As we have seen, the dynamic of artistic media for Cha is not divorced from the social context that the term instantaneously hails. Despite the desired communication, the divide between artist and audience is enabling, and part of Cha's project in her art books is to experiment with the medium such that the object before the reader becomes a means for the audience to experience dislocation and alienation from without. This unaccountable thing becomes a racial thing in its isolation of an experience that intertwines objectification and estrangement. The more we regard the book as a material object, the more unfamiliar it becomes. The otherness of the audience is not a gap to be bridged; rather, it is in some ways exceptionalized as a revelatory experience. The otherness of the audience to the art object overlaps with the experience of racial otherness. What it means to experience a book as a thing becomes a way of experiencing something other as foreign, and the experience of these foreign things calls attention to this mode of alienated seeing, of seeing that which is alien, as a kind of impaired vision.

Cha's 1980 video/film installation *Exilée* might be regarded as a companion piece to *Earth* in its exploration of an alienated vision (fig. 7). *Exilée* consists of a large film screen with a rectangle, large enough to expose the video screen mounted behind, cut out of its center. It thus employs two types of projection, which proceed from opposite directions. While a film is projected onto the screen from the front, a different video plays in the center space, projected from behind by television cathode ray tubes. If *Earth* grounds its abstractions in Asian American immigrant history by foregrounding the depersonalized figures of Chinese laborers, *Exilée* even more subtly establishes a diasporic context in its title, which is the French noun for a woman *exile*. An abiding figure in Cha's oeuvre, the condition of the exile is that of linguistic and cultural displacement, one that occupies what Elaine Kim describes as an "in-between space" or as Cha herself describes in *DICTEE*: "Tertium Quid neither

FIGURE 7. Theresa Hak Kyung Cha: *Exilée* (detail), 1980; film/video installation: black-and-white, sound, 50 min. (approx.); courtesy of University of California, Berkeley Art Museum and Pacific Film Archive; gift of the Theresa Hak Kyung Cha Memorial Foundation. 1992.4.213.6.

one thing nor the other."[47] Cha's invocation of *tertium quid*, or third thing, suggests another association for this marginalized social position—concrete physicality. At two points in *DICTEE*, this concretization of the exile's position becomes quite literal: (1) in the frontispiece, a photocopied photograph of some words that were presumably etched into stone in Korean by an exiled Korean worker outside a Japanese coal mine (they translate as: "Mother, I miss you; I am hungry; I want to go home"), and (2) a photograph of a handprint, which Josephine Park describes as "the hand of the exile, a bodily print," on a stone surface that closes the ELITERE/LYRIC POETRY section of the book.

Exilée plays on this trope, manifesting the exile as a physical thing, into which the figure herself disappears and is rendered material as a mere trace. The two modes of projections in the piece (film and video) are thus accompanied by a more metaphoric, Freudian instance, in which the psychological anxieties of the exile become projected onto material things. One of the more striking elements of the piece is a series of filmed pages with words fading in and fading out upon them, sometimes accompanied by a voice reading them aloud and sometimes without. If *Earth* imagines the page as a film screen, then *Exilée* reverses these polarities by transforming the film screen into a page. This disorientation of media then functions as an occasion to explore the condition of the female exile, which becomes manifested in physical forms as it is in *DICTEE*. In this case, the unsettled, homeless position of the exile is recast as an uncertainty about which media the audience is witnessing and about which surface should be the primary focus: screen, monitor, or page. Here, media disturbs form; what does it mean to film a poem? Does it remain a poem? How does the surface of the film screen complicate the surface of the page with which it coincides? Do words become images or mere marks? Furthermore, the filmed word images themselves connect the condition of exile with the fleeting presence of these words on the page, which become increasingly blurry, faint, and illegible as the video proceeds. At two points in the video, a poemlike block of words fades in and out, each time in parenthesis and, the second time, barely visible, as if to translate the marginalizing effect of the parenthetical into visual terms:

> (repeated as an invocation
> of that one thing
> that only thing
> the only thing and
> the one place)

Despite the insistence on the singular thing that derives from the repetition in this passage/clip, the video offers no antecedent, grammatical or otherwise, that clarifies what "that one thing / that only thing" might be. The word *thing* invokes not only materiality but also the inchoate quality of the material, as if it were imminently locatable or recognizable (I will know it when I see it), but it is difficult to describe or characterize. Nevertheless, the link between this mysterious *thing* and the coterminous *one place* subtly suggests an intimate connection between the condition of this specifically female exile and the material thing. The movement between the adjectives *one* and *only* buttresses this connection by modifying the mute nouns with a sense of singularity and solitude. As a self-reflexive statement about the installation piece itself, the would-be poem expresses the impossible wish of the exile, for the one place as a material wish, for that one thing through a multiple-media installation that paradoxically calls into question the very possibility of singularity.

Crucially, this parenthetically expressed, would-be poem is presented on screen as if in the process of vanishing. What is specifically represented by these word images is not exactly the desire of the exile but rather its disappearance. The point then is not to recover these wishes in an act of empathy or to attribute subjectivity to the unnamed exiled figure; it is to experience these wishes as becoming less accessible and more distant—to witness their vanishing just as the viewer sees the words slowly fade off the screen. In other words, central to the project of *Exilée* is to imagine the confusion and disorientation before the art object as a correlate reaction to and also of the exiled figure, which becomes more distant and whose objecthood remains sealed, as if one were meant increasingly to regard the *ineligible* (the exile) in the same terms that one understands the *illegible* (the word).[48] As if to overlay the logic of Fanon with the logic of Fried, Cha's piece expresses the ineligibility of the exile as the illegibility of the word, both of which the threat of materiality occasions. To experience the words as illegible and the page/screen as blank thus becomes tantamount to sanctioning the marginalization and erasure of the exile. Similarly, instead of granting the objectified Asian American a subjectivity, this blending of media in *Earth* instead illuminates the operations of the objectifying gaze. What we witness is the process through which human subjects disappear when understood as things (the same process by which words become things). The eligibility of the exile becomes indistinguishable from the illegibility of the exile's vanishing desires. Similarly, the potential Asian American subject whose objecthood the text earlier documents becomes repeated and reified by the privileging of textual materiality. In both cases, the objecthood of the would-be subject is doubled by the emerging materiality of the text itself. Both *Earth* and *Exilée* render media ambiguous, specifically film and book, and figure social marginality as a strange thingness. Both texts deploy their thingness not exactly in order to make visible that which would otherwise vanish (the subjectivity of marginalized figures) but rather as a means to expose the forces complicit in this disappearance.

More than reimagining reading a book as viewing a movie, *Earth* foregrounds a particular material element of film: the flicker. The flickers of light that capture Vernet's eye are primarily diegetic and come within the narrative frame of the film—from the flash of a car's headlights that a character drives, for example. They are plainly visible, and their illumination is obvious, shedding light on the entire interior space of the movie theater, the room itself along with the projector screen and audience. *Earth* indeed disorients by casting the filmic apparatus into view, but its focus, I would argue, is even more specific. Apart from Vernet's usage, flickering refers also to the fluctuating, stroboscopic effect on the screen often seen in old movies, which is the result of a problem in the film's projection or photography. These extradiegetic flashes of light and distortions of image that result not from features within the film but from its mechanical apparatus remind us of what the technology asks us to forget: These are actually a sequence of still images that the rapid-fire of the projector's shutter tricks us into seeing as moving images.[49] Like Vernet's diegetic spot of light, the flicker breaks the illusion of the cinema, but it does so in a subtler, less dramatic manner. Something seems wrong, but the flicker happens so quickly that the audience immediately regains comfort with the narrative frame. The integrity of the image is momentarily, and lightly, disturbed, but the audience—invested in the coherency of the moving image—is complicit with the projector's shutter, which covers over such imperfections. As in Vernet's account, these flickering flashes of light also call attention to the audience, but because they are so quick, this self-reflection is much more private and individual. Blink and you will miss it. Wonder if anyone else saw that? This kind of flickering also reveals the apparatus by calling attention not only to the physical apparatus of cinema but also to the forces that oppose these dynamics, that is, the audience's reluctance to depart from the illusory space of the cinema and willingness to ignore the fact of apparatus in a manner similar to how Fried described the construction of imperialistic innocence in private, subjective terms.

Cha's films have experimented with intentional flickering, but more relevant at present is her representation of flickering in a literary context, specifically in the second half of *Earth*, which attempts to replicate this visual effect or at least represent it in linguistic form. All of the printed words in *Earth* appear on the recto side of the spread, and none appear on the verso. This fact seems unremarkable until the pages themselves, as I have suggested, seem increasingly governed by a filmic logic, at which point the book as a whole comes to feel like a large version of an old-time flip book. Arguably a forerunner of film, the flip book provides a physical analog for how the technology of film creates the illusion of movement out of still images. Furthermore, there are pages on which the words are made to seem as if they were flickering, as if they were visually unstable and shaking (fig. 8). In some cases, this effect is produced by eliminating the space between the lines and overlapping the lines so legibility becomes difficult; elsewhere, words are scattered in streams across the page, as if the projector were momentarily askew. Appropriately, the diction in these cases also becomes more agitated, registering a filmic effect through the use of repeated jarring fragments, and words collide into one another and form incoherent amalgamations such as "beyondaboveground" and "writewritewrithe." In all of these cases, though, the moment one turns the page, the image becomes restabilized and the irritation dissipates.

On one hand, as an art object, *Earth* invites the viewer to experience itself as a foreign thing, critiquing the dynamics of racial objectification—Fanon's crushing objecthood—by calling attention to its own material strangeness, its thingness, as a literal manifestation of racialized figures. On the other hand, it suffuses the experience of foreignness with the compulsion to mis-see and remain within the confines of the comforting illusion. Although flickering calls attention to the fissures of the medium that reveal its illusory machinations, it also implies how the illusion requires the viewer's complicity with its artifice. *Earth* thus examines racial objecthood not only by calling attention to its own disconcerting materiality but also by foregrounding how resistant the objectifying eye can be to corrective revelation, calling attention to a powerful compulsion not to see. Whiteness in Cha's work is never unproblematically blank, just as the artistic medium is never a passive carrier to the more prominent content. In other words, blankness becomes a figure of blindness. In contrast to the deployment of blankness in Fried's account of Conrad, which authorized imperialist practices yet spared the young men engaged in them the guilt that they should feel over such violent aggression, whiteness here calls attention to and resists its own potential for producing ameliorating fictions. The compulsion to remain within the illusion, both of imperialism and of cinema, involves a powerful desire not to see.

Blinded by the Light, Seeing in the Dark

There is a moment at the end of Roman Polanski's *The Ninth Gate* (1999) that resonates powerfully both with Vernet's spots of light and with Cha's confusions of book and film. Based on *The Club Dumas* (1993), a novel by Arturo Pérez-Reverte that takes a keen interest in the history of the book as a material object, Polanski's film adaptation, like *Earth*, blurs the boundary between literary and cinematic text and makes the materiality of the film apparatus a central concern. The plot centers on Dean Corso, a rare books dealer hired to authenticate a copy of *The Nine Gates of the Kingdom of Shadows*, a book purported to have been written by the devil, on behalf of a client who seeks to harness the book's supernatural powers. Despite the literary underpinnings of the film, Corso is more coarse capitalist than a man of letters, and he treats books very much as objects and, more specifically, as commodities. Corso's investigations focus on the engravings in the book, which supposedly contain its secret.

At the very end of the film, Corso finally locates the site that inspired the final engraving, an illustration of the crumbling fortress called The Devil's Tower, which had just been the scene of the film's fairly silly climax. Just to the right of the fortress's keep, the illustration depicts a brilliant light. He holds the illustration up for the camera to close in upon, and this shot of the black-and-white engraving then bleeds directly into a full-color shot of the actual fortress in the south of France that replicates the illustration in every detail, including the brilliant spot of light. In the film's final moments just after this bleed, Corso unceremoniously walks toward the castle and into the brilliant light, which now comes from the opening gates of the fortress and eventually bathes the entire screen with a blinding white light. This final sequence is shot to suggest that, in walking through the ninth gate, he is walking directly into an image from the book and into a mirrored image of the projected light at the back of the room, as if he were walking into the apparatus of the film. Furthermore, in a moment that calls attention to the materiality of the medium, the white light that is seemingly emitted from the screen also lights up the space of the theater and provokes precisely the same effect described by Vernet. At the culmination of the film (one which might be understood as participating in the generic expectations of detective/mystery/thriller films that always end

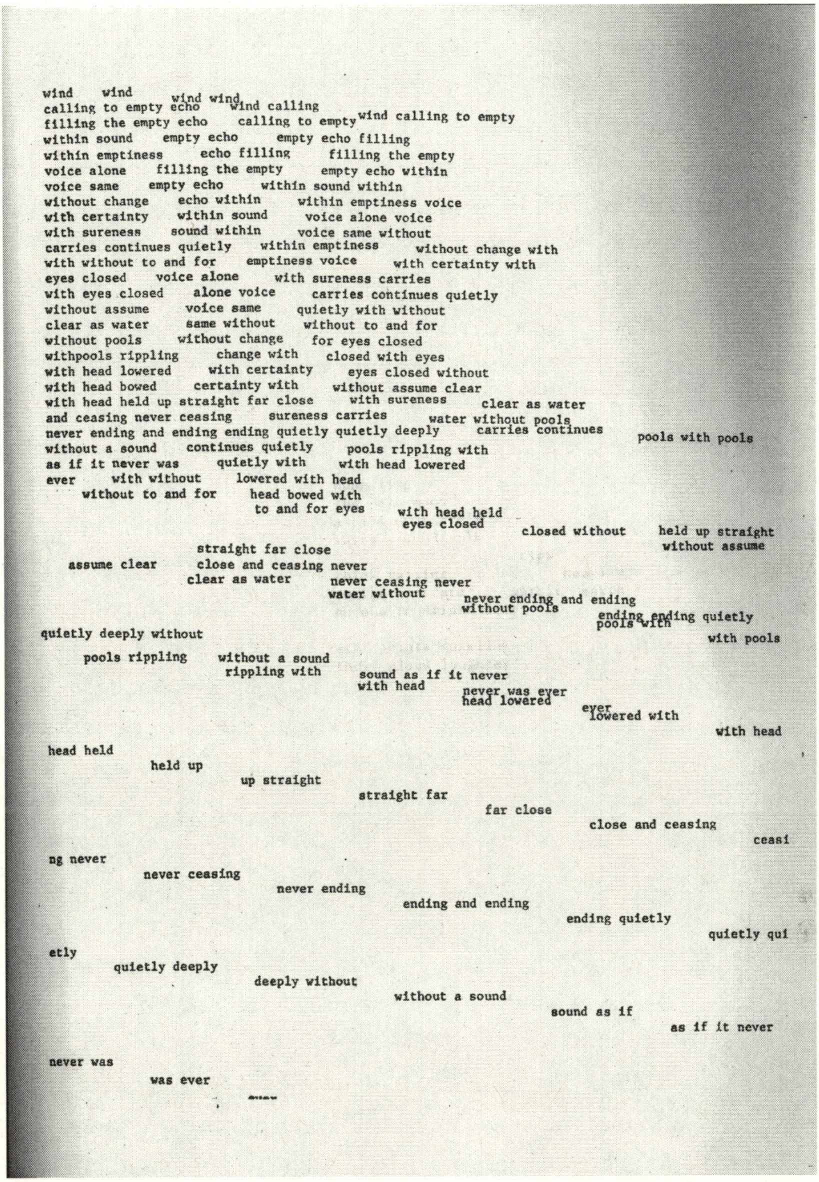

wind wind wind wind
calling to empty echo wind calling
filling the empty echo calling to empty wind calling to empty
within sound empty echo empty echo filling
within emptiness echo filling filling the empty
voice alone filling the empty empty echo within
voice same empty echo within sound within
without change echo within within emptiness voice
with certainty within sound voice alone voice
with sureness sound within voice same without
carries continues quietly within emptiness without change with
with without to and for emptiness voice with certainty with
eyes closed voice alone with sureness carries
with eyes closed alone voice carries continues quietly
without assume voice same quietly with without
clear as water same without without to and for
without pools without change for eyes closed
withpools rippling change with closed with eyes
with head lowered with certainty eyes closed without
with head bowed certainty with without assume clear
with head held up straight far close with sureness clear as water
and ceasing never ceasing sureness carries water without pools
never ending and ending ending quietly quietly deeply carries continues pools with pools
without a sound continues quietly pools rippling with
as if it never was quietly with with head lowered
ever with without lowered with head
without to and for head bowed with
to and for eyes with head held
eyes closed closed without held up straight
without assume
straight far close
assume clear close and ceasing never
clear as water never ceasing never
water without never ending and ending
without pools ending ending quietly
pools with
quietly deeply without with pools
pools rippling without a sound
rippling with sound as if it never
with head never was ever
head lowered ever
lowered with
with head
head held
held up
up straight
straight far
far close
close and ceasing
ceasi
ng never
never ceasing
never ending
ending and ending
ending quietly
quietly qui
etly
quietly deeply
deeply without
without a sound
sound as if
as if it never
never was
was ever
ever

FIGURE 8. Theresa Hak Kyung Cha: *Earth* (detail), 1976; artist's book; 11 × 8-1/2 in.; courtesy of University of California, Berkeley Art Museum and Pacific Film Archive; gift of the Theresa Hak Kyung Cha Memorial Foundation. 1992.4.137.45, 61.

with a revelation), that which is revealed is not the face of the devil, the supposed author of the text in the film, but the material apparatus of film itself. The white screen illuminates the room, and the viewer's gaze is diverted from the illusory space of the screen to the physical space of the room.

When I watched this film in 1999 in a mostly empty theater, I happened to be sitting near the back of the room underneath the projector, and the whiteness of the screen immediately produced the effect Vernet describes, drawing my gaze from the screen to the apparatus of the film in general (the projection, audience, and so on). If I had to quantify what I saw, I would say I saw more, not less, including the exasperated looks of viewers turning their befuddled faces at one another. This self-conscious turn to the materiality of the medium itself, even in a film that is obsessed with precisely this issue, felt like a betrayal of the audience's suspension of disbelief rather than a clever commentary on the very notion of revelation. The brilliant white light at the end of the film seemed more like an interruption to the act of looking, despite the fact that precisely what it allows for is increased visibility. A something experienced as a nothing: The whiteness of the screen functions as a kind of blankness, despite its ancillary effect, illuminating all the people and objects in the room. The reason visibility is associated with blindness here is not because the light itself is blinding; quite the contrary. It is because the light expels the viewer from the illusions of the cinema. The disappointment here is that revelation is not all that revealing of information, that illumination is not illuminating. What we want of the cinema at the moment of revelation is to remain within the fiction and ignorant of apparatus. Instead, in a nearly literal staging of Friedian theatricality in which the viewer is presented with the blunt fact of the theater itself, we experience the objecthood of the apparatus, and the medium becomes a thing.

In his disappointed review of *The Ninth Gate*, Roger Ebert sums up his frustrations with the film, complaining that "a film of such big themes should be about more than the fate of a few people; while at the end I didn't yearn for spectacular special effects, I did wish for spectacular information—something awesome, not just a fade to white."[50] In contrast to the ambitious themes of the film, the "fade to white," for Ebert, functions as a kind of nonevent, which fails as a matter of scale; it is not big enough for the film's big themes or relevant enough for the many people who care about such themes.

Rather than revelation, what we get is a kind of mute response. More than merely disappointing, the ending constitutes an outright refusal to offer any sort of ending at all. For Ebert, this nonending ending does not qualify as awesome because the fact of cinema's power disappoints as a supernatural force. In contrast to the big themes with which the film tantalizes its audience, the final revelation is nothing more or less than the literal revelation of the room—a sort of premature turning on of the house lights after the credits—which is understood in direct opposition to the spectacular (a word he uses twice). The spectacle absent from the screen is supplanted by a broader field of vision (the illuminated room), that is in turn understood ironically as unspectacular.

If an odd consequence to the casting of brilliant light at the end of *The Ninth Gate* is a failure of exposure, then the strangeness in Fanon is the ability to see in the dark. Fanon also goes to the movies, but he finds it impossible to lose himself in the cinematic illusion.

> The Negro is a toy in the white man's hands; so, in order to shatter the hellish cycle, he explodes. I cannot go to a film without seeing myself. I wait for me. In the interval, just before the film starts, I wait for me. The people in the theater are watching me, examining me, waiting for me. A Negro groom is going to appear. My heart makes my head swim.[51]

Reminiscent of the Invisible Man's rants in Ralph Ellison's novel (published the same year as *Black Skin, White Masks*), the paranoid tone of the passage above makes it difficult to figure out what exactly is happening. It is unclear whether Fanon is talking about what he sees on the screen, that is, the representation of black characters within the film; what is happening in the space of the theater, that people are looking at him; or if others see him metaphorically in the darkness of the room itself. Clearly, however, there is plenty of seeing going on in the dark interval before the film begins. In opposition to the theater where Ebert viewed *The Ninth Gate*, in which the bright light of the ending signified a failure of vision, Fanon's presence here is abundantly visible. Despite or perhaps because of the darkness, his visibility is already predetermined by forces outside his control. Unlike the audience in Vernet, who requires the bright light of the screen to expose the room, Fanon cannot escape the overdetermined, dark room to enter the illusion of the cinematic space, which seems to suffer from the same problems as his immediate world.

Despite the darkness of the room (and indeed because of it), blackness becomes hypervisible, whereas the materiality of the filmic medium remains invisible. The filmic apparatus thus seems a part of the larger cultural apparatus that sanctions and perpetuates racist objectification.

Whiteness, of the screen and page, in the language art of Theresa Hak Kyung Cha is never a space of absence, as Ebert imagines it to be in Polanski. Her insistence on the materiality of the medium implies a critique of willed blindness that is justified by fictions of blankness and combats the darkness of the room in Fanon's theater visit description. The two cinema scenes above seem opposed. In the first, a brilliant light illuminates the room, and everything becomes visible. In the second, the darkness of the room where literal sight is impossible ironically allows for projections of imagined sight, one even literalized on the screen. In both cases, however, there remains a discord between the act of seeing and the object of vision. In the first, that which is literally visible, the cinema, instead counts as nothing. In the second, the all-too-visible something, blackness in its myriad forms, is literally invisible. In both cases, seeing depends not on the apprehension of visual objects but on the confirmation of something already expected or anticipated. Following Cha's implicit logic, these expectations, which are built on a priori conceptions, feelings, and beliefs, confirm that a white screen or a white page is never quite blank. Rather than a space to be marked, whiteness is itself a mark. Cha thus uses the apparatus of the artistic medium and, more specifically, its thingness—as insistent as it is befuddling—as a means to demonstrate the operations of the kind of larger cultural machinery that Fanon elaborates with so much care and pain.

CHAPTER TWO

SPEAKING IN TONGUES

Myung Mi Kim's Poetics of Mouth

Defamiliarized from a bodily function that is otherwise taken for granted, a mouth that struggles with language might indeed feel severed from the organic unity of the body as it does for Myung Mi Kim in the first quotation below, as though it were a prosthetic, somehow artificial and alien. In this scenario, signification fails before it even begins, and the physicality of a tongue-tied mouth comes to embody the signifier's materiality, the recognition of which, for Paul de Man in the second quotation, dismembers language.

> No "th," "th," put your tongue against the roof of your mouth,
> lean slightly against the back of the top teeth, then bring your
> bottom teeth up to barely touch your tongue and breathe out, and
> you should feel the tongue vibrating, "th," "th," look in the mirror,
> that's better.[1]

> We must, in short consider our limbs, hands, toes, breasts . . . in themselves, severed from the organic unity of the body, the way the poets look at the oceans severed from their geographic place on earth. . . . We must consider our limbs the way the primitive man considered the house, entirely severed from any purpose or use. . . . To the dismemberment of the body corresponds a dismemberment of language, as meaning-producing tropes are replaced by the fragmentation of sentences and propositions into discrete words, or the fragmentation of words into syllables or finally letters.[2]

The avant-garde defamiliarizing gesture thus shares with deconstruction an exacting attention to the pressure points at which the organic wholeness of language devolves into unintelligible fragments, just like the poem in Cha's *Surplus Novel*. Myung Mi Kim's poem stages the physics of such dissolution. Appearing halfway through a poem that addresses immigrant citizenship and naturalization in her first volume, *Under Flag* (1991), the passage above describes the learning of language as if the act of speaking English were completely foreign to the student's body. Focused on physical mechanics, this student quite literally has nothing to say and is instead relegated to the task of making sounds. By contrast, the articulate voice here is that of the instructor, whose authority is announced by her use of imperative verbs that regulate bodily movements (lean, touch, breathe), yet the student's uncooperative mouth remains silent and unheard. Beginning in this passage with an injunction and ending with an approval, the teacher corrects not just an error in speech but also, more specifically, a physical mistake, and the more speech becomes bodily, the more language, as de Man terms it, becomes dismembered, leaving the mouth an inert object, severed from any organic context in which it becomes intelligible.

The instructor's last imperative statement, "look in the mirror," is particularly significant because it calls attention to the visuality of spoken language, imagining speech that is fragmented into the various shapes of the mouth that labors to produce the required sounds; in similar terms, de Man understands the gradual fragmentation of words into syllables and then letters.[3] Using a mirror to draw speech into the realm of the visual, the instruction in this passage reads like physical therapy in which the injured subject rehearses a series of movements intended to help repair a damaged body part. As such, the sound of speech gives way to the basic choreography of tongue and teeth within the cavity of the mouth. A native Korean speaker tends to have difficulty with the English /th/ sounds, in addition to a handful of other sounds, because there is no exact corresponding sound in Korean. This speaker thus tends to replace the /th/ sound with a /d/ or /t/ sound. "He is thirty," for example, may unfortunately sound like "He is dirty." In the first passage above, Kim calls attention to the physical aspects of language acquisition. More than learning syntax, diction, and vocabulary, the student must learn to orchestrate the tongue, lips, throat, and teeth in order to produce those sounds at all.

What comes naturally in one's native language may become quite awkward in another. Denied access to interiority or subjectivity, one might read the student's mouth as what Marjorie Perloff, in her account of language poetry, terms a "found object," which works "to deconstruct the possibility of the formation of a coherent or consistent lyrical voice."[4] In this tradition of language poetics, Kim devalues lyric identity by reimagining individual voice, a central characteristic of both lyric poetry and identity politics, as the physical operations of the mouth with a material emphasis (in the de Manian sense) that sputters incoherencies rather than producing identifiable representations.

That the mouth in Kim's poetry belongs specifically to a native speaker of Korean makes all the attention even more important because of the visual connection of mouth and script in Han'gŭl (fig. 9). Internalized into this written language are the mechanics of speech in visual terms. The written consonants of this alphabet, for example, correspond to the shape of the mouth as it produces the sound of each letter; the consonants can be divided into categories based on the part of the mouth each emphasizes: labial, lingual, dental, molar, and glottal. In addition, within each group of consonants, as the sound becomes harder, the script of the letter becomes correspondingly more complex. A visual awareness of the mouth is thus inscribed in the Han'gŭl alphabet; letters quite literally represent the mouth's shape. In her video piece *Mouth to Mouth* (1975), Cha makes a similar point. Eight minutes long, the entire video is a close-up shot of a mouth that repeats the eight Han'gŭl vowel sounds. Though the graphic marks for vowels in Han'gŭl correspond not to the shape of the mouth but instead to representations of the relationship between humans and the sun and earth (represented as an interplay of vertical lines, which represent humans, to horizontal lines, which represent the earth, and circles, which represent the sun), Cha's piece, like Kim's poetics, dilates on the physical aspects of speech and offers a visual focal point for speech (the mouth on the screen) that supplements writing. Kim, in her poetry, transfers this awareness into her dealings with English, her second language. Kim's point, however, is not to hold up Han'gŭl as a counterexample of linguistic transcendence; rather, it is to preserve in language a sense of the mouths of nonnative speakers, with all of their awkwardness, in both physical and visual terms. Often used to racialize Asian immigrants (as in the tradition of Hollywood yellow-face performances), the foreign accent of these unaccommo-

THE LETTERFORMS OF HAN'GŬL CONSONANTS

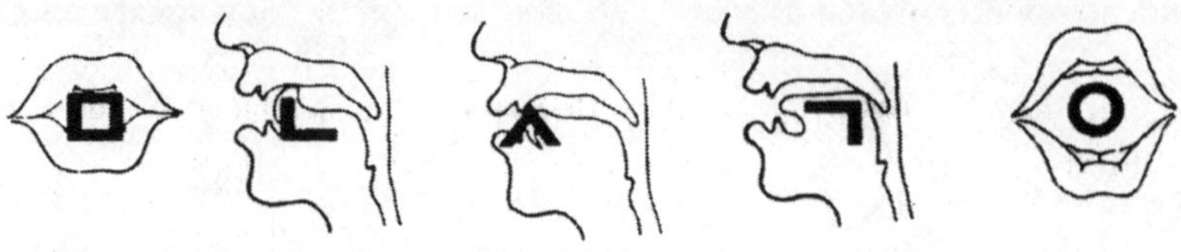

Labial (Bilabial)	ㅁ	ㅂ	ㅍ	ㅃ	
Lingual (Apical)	ㄴ	ㄷ	ㅌ	ㄸ	
Dental (Sibilant)	ㅅ	ㅈ	ㅊ	ㅆ	ㅉ
Molar (Dorsal/Velar)	ㆁ	ㄱ	ㅋ	ㄲ	
Glottal (Laryngeal)	ㅇ	ㆆ	ㅎ	ㆅ	

FIGURE 9. Han'gŭl letterforms. © 1997 University of Hawai'i Press. Reprinted with permission. Courtesy of University of Hawai'i Press.

dating mouths thus becomes a kind a physical mark and racializes the immigrant in bodily terms. Resonating with contemporary debates about bilingual education and English as a Second Language, Kim's use of mouths implicitly considers how the foreignness of an accent contributes to racialization and how differences in speech reverberate in the body-focused discourse of race.[5]

In foregrounding the physics of these nonnative mouths, Kim mines the previously articulated deconstructive possibilities and authorizes a reading of her poetics as resistant to the hegemonic assimilative forces that demand conformity in fundamental everyday activities, such as speech. Nevertheless, deconstructive refusal tells only half of the story for Kim, for whom synthetic gestures are equally important as refusals, if not more so. Although the lyric voice in this passage suffers the same ignominious fate as language, the mouth becomes neither an organ of subjective voice nor a figure of abject materiality; instead, it becomes a thing, newly unwieldy and divorced from its typical speech function and, as such, revealing of the discursive context in which it functions. For Kim, its function extends beyond the frustration of coherences. The mouth as thing not only comes to figure in bodily terms that which is inassimilable but also models alternative strategies for engaging what might be regarded as foreign entities. Although mouths abound in Kim's poems, her focus is not on speech per se but rather on the physical mechanics of speech for a nonnative speaker of English. With this emphasis, Kim recalibrates a politics of voice, usually associated with representation and expressions of subjective interiority, into a poetics of the mouth that both rejects hegemonic modes of linguistic conscription and constructs alternative coherencies out of the leftover, dismembered things. Instead of learning to speak a static language, Kim explores how languages might be changed and made more dynamic by failures or refusals to speak properly and by the revitalizing energies that nonnative speakers bring from their first languages.

Kim's poetics of the mouth is also a politics. In the quote at the beginning of this chapter, it is the body that must be disciplined in order to receive praise from the instructor, whose injunction ("no") doubles the broader denial of citizenship and the attribution of alien, nonnative status that the poem thematizes. In this poetic treatment of the process, through which one attains U.S. citizenship, naturalization demands learning the native language along with its proper pronunciation, which this passage suggests is as much physical as it is aural. The disciplining of the immigrant subject, it seems, requires a disciplined body, and the language instructor effectively functions as a kind of gatekeeper whose encouragement ("that's better") puts the student on the path toward correct speech and on his or her way to satisfying the strangely bodily demands of assimilation.

Though it does not require a scalpel, the disciplining of the mouth in this poem is invasive to the body of the racialized other in a manner similar to the plastic surgeries of D. R. Millard, as described by David Palumbo-Liu. An army surgeon sent to repair bodies damaged during the Korean War, Millard became interested in the benefits of cosmetic surgery on the eyelids of his patients. Publishing his findings in a 1955 essay entitled "Oriental Peregrinations," Millard believed that the surgeries could actually aid the improvement of East–West relations by making Asian eyes look more Western. Palumbo-Liu cites a particularly illustrative case in which Millard performed a surgery on a "slant-eyed Korean interpreter" who wanted "to be made into a 'round-eye'" because the Americans for whom he was translating did not trust him.[6] Millard's surgery is an unequivocal success, and he reports that, afterward, the patient is mistaken for Mexican or Italian, becomes a Christian, and hopes to go to the United States for religious training. Palumbo-Liu notes how the reinscription of the othered body allows a less superficial transformation, effecting a psychic and not just somatic shift:

> And with any appearance of untrustworthiness erased, the soul itself is adequately westernized and rectified, and a new "person" emerges. One notes how the interpreter is not transformed into an "American"—that would be too immodest and impossible a task. Rather, he is situated in the terrain of a positive indecideability, a flexible, albeit still ethnic, identity, that benefits from its potential confusion with other, presumably more "assimilable" ethnic types still in that liminal space of pre-Americanization, yet closer than the racially marked Oriental.[7]

That the patient is a translator is a crucial fact, because the transformative surgery performed on the body doubles the larger work of intercultural bridging. Concerned not just about the accuracy of his translations but also about his own trustworthiness, the patient feels that he must overcome linguistic and racial differences in order to perform as an interpreter. The interpreter's good will toward his American associates becomes acceptable—indeed, legible—only after it is confirmed by a bodily alteration. The physical transformation, itself an extension of translation, functions as a transubstantiation of an Oriental body into an American subject. Crucially, it is the bodily transformation, as in Kim's "Into Such Assembly," that precedes and prefigures the psychic operations of assimilation. The one case demands round eyes; the other demands a disciplined mouth. In both cases, though, linguistic difference becomes deeply imbricated with racial difference. Language becomes a bodily matter. As Palumbo-Liu articulates, "Assimilation, then, was both a psychic *and* a somatic phenomenon, the latter now presenting in concrete form the actuality of Americanization (and, conversely, if certain bodies *won't* change, or do so only recalcitrantly, then it is taken as an index to their resistance or inability to assimilate)."[8]

With this emphasis on the physicality of mouths, Kim's poetry attempts to dramatize not how an immigrant speaker learns to speak a new language but how the languages themselves learn to speak each other as a rejoinder to the kind of somatic assimilative demands that Palumbo-Liu describes. Although Kim's concern is not exactly translation, her poetics takes up the task of the translator, as famously conceived by Walter Benjamin. Benjamin resists the conception of translation as an act of transcription, which seeks to reproduce the equivalent of the original in another language. Rather, translation aspires to find a kinship between languages, and the transaction between them is mutually transformative. Accordingly, Benjamin's descriptions of languages are filled with anthropomorphisms:

> Translation thus ultimately serves the purpose of expressing the central reciprocal relationship between languages. It cannot possibly reveal or establish this hidden relationship itself; but it can represent it by realizing it in embryonic or intensive form. . . . As for the posited central kinship of languages, it is marked by a distinctive convergence. Languages are not strangers to one another, but are *a priori* and apart from all historical relationships, interrelated in what they want to express. . . . The kinship of languages is brought out by a translation far more profoundly and clearly than in the superficial and indefinable similarity of two works of literature. . . . [In translation's] afterlife—which could not be called that if it were not a transformation and a renewal of something living—the original undergoes a change. Even words with fixed meaning can undergo a maturing process. . . . Translation is so far removed from being the sterile equation of two dead languages that of all literary forms it is the one charged with the special mission of watching over the maturing process of the original language and the birth pangs of its own.[9]

This passage describes languages as if they were living beings capable of growing and maturing, and the mention of "birth pangs" momentarily offers the faint suggestion that they have bodies as well. Accordingly for Benjamin, translation seeks not only accuracy but also, more importantly, kinships between and among languages, as if it involved the search for familial connections among strangers. The stakes of this search resonate powerfully with Kim's poetics. Toward the end of the essay, Benjamin quotes Rudolf Pannwitz, who critiques the practice of translation in Germany:

> Our translations, even the best ones, proceed from a wrong premise. They want to turn Hindi, Greek, English into German instead of turning German into Hindi, Greek, English. Our translators have a far greater reverence for the usage of their own language than for the spirit of the foreign works. . . . The basic error of the translator is that he preserves the state in which his own language happens to be instead of allowing his language to be powerfully affected by the foreign tongue. Particularly when translating from a language very remote from his own he must go back to the primal elements of language itself and penetrate to the point where work, image, and tone converge. He must expand and deepen his language by means of the foreign language.[10]

The challenge of translation for both Benjamin and Pannwitz is the ability to embrace a larger challenge of the foreign, and this eager acceptance of difference—though Benjamin is not explicit on this point—implies a broader cultural openness.[11] Certainly, German anti-Semitism and xenophobia inform the critique of German translation here, which subtends a critique of a cultural unwillingness to incorporate the foreign. Kim's poetry aspires to locate this sort of kinship—not only of languages but also of mouths—and uses this linguistic convergence of would-be strangers, of languages, as a means to think about the social integration of strangers in another sense: immigrants. As in Benjamin, this integration occurs in a mutually transformative encounter between languages. As opposed to the logic of bodily transformation in Millard, which doubles a broader assimilative logic that subordinates one kind of body to another as well as one kind of language to another, Kim's poetics, like Benjamin's model of translation, utilizes instead of suppresses the otherwise strange thingness of the mouth. Not simply an inassimilable entity, the mouth as a thing sketches out the terrain for a new interlinguistic kinship, transforming a would-be racial mark into a figure of connection that reveals relational energies.[12]

Kim's "And Sing We" is about immigration and assimilation; it is about how immigrants might overcome the challenges of a new place and culture and how their voices might be included in the national collective subject position (*we*). It confronts the familiar themes of immigrant literature—loss, dislocation, and displacement—and, in particular, it engages what critics such as Patricia Chu foreground as a primary ideological task of Asian American literature: "to resolve the contradictions of being Asian American in a country that has historically construed the terms *Asian* and *American* as mutually exclusive."[13] This transformational exercise becomes reimagined in "And Sing We" as a poetic task that deals less with foreign and native identities and more with foreign and native languages, less with immigrant subjectivity and more with their tongues (both figuratively and literally). Though the emphasis shifts from social to linguistic and from subjectivity to thingness, it remains engaged with the revisionist project that Chu describes. In Kim's poem, the marginal becomes fundamental; the mouth of the native Korean speaker, whose awkwardness in English functions as a bodily mark of racial difference, becomes the basis for the work of bridging that the poem undertakes. If Cha's work calls attention to the dynamics of racial objectification, then Kim's work combats these dynamics and incorporates inassimilable, foreign things into the category of the native—not through nationalistic assimilative strategies nor through corporeal reinscription but by reconfiguring the discursive categories of naturalization that separate alien from citizen and foreign from native.[14] Kim attempts to reconcile otherness by reconciling the foreignness of these mouths that stumble so awkwardly through a nonnative language. Whereas Cha's material concerns foreground the ideological implications of racialization, Kim's interest in physical mouths reworks abject materiality into a suturing figure that offers an alternative to the instructor's offer of assimilation ("that's better"). Her poetics insists on a bodily thingness that subsumes lyric identity by refiguring voice as a physical rather than subjective operation. By supplanting identity with language, Kim's poetics takes on the task of bridging and resolving the historically conflicted categories of Asian and American by attempting to reimagine English as if it were Han'gŭl and Han'gŭl as if it were English.[15]

Voicing the Mouth

Appropriately, "And Sing We" in its very title foregrounds the conjunction *and* as a figure of connection, which reflects the poem's interest in acts of bridging that redress dislocation. In its opening lines, the poem addresses this problem by foregrounding gaps and lacunae of various kinds, both literal and figurative. The immigrant's emotional dislocation is in turn doubled by some of the poem's stylistic features:

> Must it ring so true
> So we must sing it
>
> To span even yawning distance
> And would we be near then
>
> What would the sea be, if we were near it[16]

The opening, unrhymed couplet divides ten monosyllabic words evenly between two lines. The first seems to be more of a question, whereas the latter is an imperative statement, but both use the same word, *must*, in lines that produce opposite effects: doubt and urgency. The couplet suggests but falls short of asserting a causal relationship, as in "In order for it to ring so true, we must sing it." Instead, the lines seem simultaneously to be part of the same thought and the product of conflict, equally divided (like the syllable count) between question and answer. Invoking the physicality of the mouth as a mark of difference, the second couplet names this disparity a "yawning distance" and ushers in talk of spanning and nearness that might close such a gap. As in the first couplet, each of the two sentence fragments here sits in an uncomfortable relationship to the other. The first of the two lines seems to complete the thought begun in the second line of the first couplet, as in "We must sing it in order to span even yawning distance," but these lines are of course separated on the page by a gap. Finally, the last line of this opening section repeats the oscillation between doubt and certainty from the opening couplet: "What would the sea be, if we were near it." Like the opening couplet, this line also divides ten monosyllabic words equally between two clauses, though here they are not separated by a line break. The caesura forced by an oddly extraneous comma, however, divides the line into question and condition, calling attention to the metaphysical question of how one's position affects one's knowledge. Where one is located here becomes a condition of how or what one knows, and dislocation seems to trouble knowledge in general.

The task of Kim's poem becomes finding a way to bridge the gap that dislocation and displacement leave exposed. The key to this work of bridging in the poem has to do with speech. This process, however, begins not with a celebration of the voice's strength as a vehicle for communication but with a meditation on the way speech becomes reduced merely to the sound the mouth makes:

Voice

It catches its underside and drags it back
What sound do we make, "n," "h," "g"
Speak and it is sound in time[17]

In this passage, the voice is not a figure for representativeness. It does not signify a capacious Whitmanian subject speaking on behalf of a larger body; neither is it a representative Asian American or Korean American voice that seeks recognition. This voice scarcely seems to express the thoughts of an individual at all, and it seems rather to represent merely the sound of a mouth. Speech becomes reduced to "sound in time," and the physicality of the mouth echoes its function in "Into Such Assembly." "Voice" is marginal, but this seems more a typographical than political condition; placed at the literal margin of the page, it shies away from the burden of representing a minority group.[18] For example, the three consonant sounds in the third line (/n/, /h/, /g/) obliquely refer to the Korean word 나가 (*naka*), which is the imperative form of the verb *to leave*; it is also the word that angry Korean protestors have shouted for years at various unwelcome occupants (including the U.S. military): "Leave."[19] The presentation of the word as a series of consonant sounds, however, does not so much voice angry protest as it locates protest in the very operations of the mouth. The would-be representation of protestors becomes reduced to sound in time, and the efficacy of their political voices registers obliquely at best. Quite literally, it does not translate.

The second stanza locates these issues more explicitly within a historical context. Here, the poem offers fragments of a remembered past, which is initially remembered as violent:

Depletion replete with barraging

Slurred and taken over

Diaspora. "It is not the picture

That will save us."

All the fields fallow

The slide carousel's near burn-out and yet

Flash and one more picture of how we were to be[20]

From the larger context presented in *Under Flag*, one infers that the siege described in this stanza refers to the Korean War. War, however, functions less as the primary subject of the poem and more to contextualize the poem's earlier contemplation of language. The opening line, "Depletion replete with barraging," sutures the contradictory meanings of its first two words, which respectively suggest emptiness and abundance, into a familiar denouncement of the emptiness of excessive violence, of pointless barraging. The use of sound in this line is more remarkable. The delicate repetition of the *-eple-* sounds in the first half of the line collides into the echoes of the /r/ sounds in the second half. The former seem weightless, voiced in the front of the mouth, especially compared to the latter, which are heavier and voiced farther back in the cavity formed behind the raised tongue. The heavy /r/ sounds continue into the next line with the word *slurred*, which itself describes an act associated with the mouth. If the siege described in these lines concludes when the enemy has "taken over," then the result seems to be a compromised voice, slurred and indistinct, with its language forced into "diaspora." This dispersion, in turn, corresponds to the fallow fields and old slide-projected photographs that now signify loss and absence instead of the promise and potential that they might have once implied—pictures of "how we were to be." Even the anonymous voice of the curiously unattributed quotation in the middle of the stanza seems unconvinced of what, if not "the picture," offers hope.[21]

The next section of the poem tests memory, particularly nostalgia, as a strategy of bridging gaps between past and present. These fragmentary stanzas, voiced perhaps by the "fable(d) voices" that the poem names, take the form of comforting memories and the most pleasantly anesthetizing forms of nostalgia: invocations of food and childhood games. However, the final line of the fourth stanza, "Once we leave a place is it there," undermines this effect.[22]

Without punctuation to resolve the ambiguity between assertion and question, the line doubles this uncertainty with the word *there*. It might signify a faraway locale, thereby expressing sadness over the loss of a once familiar and now distant place. On the other hand, the line could also be read as an indulgence in a kind of playful Faulknerian ontology: When one leaves a place, it is no longer *here* but *there*.[23] In either case, nostalgia and memory prove to be faulty bridges. However fondly remembered, the past feels distant and remote, irrelevant to the challenges of dislocation and diaspora, and the failure of memory reflects a larger ambivalence in the poem to more subjective modes of facing these problems, which might describe them as personal experiences.

Instead, the poem turns specifically to the mouth. Even though "And Sing We" lacks any explicit discussion of physical mouths, it calls attention to their operations—first, by reducing speech to the status of mere sound; second, by orchestrating the sound of words in order to call attention to the way in which these sounds form a level of coherence that supplements the poem's semantic content. A nonnative speaker often thinks of a language along similar lines when he or she is first learning to speak it. One first learns how to make the sounds before learning what they mean, and one way of learning to say these sounds is by rehearsing and repeating different words that contain them. It is too much to say that this learning happens independent of the recognition of semantic content, but it is not too much to suggest that one thinks little of meaning when one repeats aloud the words *cat*, *color*, and *couch* in order to learn how to pronounce the sound of the hard *c*.

Much of Kim's earlier poetry, including *Under Flag*, attempts to politicize the sound of spoken language without necessarily relying on the content of this speech; it often does this by focusing on how a nonnative speaker of English might make the language his or her own. Kim's own intricately crafted poetry displays an intense intimacy with its idiom, well beyond the kind of proficiency sought by the awkward speakers of English presented in her poems. Although her poems often integrate prose fragments, they more typically offer complexly crafted abstractions filled with flights of sound in which words and phrases are rarefied objects, strange to behold in their uniquely imagined, phonetic complexities. This is evident in "Chart," which appears in Kim's third volume of poetry, *Dura* (1998):

Brittle afford
Nerve branch
Heir inculcate
Apparent corona
Muffled trace
Derelict summation
Jutting shaped
Baffle flung[24]

Kim offers a list of seemingly random, mismatched pairs that only hints at two underlying governing logics. On one hand, the unattributed list presents a series of perceptions that suggests a keen, observing mind. The eidetic imagery in lines such as "brittle afford," "nerve branch," and "muffled trace" flash the concerns of a sharp observer with a refined sense of detail. On the other hand, the passage intersperses these subtle descriptions with what seem nearly political abstractions. Lines such as "heir inculcate" and "derelict summation" stand apart from the world of perception and seem part of a larger, unnamed ideological critique. Although this excerpt is not devoid of semantic content, it leaves these themes provisional and unrealized. The fragmentary perceptions fail to define a given point of view, and as political abstractions, they fall short of making any intelligible ideological claims. Lacking any logic of organization in either of these two directions, the logic of the passage instead seems governed by a concern for how the words of each pair resonate phonetically with each other. Particularly prevalent in this sequence (and, as we shall see, not uncoincidentally) are the repeated /r/ sounds. Prosody and sound step center stage, but because of the poem's politicized (if unnamed) energies, their reverberations seem political in some inchoate sense.

Recombinant Mouths

One important context for Kim's preoccupation with the sound of words is her interest in the transliteration, or Romanization, of Han'gŭl into the English alphabet. For Kim, this interest is rooted in the nature of Han'gŭl itself. For example, "Primer" in *The Bounty* (1996), her second volume of poetry, begins:

1443

– to represent 14 single and 5 double consonants, Hangul starts with five basic symbols, which are shaped to suggest the articulators pronouncing them. For example, a small square depicts a closed mouth pronouncing /m/.

This is the study book.[25]

The date that begins the poem refers to the year that King Sejong is said to have invented the Korean alphabet.[26] The bulk of the poem consists of fourteen sections, which correspond to the fourteen single consonants in Han'gŭl. Each section is titled with one of the Han'gŭl consonants, and the corresponding English sound is presented in brackets. The poem thus imagines itself as a language primer and a definitive one at that ("*the* study book"). However, even though it is written in English, it is unclear which language it means to instruct.

This ambiguity opens the possibility of a metacritical function within the genre of language primers, and Kim's primers serve not as guides for potential speakers of English but as means of creating a Benjaminian encounter between languages—putting English and Han'gŭl into conversation with each other. This encounter pivots on the mouthing tendencies of native Korean speakers. The above passage also points out, as I discussed earlier, that the shape of the letters in Han'gŭl matches the shape of the mouth speaking it, and the poem proceeds to contemplate pronunciation in the form of a Han'gŭl language primer. For example, the section of the poem entitled "[r] [l]"—both of which are sounds that roughly correspond to the Han'gŭl letter ㄹ (*riŭl*)—presents a Korean sound in English:

given tape to cover ears clear
rescind regroup the letters and gauntlets
that which comes to abbreviate lion and rat
concomitant hard and grueling work[27]

Like the quotation from *Dura*, this passage seems faintly guided by a thematic logic, and it expresses a vague concern perhaps for communicative labor—

listening and letters. Alongside this effort, however, the passage also behaves as a primer that might instruct a nonnative speaker in how to produce certain sounds. Note the preponderance of the title sounds (/r/ and /l/) in this excerpt; this particular sound in English, like /th/, is a difficult one to transliterate because the actual pronunciation of ㄹ falls somewhere between the English sounds. One can imagine a native Korean speaker stumbling through the difficult alternations of /r/ and /l/ sounds in hopes of training his or her mouth to utter the sounds properly. This iteration of a language primer also functions to cast into relief the difference between the poem and its imagined speaker, which in this case is a reader who recites the lines of the primer. In contrast to the difficulty experienced by this reader/speaker/student who tries to pronounce certain sounds, the poem displays a kind of poetic mastery of precisely these sounds, as in the subtle consonance in "cover ears clear," which is magnified by the collapse of the difference between /l/ and /r/ sounds in Korean. The passage thus stages a tension between its status as a language primer versus that of a poem. In the first case, the imagined voice that speaks is that of a novice stumbling over the foreign words. In the second, the words on the page display, beyond mere comfort, an adroit sensitivity toward, and an intimacy with, the language. Not coincidentally, it is precisely at the point of difficulty for the would-be student that the primer-as-poem locates its sonic intricacies.

Kim's primers both invoke and adapt the function of the more well-known language primers in Asian American literature: those of Theresa Hak Kyung Cha in *DICTEE*. Cha's language primers contemplate and resist the political ramifications of the dictations that one engages in when learning a new language. As Lisa Lowe argues, dictation in Cha "is at once a sign for the authority of language in the formation of the student, a model for the conversion of the individual into a subject of discourse through the repetition of form, genre, and example, and a metaphor for the many regulating reproductions to which the narrator is subject in spheres other than the educational."[28] In resistance to the authority represented by this pedagogical imperative, the subject of *DICTEE*, as Lowe suggests, "recites poorly, stutters, stops, leaves verbs unconjugated. She fails to imitate the example, is unfaithful to the original."[29] This unfaithfulness registers an unwillingness to submit to the ideological mandate implicit in these language exercises. Like Cha's language primers in

Lowe's account, Kim's language primers change, adapt, and revise the original into a form more suited to the strategy of her own text. Whereas Cha calls attention to the difference between dictation and original in order to assert the resistance of the speaking subject, Kim foregrounds the disparity between the difficulty the text poses as a language primer to a native speaker of Korean and the ease with language exhibited by her skill as a poet. Furthermore, she locates the ideological content of the primer less in its semantic content or approach to this content by a particular speaker and more in the mechanics of voice and pronunciation called attention to by the juxtaposition of languages. For Cha, the learning of a language is a site of contestation, as is evidenced by her concern for translation throughout her text. For Kim, it is also a site of synthesis, and its mode is transliteration.[30]

As in "Primer," "And Sing We" foregrounds its awareness of the difficulties that typify the experience of a native Korean speaker by rehearsing many of the sounds that such a speaker would find most difficult to say. The poem similarly displays a mastery over these sounds and thus produces a kind of tension between the voice of a tongue-tied native Korean speaker and that of the poem's speaker. This often takes the form of executions of precise sonic intricacy:

> What would the sea be, if we were near it . . .
> Depletion replete with barraging . . .[31]

> Prattle done trattle gone just how far . . .
> Callback fallback whip whippoorwill . . .[32]

In all of these cases, the deft repetitions and modulations of consonants and vowels emerge as the obfuscated semantic content recedes. Especially since some of these lines seem to lack semantic coherence altogether, they continually invoke a nonsemantic register as the reader proceeds through the poem. In order to be spoken, the sounds require an exercise of the mouth, a veritable workout of the tongue for any speaker of English, no matter how experienced. In such lines, the poem jumps into the English language not only as a vehicle for communication but also as an opportunity for sonic exploration.

Given Kim's interest in the sound of English words and the sounds native Korean speakers tend to mistake in English, a useful context for her poetics is the controversy that developed during the last twenty years over choosing a standard system for Romanizing Han'gŭl. Like Kim's poetry, the debate about Romanization considers how best to represent Korean sounds in the English alphabet. In the 1980s and late 1990s, separate debates arose about whether systems such as the McCune-Reischauer, Ministry of Education, Yale-Martin, or one of a few others was the best way to transliterate Han'gŭl. The dates are not arbitrary; the discussions occurred in the years leading up to the Seoul Olympics in 1988 and the FIFA World Cup in 2002, both of which promised a large number of foreign visitors to Korea. The debate in the 1980s boiled down to a selection of either the McCune-Reischauer or Ministry of Education system. The former was used more prevalently in English language newspapers and tourist pamphlets; the latter was used for road signs and other government applications. Although the specifics of the debate are not pertinent to my discussion here, one of the cruxes of the debate, the question of whom Romanization serves, provides a useful context for Myung Mi Kim's interest in transliteration.

On this point, most of the articles in the August 1982 issue of the *Korea Journal*, which is entirely devoted to the Romanization debate, more or less agree with guest editor Lee Sang Oak: "The convenience of foreigners should be considered first since the Romanization itself is for foreigners."[33] Lee Hyun Bok points out that Koreans also benefit from Romanization—for example, when "a man in the head office in Seoul is to send a cable to someone in the London branch, he has to rely on some Romanization system"[34]—and Edward Klein, extending communicative concerns to economic ones, suggests that "Romanization is for Koreans who want to present their culture, their history, and indeed their products to the outside world."[35] None of these critics imagines any sort of political implications for Romanization. To be fair, the linguists who appear in this issue of the *Korea Journal* were thinking of street signs, tourists, and logistics more than the implications of Romanization to individual and national identity, and the need for simplicity often outweighed strict demands for accuracy: "When a Korean Romanizes the Korean language, he is likely to be an intellectual who can bear some burdens of this complicated system. On the contrary, when foreigners are exposed to Korean Romanization, they may even be tourists and peasants who need a simple and convenient system."[36]

Unlike any of the Romanization systems mentioned above, Kim's poetry uses transliteration as an occasion to investigate all of the political complexities involved in such an act. Certainly, she holds a distaste for standardization in general, specifically for the way it trumps individual mouths and ears in favor of a totalizing system. In "The idea of romanization," from her volume *Commons* (2002), Kim writes of the inadequacies of standard practices of Romanization.[37]

> Practices in transliteration: comparing the standard to what [I] might be said to be hearing: "sesang sarămdŭr-a" next to "sae sahng sah rham deul ah." Whose ears are at work? Where does the authority of romanizing reside?[38]

Here, the problems surrounding transliteration seem similar to the issues of authority and compliance that Lowe argues Cha addresses through her experiments with dictation. Kim offers alternative Romanizations of a Han'gŭl phrase that roughly translates as "to the people of the world," invoking the concern for foreign visitors in the aforementioned Romanization debates. The first of the two is the McCune-Reischauer system, one of the most prominent systems, and the second is Kim's own. The subject referred to by the bracketed "[I]" seems dissatisfied with the clipped vowels of the first version and happier with the broader ones in the second. As in Cha, standardization subtends authority, which compromises the individual.

Kim takes on the issue of Romanization most directly in "Siege Document," in which the pair of Romanizations from "The idea of romanization" appears in the first stanza. Echoing the kind of ideological refusals in Cha's language exercises, the poem explores the difference between official and personal transliterations. Except for the final line, the poem follows the sequential form of a McCune-Reischauer Romanization, followed by the phrase in Han'gŭl, followed by a personal Romanization:

> sesang sarămdŭr-a
> 세상사람들아
> sae sahng sah rham deul ah.
>
> i nae mal tŭrŏ poso
> 이네말들어보소
> e nae mahl deul uh boh soh

naj-i myŏn-ŭn mur-i malkko
낮이면은물이맑오
naht e myun eun nul e mahl ggo

pam-i myŏn-ŭn pur-i palga
밤이면은불이발가
bahn e myun eun bul e bahl gah

ttae-nŭn mach'um onŭ ttae-nya?
때는맏침어느때냐?
ddae neun maht chim uh neu ddae nyah?

This time what time does it happen to be?[39]

Transliteration here takes precedence over translation. For the nonreader of Han'gŭl, the Han'gŭl script in each stanza represents a phonetic ideal to which Romanization can aspire but never really attain. I have included a translation of the poem in the endnotes,[40] but the meanings of the words, I would suggest, are somewhat secondary. Given the emphasis on transliteration, the audience that the poem imagines consists largely of readers who cannot read Han'gŭl—indeed, I would argue that the poem is addressed as much to readers who do not speak or read the Korean language as it is to those who do. In fact, one could argue that knowledge of Han'gŭl does not dramatically change the reading experience, since the central preoccupation is about sound. Readers unacquainted with Han'gŭl read through the pairs of Romanizations and, as suggested in "The idea of romanization," compare the standard to the individual. The conflict is staged not so much between English and Han'gŭl as it is between different Romanizations of Han'gŭl.[41] The "siege" in the title refers to the way in which standardization elides the individual speaking mouths and the full resonance of their sounds in favor of convenience. The poem thus defends the individuality not of the lyric subject but of the individual's mouth. What ultimately gets translated here is not language but the mouths that speak it.

If the individual is under siege by the practice of standardization, resistance for Kim is only the first step in a larger project that sees the sometimes fractious intersection of languages as a site of possibility. In "The idea of romanization," she asks, "What *is* English now, in the face of mass global migrations, ecological degradations, shifts and upheavals in identifications of gender and labor?"[42] Kim's emphasis on the present undermines the tight association between language and national identity, between English and American identity. The myriad destabilizing forces that characterize the *now* allow for a reexamination of the historical constructs that, to return to Patricia Chu, "construed the terms *Asian* and *American* as mutually exclusive."[43] Whereas for Chu, this project occurs by revisiting and revising narratives about American identity, Kim sees the limits of identity as tied to the problems of lyric voice, and she instead treats the categorical problem as a language issue. "The idea of romanization" thus offers an insight into how her poetry might participate in this venture, and it serves as a rejoinder to Chu's formulation of the problem. According to Kim:

> It is not the actual translation or even the state of translatability between the two texts that is intriguing but the possibilities for transcribing what occurs in the traversal between the two languages (and, by extension, between the two "nations," their mutually implicated histories of colonization, political conflicts, and so on). What is the recombinant energy created between languages (geopolitical economies, cultural representations, concepts of community)?[44]

In this passage, the emphasis shifts away from translation and moves toward transcription. Though Kim does not name transliteration here, she describes the idea of Romanization as implicated in the "traversal" and "recombinant energy" that she finds so intriguing about the process of transcription. This shift recalls the trajectory of "And Sing We," which moves from the dislocations caused by immigration to the bridging required to reconcile *American* and *Asian*. The final line of the poem, "Mostly we cross bridges we did not see being built," represents the culmination of this process.[45]

For Kim, the recognition that transliteration has its shortcomings is not simply an opportunity to register an unruly subversive statement or a resistant unfaithfulness to the notion of originality or authenticity in a kind of across-the-board deconstructive gesture. Rather, she is interested in the way that the conditions of transliteration can be manipulated so that language seems already transliterated and translated and so that different languages seem to synthesize and learn from one another. The real student is not the native Korean speaker learning to speak English; rather, the languages themselves are learning one another in an idealized vision of mutually transformative exchange. In this poem, the work of bridging engages in precisely this labor. Particularly toward the end of the poem, there seem to be odd cross-articulations and exchanges that take place not between speakers but between languages. The point is not so much to represent an English speaker learning to speak Korean sounds, or a Korean speaker learning to speak English, as it is to represent English itself learning to speak Korean—as if Kim's poetry were laboring to foment a new synthetic language. Although "And Sing We" does not partake in actual transliteration, its style certainly is invested in the idea of Romanization as Kim conceives it and in the recombinant energy it subtends.

This focus on recombinant energy also echoes Benjamin's notion of "pure language," which is the ideal goal of a good translation. In this term, Benjamin seems to imagine a fundamental characteristic that might connect all languages to an idealized pre-Babelic or divine language: "All suprahistorical kinship of languages rests in the intention underlying each language as a whole—an intention, however, which no single language can attain by itself but which is realized only by the totality of their intentions supplementing each other: pure language."[46] For Benjamin, pure language is an impossible ideal whose impossibility compels one to seek it:

> Although translation, unlike art, cannot claim permanence for its products, its goal is undeniably a final conclusive, decisive stage of all linguistic creation. In translation the original rises into a higher and purer linguistic aim as it were. It cannot live there permanently, to be sure, and it certainly does not reach it in its entirety. Yet, in a singularly impressive manner, at least it points the way to this region: the predestined, hitherto inaccessible realm of reconciliation and fulfillment of languages. The transfer can never be total, but what reaches this region is that element in a translation which goes beyond the transmittal of the subject matter.[47]

Although the ideal of translation remains beyond the reach of the translator, the effort of translation seems to move one closer to this "inaccessible realm." As in the case of Kim's "recombinant energy," Benjamin's vision of translation aspires toward a richer, fuller conception of language, which, though inchoate, invigorates language in general. In addition, Benjamin in this passage dabbles with metaphoric invocations of travel and traversal, as if to suggest that translation were a journey; languages themselves are like explorers who seek out hidden regions and realms, travelers in unfamiliar territory. Perhaps it is not too much to say then that languages for Benjamin are like racialized immigrants.

Mouth Bridges

Following a similar trajectory to Benjamin's formulation of translation, "And Sing We" begins by calling attention to the gaps caused by immigration, and it ends with a figure of traversal in the last line: "Mostly, we cross bridges we did not see being built."[48] The equivocations in this line, however, mediate against any sense of achievement on the part of the bridge crosser. Although the bridging at the conclusion of the poem closes the yawning distance with which it began, we find that the work of bridging has already been accomplished prior to our arrival, and so it is not this arrival that guarantees the bridging but some prior unseen agency. The qualifier in the last line mostly undercuts any sense of successful finality, which seems to revolve not around traversal (where the bridge can take us) but around the unseen work of bridging itself.

Central to this work is Kim's mouth poetics. After establishing and fleshing out the gaps and disparities that represent immigrant dislocation in its first half, "And Sing We" in the penultimate stanza reimagines the voice as a mouth that often produces meaningless sounds—"Prattle (heard, found, made) in the kitchen," "Prattle done trattle gone just how far / Do voices carry."[49] As a noun, *prattle* refers to "trifling or empty talk" or "a sound that is meaningless, repetitive, and suggestive of the chatter of children." Here, the quasiword *trattle*, though it invokes travel and traversal, functions as an example of prattle, a meaningless (though perhaps affectively suggestive) sound that has no actual signification except as an instance of prattle. The subsequent question, "do voices carry," then becomes a meditation not so much on the ability of voices to speak intelligibly but on the capacity of sounds themselves to span across distance; it is less about the communicative potential of words and more about the likelihood of sound waves extending into space. In the poem's final stanza, the attention to sound both complements and revises the function of the semantic content; indeed, there is much in the way of prattle to be heard:

> What we might have explored, already discovered
> Falling down falling down
> Callback fallback whip whippoorwill
> Not the one song to rivet us trundle rondo
> Not a singular song trundle rondo
> What once came to us whole
> In this we are again about to do
> In the times it takes us to dead dead dead la la la
> Trundle rondo for a long time it stood marker and marked
> Mostly, we cross bridges we did not see being built[50]

The content here is willfully obscure and unsettling. Thematically, the stanza describes the futility of effort and hope at a point in time that seems too late to do anything that might change the course of events; the possibilities of the future seem determined—"already discovered"—as if one could now only hopelessly retread predetermined paths. The options seem limited: "Not the one song to rivet us . . . Not a singular song." This lack of strength parallels the immigrant's object status; immigrants are unable to determine their fate because they are bound by contexts they have no hand in building. The foreclosure of possibility suggested by the negative syntax ("Not the one song . . . / Not a singular song . . .") seems emphatically confirmed by repetitive banter that links death to unintelligibility: "dead dead dead la la la."

This nonsensical line, however, as well as the repetition of "trundle rondo," offers the possibility of an excess to the thematics in the form of prattle, sounds that resist signification. The passage sketches out the thematics of helplessness, but the sketch is not fully realized in any explicit way because so much of the passage fails to make any sense at all. So, though the phrases "Not the one song to rivet us" and "Not a singular song," for example, seem to register resignation and despair, the addition of "trundle rondo" at the end of these lines not only muddies the syntax but also negates the negations by offering a figure that suggests the singularity of song (trundle as in trundling, which infers rotating or revolving, and rondo as a musical form that repeats its principal subject). Nonsense and frustrated coherency seem the rule in this stanza, but this does not mean that it remains entirely unintelligible.

First of all, though obtuse, the stanza itself is extremely patterned. Echoing the ten-word opening couplet that begins the poem, this stanza consists of ten lines. Like the opening couplet, it also foregrounds gaps through various stylistic strategies of division. The first and last three lines here are divided into halves in various ways, and the second, third, seventh, and eighth lines are halved by different sorts of caesuras. The middle four lines form a pair of couplets, each organized by an initial assertion that is followed by a modification of the original statement. In many ways, the entire stanza resolves into an overall symmetry with the last five lines acting as a mirrored reversal of the first five lines. The stanza's divided structure thus extends the effort begun in the very first lines of the poem and stylistically represents the literal and psychic dislocation of the immigrant: "Once we leave a place is it there."

Second, the consonant sounds that are difficult for native Korean speakers to pronounce are extremely prevalent. In a sense, this final stanza is a kind of torturous rehearsal of all these sounds. In *Native Speaker* (1995), Chang-rae Lee offers a simplified linguistic account of how and why these consonants are difficult for such speakers, offering his protagonist's father as an example of the resulting comic potential:

> I didn't know what a difference in language meant then. Or how my tongue would tie in initial attempts, stiffen so, struggle like an animal booby-trapped and dying inside my head. Native speakers may not fully know this, but English is a scabrous mouthful. In Korean, there are no separate sounds for L and R, the sound is singular and without a baroque Spanish trill or roll. There is no B and V for us, no P and F. I always thought someone must have invented certain words to torture us. *Frivolous. Barbarian.* I remember my father saying, Your eyes all *led*, staring at me after I'd smoked pot for the first time, and I went to my room and laughed until I wept.[51]

The final stanza of Kim's poem relentlessly rehearses Lee's examples—/l/ and /r/, /b/ and /v/, and /p/ and /f/. If spoken with the typical accent in which native Korean speakers speak English, the /b/ and /v/ sounds in "have" and "discovered" of the first line are inflected in the "bridges being built" of the last line, and the /p/ and /f/ sounds connect "Falling down falling down /

Callback fallback" to "whip whippoorwill." In this second example, the consonants in *fall* are thrice repeated and sound nearly indistinguishable from those in the middle syllable of *whippoorwill.* The former are pronounced something like *pall* and the latter something like *pool* because of both the *p/f* overlap at the beginning of the syllable and the *l/r* ambiguity at the end of it. If it were to be written in Han'gŭl, only the vowels would be different. Just as the second two lines are linked by this sort of sonic kinship, so are the eighth and ninth; because of the *l/r* conflation, "la la la" finds an echo in the /r/ sounds in "marker and marked." This final overlap of sound between /l/ and /r/ becomes the most prevalent sound in the entire stanza: "explored, already discovered / Falling," "falling," "Callback fallback . . . whippoorwill," "rivet . . . trundle rondo," "singular . . . trundle rondo," "whole," "are," "la la la / trundle rondo," "long . . . marker and marked, Mostly . . . bridges . . . built." Every line in the stanza features the sound at least once, and most of them do so more often. Indeed, the thrice-repeated "trundle rondo" is a perfect example of Lee's description of English as a "scabrous mouthful" for nonnative speakers, and it is extremely difficult for many native speakers of Korean to pronounce.

By insistently invoking the tendencies of the native Korean speaker when speaking English and by using these tendencies as a way of establishing phonetic cohesion throughout a stanza that seems explicitly about despair and disparity, the stanza balances mistake and mastery. The value of mispronunciation (though this would be a misnomer for Kim) thus parallels Bill Brown's "mis-use value" of things by offering an alternative criterion for linguistic coherence.[52] Instead of yielding to the kind of assimilative demands for bodily reformation or reinscription seen in "Into Such Assembly" or Palumbo-Liu's account of plastic surgery, Kim positions the unassimilated body, specifically the mouth, at the pivot point for her poetics. Historical crossings are thus enacted by linguistic cross-ups. On one hand, the stanza calls attention to the typical mistakes and failures of a native Korean speaker; on the other, the poem uses precisely these mistakes as the raw material with which to build its stylistic bridges. In contrast to the speaker's clumsiness, the poem demonstrates its command of the language. The recognition of the tendencies of this speaker offers an entirely different kind of coherence that challenges the dislocation that the passage seems to foreground on a thematic level. The prattle of the native Korean speaker's mouth is thus not merely a resistance to signification; it also functions to superimpose an alternative logic of connection and bridging over the otherwise incomplete operations of language. Instead of marking racial difference, these mouths function as figures of cohesion. The poem thus bridges the gap that Kim, in the opening lines, refers to as a "yawning distance." The mouths of these speakers, though foreign to the language, become central to the poem's style. Kim's mouths do not become absorbed into English as much as English becomes absorbed into them, as if the very effort to incorporate the sound of a Korean speaker's mouth into English claims a natural status for it—that it preceded the heretofore new language it was trying to learn since it is already woven into the fabric of English.

The point of Kim's stylistic experiments is to treat the demands of assimilation as water under the bridge (of the mouth). By refusing the entire project of incorporating a foreign entity into a native one, Kim enables her own project of recalibrating the relationship of racial other to native speaker. The project is one of both deconstruction and synthesis; it negates the categories of foreign and native, altogether refusing the underlying nativist models of citizenship and naturalization, but it also imaginatively seeks alternative modes of refusing these heretofore antithetical categories. She humorously sums up the first aspect of the project in "Into Such Assembly": "Who is mother tongue, who is father country?"[53] In this ostensibly lighthearted question, Kim toys with the various idioms in English that link both speech and place to parentage. Specifically, the false naïveté of the personification in this line ("mother tongue" and "father country") troubles the foundational notions that underlie such idioms. The speaker's quasi-innocent question about the identity of these mysterious parents pokes fun at the notion that language and place are more than arbitrary signifiers, which might be part of a specific familial or cultural heritage, and it reduces them to, say, Mother Goose and Father Time—benign characters that are the subjects of fairy tales. The poem constructs in its place, however, a bridge uninterested in origins and destinations but interested in the work of bridging itself, which offers unique opportunities to transform something foreign and marginal into something fundamental.

In "And Sing We," the first-person plural of the poem's title, which had been absent from the penultimate stanza (only), returns in the final stanza. The pronouns *we* and *us* are used differently here than they were earlier in the poem when they represented a more historically contingent body of immigrant subjects objectified and rendered helpless in an unfamiliar, foreign environment. By the end of the poem, their voices, via the logic of prattle, are integrated into a network in which their voice sounds are not foreign and external but central and primary. In this way, the voices of native Korean speakers, once incapable of speaking properly, become the vehicles through which the song becomes intelligible, not because they have learned "proper" speech but by becoming figures of kinship and cohesion—rather than of displacement and loss — that build bridges we did not at first see. Although style cannot be considered representative of the mouths of native Korean speakers, neither can it be properly understood apart from them.

In his attempt to outline the task of the translator, Benjamin makes a distinction between this task and, relevant to the present discussion, that of the poet. Here again translation is figured as travel:

> The task of the translator consists in finding that intended effect [*Intention*] upon the language into which he is translating which produces in it the echo of the original. This is a feature of translation which basically differentiates it from the poet's work, because the effort of the latter is never directed at the language as such, at its totality, but solely and immediately at specific linguistic contextual aspects. Unlike a work of literature, translation does not find itself in the center of the language forest but on the outside facing the wooded ridge; it calls into it without entering, aiming at that single spot where the echo is able to give, in its own language the reverberation of the work in the alien one. Not only does the aim of translation differ from that of a literary work—it intends language as a whole, taking an individual work in an alien language as a point of departure—but it is a different effort altogether. The intention of the poet is spontaneous, primary, graphic; that of the translator is derivative, ultimate ideational. For the great motif of integrating many tongues into one true language is at work.[54]

In this remarkable passage, translation, described as if it were an allegorical pilgrim, calls into a wooded ridge in an alien tongue, seeking a harmonic echo, a kind of song for the barbarian reed pipe that unites, however provisionally, center and margin, native and alien. "And Sing We" works in an analogous manner; however, rather than translation, it deals in transliteration. It replaces Benjamin's pilgrim with a native Korean speaker armed with a language primer, a speaker who fumbles through a language he or she has difficulty pronouncing. Rather than imagining the poet's task and that of the translator/transliterator as diametrically opposed, Kim collapses the two and combines native and alien into an amalgamated mixture, skewing the view so that one can no longer see the forest for the trees nor the language for the mouths.

Ante-English

Myung Mi Kim's chapbook, *River Antes* (2006), revisits the consideration of race and language developed in *Under Flag*. Instead of using literal mouths to defamiliarize English, *River Antes* uses difficulty and objecthood. The book is a thorny experience for readers because it immediately tries to cancel our expectations of poetry and of books in general. One wonders if these arrangements of words can really be called poems at all. There are no titles, except for a few cryptic titlelike captions that unobtrusively appear at the lower-right corner of the pages. Lineation and typography are irregular at best. Filled with elliptical phrases and words often juxtaposed in seemingly random patterns, one tends to gravitate toward the fewer coherent phrases and more stable images that are interspersed throughout the text before realizing that these feel more like found fragments than they do recognizable articulations by a subject with a clear sense of intention of direction.[55]

Recognition in fact becomes one of the central issues of *River Antes*, which is highly preoccupied with obfuscation and hiddenness. One page, for example, consists of five poetic lines each divided in the middle by a pair of vertical lines (a typographic trope that appears throughout the volume), but most of the words in each line are rendered illegible, as if someone had employed the old-time typewriter technique of overtyping in order to effectively cross out a word. On another page, fragments of words that seem to have been cut sloppily with scissors, some more identifiable than others, float free of lineation in three loose clusters. The book also seems to foreground found textual fragments. Early in the volume, a series of four of the aforementioned titlelike phrases appear italicized at the bottoms of pages: "*house installation partial slab*," "*small business transcript*," "*Tablet V Panel 53 / 692 B.C.*," and "*transcript 205*." The titles ask readers to reimagine the poetry as found documents and to assume a nearly archeological stance toward the text on the page. It is not enough to attempt to figure out what the words on the page might mean; one must also imagine a context in which the words become properly intelligible. This is not to say that one cannot appreciate the word arrangements as discrete poems that are themselves often striking and wonderful, but because the text frustrates readerly recognition, one remains suspicious of one's own interpretive attempts at deriving coherence from Kim's presentations of language.

Perhaps the most striking feature of *River Antes* is the series of four triptychs that make up the second half of the book. When the reader first turns to the any of these triptychs, he or she sees only a pair of puzzling pages that are blank except for a small set of three graphic marks that consist of one period and a number of slashes. The right-hand page folds out, however, and reveals a hidden page that in turn folds out to the left, exposing three separate poems on the now upward-facing three pages. The design feature parallels one of the book's central preoccupations: to protract the experience of reading and to delay its most basic operations—from the apprehension of letters to the turning of pages to the recognition of familiar modes of poetic practice—such that the reader is put in a position not unlike that of a foreigner coming to a new language.

By defamiliarizing the text and making it elliptical, and by fostering interpretive attempts to build coherence only to frustrate them, Kim returns us to her central question from "The idea of Romanization": What is English now? Disarticulating it from questions of nativisim and racialization, Kim treats the English language as if it were recovered from a context we can no longer identify and recognize and in which we can no longer take its grounding assumptions for granted. The enigmatic title of the volume *River Antes* returns us to the issues that animated *Under Flag*. This title, containing a paradoxical figure of both separation and connection (river) as well as invocation of a prior time (*antes* as in the Spanish word for *before* or the Latin prefix *ante*), seems to echo the sentiment that underlies the line "Mostly we cross bridges we did not see being built." Implying figures of crossing and mitigating against these figures with complications of time, *River Antes*, in the context I have tried to elaborate here—in which language problematizes models of assimilation and naturalization—subtly considers various historical crossings of frontiers, both racial and otherwise (to invoke Palumbo-Liu's subtitle), through its attempt to imagine English in foreign terms. The spatial-temporal emphasis on what becomes implicit in *Antes* is thus crucially distinct from the prefix it resembles (*anti-*). To be anti-English is to be oppositional and defiant; to be ante-English is to fold resistance into a claim of inclusion and belonging. English itself becomes a temporal entity that is constantly renegotiated in the now, and it becomes continually transformed, even by the mouths that mispronounce it.

CHAPTER THREE

THE BODY OF THE BOOK

Positioned Phenomenology in Mei-mei Berssenbrugge's Art-Book Collaborations

Mei-mei Berssenbrugge's two major art-book collaborations, *Hiddenness* (1987) with Richard Tuttle and *Endocrinology* (1997) with Kiki Smith, share a curious feature: They both have tails. Specifically, in each book, a colored bit of paper extends past the bottom margin of the page (itself called a "tail" in bookmaking parlance), forming a bit of excess that hangs off the edge and remains visible even when the book is closed (figs. 10 and 11).[1] In both cases, the tail is an extension of an image whose distinct color it shares, distinguishing it from other anomalies at the page's rough, uncut edge. In *Hiddenness*, for example, a green cloudlike form opposite the poem's third section narrows into the tail, which is green on both sides, unlike the rest of the shape. The longer of the two tails, it tends to fold and crumple when the closed book is stored or shelved. In *Endocrinology*, the tail extends from a depiction of the bones in a human forearm. Appendages uncontained by the frame of the page, both tails seem to jump off the margin of the page's flat pictorial space into a third dimension, as if to become more shape than image (not coincidentally, both of Berssenbrugge's collaborators also work with sculpture). By invoking this bodily figure, the books recall a fact often forgotten in an age of mass reproduction: Books have always been associated with bodies—medieval manuscripts were written on vellum, a treated animal skin, and bookmaking terminology has long appropriated the names of body parts and functions to describe physical elements of the book (heads, tails, spines, bleeds, and so on).

FIGURE 10. Mei-mei Berssenbrugge and Richard Tuttle, *Hiddenness* (detail), 1987. Published by the Library Fellows of the Whitney Museum of Art. Accessed at the Milton S. Eisenhower Library, Sheridan Libraries, the Johns Hopkins University. Courtesy of the Whitney Museum of Art, the Sheridan Libraries at Johns Hopkins University, and the artists.

Reminding us of this tradition, Berssenbrugge's books explicitly foreground our bodily relationship to the books we read. Both are much larger than the typical trade book, and one's encounter with them is much more physical, not only because they incorporate modes of viewing that one associates with looking at art in public places but also because they demand that the reader/viewer handles the text deliberately.[2] Too rare or expensive to purchase easily, these books typically require travel to a particular location in order to view them (in my case, Baltimore and Houston). We experience them not at our office desks or in our familiar reading chairs but in museum cases or under the watchful eyes of curators or librarians in quiet, rare-book rooms, where the turning of delicate pages in these limited-edition volumes requires more than a thoughtless flick. In this context, books seem to recover an aura otherwise lost late in the age of mechanical reproduction.[3] In the case of *Hiddenness*, because of its accordion binding, one must actually walk a few paces to view the entire text when it is laid out flat (fig. 12).

FIGURE 11. Mei-mei Berssenbrugge and Kiki Smith, *Endocrinology* (detail), 1997. Published by ULAE, Inc. © Kiki Smith, courtesy of The Pace Gallery. © Mei-mei Berssenbrugge. Accessed at the Woodson Research Center, Fondren Library, Rice University. Photo: Katherine Sullivan. Courtesy of ULAE, Inc., and the artists.

More than simply calling attention to our physical proximity to objects we might take for granted, Berssenbrugge's art books also function as figurations of human bodies. As such, they invite us to consider how we regard bodies in human interactions. In a 2005 interview, in which she discusses *Hiddenness*, Berssenbrugge cites Tuttle's plain view of the matter: "Richard says that a book is like the body, that it is a metaphor for the body. A book has a spine, and its cover is like the skin. And it has a heart."[4] Smith's oeuvre is even more explicitly invested in these issues; her work often focuses on abject bodies. Known for her experiments with paper, which she uses to represent skin and bodily forms, Smith chose for *Endocrinology* a Nepalese paper for its skinlike color and texture. By forcing the reader/viewer to imagine them as abstracted forms of human bodies, both texts demonstrate Berssenbrugge's interest in how we view one another as well as how we view ourselves. Furthermore, the invitation to focus on such acts of perception dovetails with the interests of phenomenology, particularly its iteration in the work of Maurice Merleau-

FIGURE 12. Mei-mei Berssenbrugge and Richard Tuttle, *Hiddenness*, 1987. Published by the Library Fellows of the Whitney Museum of Art. Accessed at the Milton S. Eisenhower Library, Sheridan Libraries, the Johns Hopkins University. Courtesy of the Whitney Museum of Art, the Sheridan Libraries at Johns Hopkins University, and the artists.

Ponty, which places a particular emphasis on embodiment in the operations of human perception. Berssenbrugge's tails subtly announce her phenomenological engagements, which are staged as the interaction of the reader/viewer with the unusual book/body placed before him or her. Denied the more familiar trappings of reading, this reader/viewer is faced with a newly estranged thing, an encounter that exemplifies the primordial perceptual operations that occur in all human interactions.

Of course, tails refer not just to bodies in general, in a universal human context, but more specifically to human bodies that are regarded as somehow aberrant. In modern literary and intellectual discourse, the tail varies as a symbol—standing in for everything from genitalia, to scatological operations, to repressed homoerotic desire, to trickster whimsy, to shame. One common implication, however, through this range of symbolic registers, is that the tail often marks that which is seen against a desire for invisibility. It often functions as a kind of embarrassing, indelible mark, as it does for the very last

Aureliano Buendía (in Gabriel García Márquez's *One Hundred Years of Solitude*), who is born with a pig's tail that is, presumably, the shameful mark of generations of intermarriage by a tragically cursed family. As in García Márquez, the tails in Berssenbrugge's books serve as visible indices of contingency and of position within a specific social, cultural, or historical discourse —that which opposes the normative and universal. In this regard, they are like racial marks in that they signify a nonnormative, bodily difference. By marking the human body with a characteristic of an animal body, tails imply something primitive or subhuman that cannot remain hidden from view; in so doing, they evoke racist perceptions of the nonwhite body. Though not reducible to any specific social position in this register, these tails figure positionality itself as a kind of irreducible thingness that opposes the immaterial blankness (or whiteness, as it was in Cha) associated normative universalism.

On the broadest level, then, tails in these books have contrary implications. On one hand, they signal an imperative toward phenomenological investigation, through which one can consider universal human operations such as perception and embodiment, abstracted from socially specific contexts (not *my* perceptions, but perception writ large). On the other hand, they mark bodily aberrance, racial or otherwise, which prevents them access to the kind of a priori, universalized forms of knowledge that phenomenology aspires to adumbrate. If, on some level, we are to regard both books as representations of bodies, an important set of questions emerges from Berssenbrugge's vectoring of alternative modalities. What kind of bodies are we examining? Are these the kind of universalized, abstracted bodies often formulated proverbially as "the body" in medical or philosophical discourse? To what extent are these bodies marked by race or gender? To what extent are they contingent bodies? In short, to what extent are they positioned bodies?

The tails thus mark an important fault line in Berssenbrugge's philosophical engagements. On one hand, *Hiddenness* and *Endocrinology* are interested in phenomenological modes of bodily perception and accordingly investigate the subtleties of bodily experience in their uncertain, nascent moments before conceptual knowledge and understanding stabilizes, reduces, and erases them. In so doing, they echo Merleau-Ponty's attempt to incorporate the role of the body as the fundamental means through which one engages with the world in phenomenology.[5] On the other hand, they respond to what critics have identified as problematic in Merleau-Ponty—that his interest in bodies often seems to obviate a concern for particular bodies. One typical critique has been that the universalized body of phenomenology is actually an unacknowledged contingent body, and any claims to universality are thus false. Reflecting on the dangers that phenomenology poses to feminism, Judith Butler argues that Merleau-Ponty's examples "reveal the impossibility of [his] project."[6] Specifically, she claims that the subject of phenomenology in Merleau-Ponty is a concrete masculine subject posing as a universal subject and that his model of perception fails to recognize its own contingent positionality.[7] Hal Foster, in his critique of minimalist art, makes a broader, but similar, point: Phenomenological endeavors by definition lack historical specificity since the perception they seek to circumscribe is positioned outside a symbolic order and imagined as outside of history, and it thus indexes a larger ideological ambivalence.[8] A universal view of human perception is thus purchased at the cost of historical contingency. In this context, these tails, which figure the idiosyncratic visibility of marked, nonnormative bodies, seem out of place in texts that are otherwise concerned with phenomenological explorations of perception; thus, they signal a divided commitment to potentially contradictory polarities. One wonders if there can be such a thing as positioned phenomenology.

Since the mid-century attempts of Frantz Fanon and Simone de Beauvoir to incorporate a concern for race and gender into phenomenology, the possibility of a positioned phenomenology has been an open question, and it is in this tradition that I wish to locate Berssenbrugge's poetic experiments. As I discussed in chapter 1, Fanon demonstrates a tension between racial position (the fact of blackness) and the aspiration toward a bodily schema that might allow for reflection on the operations of perception. In Fanon's account, the problem of positioned phenomenology is that it is itself a conflicted term; for a person of color, bodily consciousness or a "third person consciousness," is "solely a negating activity," and, as such, it seems anathema to the underdetermined blankness of the phenomenological subject.[9]

Complicating the position taken by Butler and Foster, who argue that the body in Merleau-Ponty is subsumed by ideological forces he does not acknowledge, Linda Alcoff reappropriates Merleau-Ponty in service of progressive politics through his notion of the habitual body. Instead of simply functioning as a descriptor of "motor habits of perception and movement" in physical acts such as typing, Alcoff suggests the idea also "can be easily applied to postural attitudes and modes of perception" involved in interactions involving cultural otherness, and she argues that the lived experience of the habitual body includes a "tacit knowledge about racial embodiment."[10] For Alcoff, race is part of the background perceived by phenomenology, and she goes on to compare Merleau-Ponty's famous description of phenomenological perception as a blind man using his stick to find objects to habitual reactions to otherness in which racist sentiment is internalized as inclination. In both cases, Alcoff suggests that perception operates independently of interpretation and without any reliance on "historico-cultural schemas of meaning."[11] Unlike Foster, who implies that any consideration of positionality—the place of a body within ideology—already enters a symbolic discourse and thus compromises the phenomenological imperative toward recovering primordial experiences, Alcoff locates awareness of positionality in a brand of instinctual habit within the primordial itself. Alcoff wishes to bracket off the tacit quality of habit from the tacit nature of ideology and thus challenges the "completeness" of interpellation.[12] Although Alcoff's account is compelling as part of her larger defense of identity as a useful political construct, the question becomes how firmly the line between habit and interpellation can be drawn and how "easily applied" motor habits are to social behavior. At stake is not whether or not Alcoff's argument is useful as ideological critique but whether or not it still counts as phenomenology, given phenomenology's commitment to isolating perception itself a priori to discursive determinants.

Sara Ahmed's formulation, which she terms *queer phenomenology* and admits is an improper appropriation of the philosophical tradition, addresses this sticking point by demonstrating that this entire temporality, the conceit that there can be something prior to discourse, is false and that the notion of neutral, prediscursive perceptions and movements of the body in phenomenology are fictitious as well. This is because the objects of phenomenology are never arbitrary or innocently hypothetical; they are always certain objects and not others. Phenomenology, Ahmed argues, "always faces a certain direction, which depends on the regulation of other 'things' to the background."[13] Thus, rather than imagining how phenomenology might work from a racial or gendered perspective, Ahmed demonstrates how all phenomenology is inherently positioned or, as she terms it, *orientated*. As such, the drama of orientation in phenomenology—the positioning of the body within space with regard to the perceptual relationship to objects within that space—is impossible to imagine in universal terms because of the inevitable particularity of those spaces and objects, in addition to the ideological content inscribed and embedded within them. Queerness in this regard involves not only a nonnormative sexual desire but also an alternative phenomenological mode of being in the world—quite literally, another orientation.

Berssenbrugge's project might be situated in terms proximate to those of Alcoff and Ahmed: *Hiddenness* and *Endocrinology* negotiate within the conflicts of a positioned phenomenology. Both texts seem attracted to the kind of middle ground articulated in Alcoff's account of the habitual body. At the same time, however, both texts also seem wary of the implicit danger that the habitual body might lapse into a full-blown, interpellated subject and thus foreclose on the kind of primordial perception that is central to phenomenology. They thus repeatedly call attention to more contingent, positioned bodies—paradoxically hidden and insistently visible, like the tails—that challenge and broaden the limits of the phenomenological gaze in the manner that Ahmed proposes. In *Hiddenness*, attention to color encapsulates this central conflict, marking both a phenomenological aspiration to perceive that which is ostensibly hidden as well as a commitment to acknowledge positionality. My usage of the term *woman of color* thus invokes both the phenomenological encounter with literal color in visual art and the racial sense of the term, and it becomes a mode of seeing in addition to a mode of being. In *Endocrinology*, illness similarly functions as a limit to the desire to wrest the body away from scientific, medical discourses, which supplant phenomenological, bodily experience with a cold, hard language that, in explaining bodily functions, threatens to explain them away. Illness marks the boundary between the body in phenomenological thought and the physical body that, when it is sick, resists such abstractions with its stubbornly viral insistence. Although she never addresses race directly in these texts, Berssenbrugge does reduce to elemental form an interest that is otherwise pervasive in her oeuvre. In both cases, though the immediate context becomes increasingly abstract, Berssenbrugge reimagines the problem of visualizing race in contemporary American life that she addresses in her earlier work as a problematic conflict between perception and position. In this context, color in *Hiddenness* and illness in *Endocrinology* do not function so much as analogical codes for race but rather as elemental manifestations of bodily characteristics. By tracking the way in which these bodily phenomena are perceived, Berssenbrugge's art books interrogate the social dynamics of other more complex forms of human interactions, including racialization. In short, the body in these books becomes a means to isolate and expose the root elements of more complicated examples of human behavior.

X-ray Vision and a Woman of Color

Despite Berssenbrugge's explicit embrace of the moniker "Asian American poet," critics have had difficulty reconciling this stance with her antilyrical poetics, deep commitment to abstraction, and general avoidance of conventional Asian American themes. In a 2002 interview, Xiaojing Zhou presses Berssenbrugge on the disparity between the obvious political awareness of Asian American issues that become readily apparent in their discussion and a poetics that does not seem to match. Though she refuses reductive categorization in general, Berssenbrugge, who has a mixed-race background, responds that she enjoys being defined as Asian American because she tends to be excluded from the category.[14] She reasons that this exclusion is based on the perception that her poetry and sensibility appear assimilated, derived perhaps from her unwillingness to use the rhetoric of identity and her philosophical inclinations, which are not usually associated with racially positioned writers.

Earlier in her career, the moniker was less problematic. She was active in the multicultural political movements of the 1970s and was friends with, among others, Frank Chin, who even directed her play "One, Two Cups" (1974). Her work was anthologized in Joseph Bruchac's *Breaking Silence: An Anthology of Contemporary Asian-American Poets* (1983), L. Ling-chi Wang and Henry Yiheng Zhao's *Chinese American Poetry* (1991), and Garrett Hongo's *The Open Boat: Poems from Asian America* (1993). Published in 1987, *Hiddenness* might then serve to mark a turning point in Berssenbrugge's career. Though her work continued to be included in later anthologies of Asian American poetry, it was generally her earlier work, written before this point, that was chosen for its more explicit Asian American themes.

In 1974, however, it would have been far less controversial to label Berssenbrugge an Asian American writer. Although this work never approaches the activist lexicon of the period, it nevertheless explores familiar Asian American themes such as stereotypes, racial positions, and identity crises. In a section of "Farolita," for example, which was included in her volume *The Heat Bird* (1974) and anthologized in various forms in two of the aforementioned collections, Berssenbrugge presents a scene in which race suffuses all aspects of the human interactions at a party:

> The Eurasian at the party would not speak to her. Little lights
> inside paper sacks cast willow flames on the snow
> the little lights that line paths
> of the courtyard. You have to assume each is the same, so
> the maze recedes and is not a vertical map of varying sacks
> on a blank wall, since it is dark, oh
> Mei-mei, you've walked in that garden before. I'm sick of
> these dry gardens. Everyone tells me I should get angry at him
> The nun's voice quavered behind a screen. There was a shadow
> voice to hers of another one singing quietly and
> a little off. I prefer to think it was the light back
> How can he dream of tying me to his bed, in a blizzard
> with snow to my thigh? He tells me I am flirting
> with the void. I am not Chinese. I invite him to step
> out to the garden for plum blossoms. They would be
> very beautiful, now. Their petals would blanket the snow on sand
> but it is morning.[15]

Beginning with an account of a social affront, the poem here stages a human interaction in a social setting in order to examine how racial codes inform these encounters. The refusal of the Eurasian at the party occasions this section of the poem and establishes a context of rejection. We do not know for certain why he refuses her, but the racial indicators in the poem hint at the reason. The poem proceeds speculatively, toying with Orientalist fantasies of plum-blossom gardens that aestheticize and objectify Asian femininity. Concerned with the ambiguity of perceptual experience, the poem is animated by the play of racial assumptions and expresses frustration with how these assumptions prevent intimacy; the thwarted would-be sexual encounter stands in for broader forms of failed engagements.

Race becomes increasingly illegible, an ambiguity that becomes literalized by the use of pronouns with unclear antecedents. The second person addresses the position of the poet by name ("Mei-mei, you've walked that garden before"), but the next two sentences ("I'm sick of . . . ," and "Everyone tells me I should . . .") leave unclear the precise moment when the position of the poet regains the first-person speaking function. Soon after, it seems that the Eurasian, who originally had refused to speak to her, changes his mind, or else this is the speaker imagining a conversation: "He tells me I am flirting / with the void." By the time we arrive at the clearest declaration of identity, in the negative form ("I am not Chinese"), it remains uncertain who is making the pronouncement (in other words, who the *I* is) until the next line where the referents are stabilized ("I invite him to . . ."). Is the Eurasian describing himself as not Chinese? Is he declaring that she is not Chinese? Is she saying this to describe herself? That Berssenbrugge herself might be classified as Eurasian further complicates matters. The way in which race informs this interaction remains unclear, but the poem seems to search unsuccessfully for material manifestations or objective correlatives, which might give concrete physical form to the sense of race that seems both pervasive and inchoate. These figures, namely the plum blossoms and its petals, tentatively formulate the body of the poem's central persona in sexualized racial terms, but these clichéd forms prove inadequate. Instead of a clear statement about identity (such as *I am not . . .*), this section of the poem ends only in speculation about a visit to a garden that seems never to have happened.

Berssenbrugge's play "One, Two Cups," addresses the issue of Asian American identity is similarly physical terms. Alternating between scenes set in present-day New England and 1940s China, the play deals with how the old Asian culture is remembered and transmitted, if at all, to the new American context. It ends with a voice-over monologue that echoes the attempt to locate material forms of race in "Farolita" and anticipates her art-book tails along with the terms through which she later explores positioned phenomenology:

> They put the stories inside you, wrapped in cloth. But then the threads began to rot away, and the stories and the rags lie jumbled in the bottom

of the jar. Spring the dogwood blossoms. The man rakes the dirt yard. He has hung his birdcages out on a branch near him. The young women wore light-colored spring dresses and white shoes, in a western style.[16]

Distinguishing between that which adorns the body (Western dresses and shoes) and that which is hidden internally (stories and rags that lie jumbled in the bottom of the jar), the monologue formulates race as a material inheritance that rots away in some unseen corner of interiority. Contrasting against the "light-colored" and "white" Western clothing, this racial materiality persists as a trace, like the tail in her later work, which cannot be completely hidden or thoroughly expelled. In this passage, this tension seems unresolved and perhaps tragically irresolvable, whereas in later work, it becomes necessary and valuable—expressive of both her attraction to phenomenology and her discomfort with it.

Modulating the more positioned inquiries of "Farolita" and "One, Two Cups" into more abstract registers, *Hiddenness* is a text about human interactions in which unspoken, invisible determinants shape the experience of one person engaging with another. Modeled on the idea of collaboration itself, specifically the collaboration between Tuttle (plastic artist) and Berssenbrugge (poet), *Hiddenness* immediately places the visual and the verbal at odds, self-consciously staging its own conditions of production as a model for phenomenological encounters between and among people. The explicit racial markers in "Farolita" give way to more abstract manifestations of decidedly material forms, which are emblematized by the book's tail.

In this spirit, the book itself presents itself as a thing. Published by the Whitney Museum in a high-priced, limited edition, *Hiddenness* is the sort of book that tends to be displayed in a glass case, as it was for the Tuttle retrospective at the San Francisco Museum of Modern Art (SFMOMA) in 2005. As a result, it is difficult to read, and SFMOMA's crowded arrangement of his art books did nothing to help matters. Having long experimented with book making, Tuttle is interested in the book that, as Miguel Fernández-Cid puts it, "ceases to be a support for explaining ideas in words."[17] This rejection of signification is perhaps clearest in Tuttle's 1974 book entitled, simply, *Book*, which consists of bound square, gray pages, with a single letter of the alphabet printed at the center of each page. *Book* asks the viewer to treat letters as defamiliarized objects not only because they do not form words but also because their materiality becomes a point of emphasis, either as figurations of de Manian signification or, more literally, as inked physical imprints. In a context where words become mere objects, a context that would seem structurally hostile to literary art, poetry itself becomes that which is hidden. Though Berssenbrugge and Tuttle collaborated because of what they perceived to be a shared aesthetic, the book itself, at least provisionally, seems to play out a conflict between conflicting modes of vision, which might be analogized but not reduced to the conflict between word and image.

In this context, Berssenbrugge stages these conflicts in collaboration as a battle, not between words and images—between visual artist and poet—but between two kinds of visuality. Committed to visual poetics in general, Berssenbrugge embraces the visual characteristics of words, and her compositional method, in fact, resembles that of a visual artist. Typically, Berssenbrugge writes thoughts and phrases on paper, cuts them out, and then reassembles them, creating associations and resonances in her typically lengthy lines that might not arise from more conventional forms of composition. In interviews, she calls attention to the "surface" of her poems, as if they were primarily visual artifacts.[18] Her writing occupies what Johanna Drucker identifies as the middle ground between poetic and visual arts. Though Drucker focuses on modernist typographic experimentation, her description of "the messy, boundary blurring practice which included both formality and reference, image and language, present signifier and absent signified" encapsulates Berssenbrugge's work as well.[19] Accordingly, the fight for visibility in *Hiddenness* is reimagined as a conflict over visuality rather than one of simple recognition; the question becomes how we see one another in human interactions rather than whether we see one another at all.

In the opening stanza of *Hiddenness*, Berssenbrugge lays claim to visuality within poetic space and immediately distinguishes between the visible and the hidden as requiring different degrees of attention. This distinction in turn helps demonstrate the challenges to intimacy in human interactions. Phenomenological perception is valorized as a useful mode of meeting those challenges and of attending to hiddenness:

Though relations with oneself and with other people seem negotiated in terms secretly confirmed
by representations, her idea of the person's visibility was not susceptible to representation. No matter
how emphatically a person will control his demeanor, there will be perspectives she cannot foresee or direct,
because there is no assignable end to the depth of us to which representation can reach,
the way part of a circle can be just the memory of a depth. The surface inside its contour,
like the inside of a body, emits more feeling than its surroundings, as if
the volume or capacity of relations would only refer to something inside, that I can't see,
that the other person and I keep getting in the way of, or things in the landscape while they are driving,
instead of the capacity being *of* your person.[20]

This passage tracks the failures of self-representation in human interactions, which fails because it is not fine enough to convey other hidden, obscured regions of thought and feeling. Ironically, that which is hidden, though "not susceptible to representation," remains understood here in visual terms: "her idea of a person's visibility." Visuality, in this case how we perceive one another, thus becomes understood as a contest not between the visible and invisible but between the easily visible and the hidden, and that which is hidden becomes associated with uncertainty in an unanticipated future ("perspectives she cannot foresee or direct"). Furthermore, time and space subtly conspire to distance the perceiver from the hidden object of perception, further challenging vision. It is not enough that things in the landscape are distant; using driving as a model, Berssenbrugge suggests that we are also distracted transients in that landscape, with our concerns presumably directed elsewhere (turns in the road, speed, other cars, and so on) and thus not attentive to hidden things. Associated with the application of force, that which is easily visible later in the poem is represented as a doll, a reductive figure in which complex feelings are reduced into an objectified, all-too-legible object: "He / has a doll in his mind on which he can predict what she will be feeling, as if he would not / touch the doll, until her actual feeling would make contact with the object of his thought." A reified object, the doll makes these feelings visible by presenting them as if they were static and stable, but in so doing, it loses all the complex textures of feeling. In the terms I have developed, it is the opposite of a thing because it foregrounds reductive recognition rather than defamiliarized attention.

This distrust of the easily visible and concomitant embrace of a more difficult form of vision reflects the poem's commitment to phenomenological imperatives. In his reading of *Empathy* (1989)—the volume in which a heavily revised, unillustrated version of *Hiddenness* appears (retitled as "Honeymoon")—Charles Altieri makes precisely this connection, calling attention to Berssenbrugge's emphasis on "the ways that efforts at representation and self-representation seem to elicit intimacy but in fact block access to many dimensions of the psyche that might enable intense closeness between people."[21] Altieri foregrounds Berssenbrugge's attentiveness to that which these explicitly articulated representations obscure in human relations. Because they "purchase self-confidence at the cost of entering self-protective illusions" and stabilize by erasing the many uncertainties involved in human interactions,[22] these representations trade certainty for access to other more ideal dimensions of the psyche and more intense closeness. One hears echoes of Merleau-Ponty's critique of naming: "To name a thing is to tear oneself away from its individual and unique characteristics to see it as a representative of an essence of category."[23] Like Merleau-Ponty, Altieri elucidates the price of articulation: Representation, like the act of naming, jettisons uniqueness for the sake of clarity. Both critics ultimately valorize a kind of phenomenological walk in the dark; though one blindly fumbles through a room of unseen objects, one's senses are sharper when such unfamiliarity pervades.[24]

Tuttle's use of layering complements this phenomenological vision. Like palimpsests, his illustrations reimagine layers behind or beneath as visible on the surface; unlike palimpsests, this capacity is not attributed to an imperfect erasure in the past, and what remains legible is much more than a trace.[25] Instead, layering embraces a fantasy of transparency; rather than occlude what is behind, the surface becomes capable of representing that which is hidden beneath and that which has preceded the top layer in the temporal sequence of imprints. The volume's first image, which appears on the verso

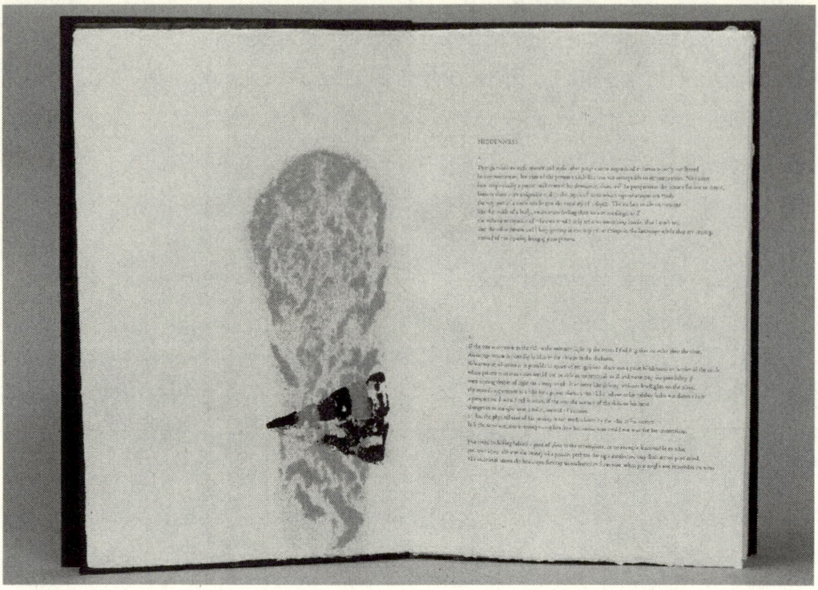

FIGURE 13. Mei-mei Berssenbrugge and Richard Tuttle, *Hiddenness* (detail), 1987. Published by the Library Fellows of the Whitney Museum of Art. Accessed at the Milton S. Eisenhower Library, Sheridan Libraries, the Johns Hopkins University. Courtesy of the Whitney Museum of Art, the Sheridan Libraries at Johns Hopkins University, and the artists.

FIGURE 14. Mei-mei Berssenbrugge and Richard Tuttle, *Hiddenness* (detail), 1987. Published by the Library Fellows of the Whitney Museum of Art. Accessed at the Milton S. Eisenhower Library, Sheridan Libraries, the Johns Hopkins University. Courtesy of the Whitney Museum of Art, the Sheridan Libraries at Johns Hopkins University, and the artists.

across the fold from the previously quoted first section, attempts to spatialize time such that sequential layers appear immediately visible on the surface (figs. 13 and 14). This is a pink cloudlike shape, formed by adding colored pulp into the paper as it was being made. It shares the same texture as the paper itself, thus creating—and undermining—a subtle sense of depth; the colored image seems *on* the page, but because it was formed as part of the paper-making process itself, it also *is* the page. On top of the pink cloudlike form sits two elongated triangles. The first consists of overlapping green, yellow, and black hand-stamped shapes, apparently imprinted in sequence from darkest to lightest color. On top of the second, blue triangle, which becomes less defined toward the leftmost and sharpest angle, there is a clear, shiny substance that imperfectly traces this angle and covers most of the blue of the triangle, making it appear shiny and wet. The shiny covering also makes the darker blotchy shapes within the blue form more visible. Taken as a whole, the layering of shapes on the page occupies physical depth, subtly registering in three dimensions, and it represents the passage of time by making sequence legible, in a manner similar to sediment in a riverbed. Lighter colors tend to be layered on top of darker ones, and even when this is not the case, such as the blue triangle over the pink cloud, the darker forms are porous, more like veils than shields. Even the pink cloud, which is the largest and most visually dominant form on the page, seems diffuse, almost transparent. In this image, Tuttle represents the kind of phenomenological vision that is capable of seeing hiddenness as protracted over time and capable of looking both *at* and *through* objects. Diachrony manifested as synchrony, the conceit here is that all the layers are visible at once.

Appearing on the verso opposite the poem's third section, the second image in the volume demonstrates a similar fantasy: Everything beneath is visible on the surface, and flatness is not antithetical to depth. A long green cloudlike form, narrower and longer than the pink form, spans the right side of the page and extends off the bottom margin of the rough-cut page to form the previously discussed tail. Positioned near the margin, a small portion of it breaches the divide marked by the fold of the page. Also produced by the adding of colored pulp into the paper mixture, it has a similar texture to the pink cloud; though it is denser in composition, it maintains a porous, semitransparent look. Three-fourths of the way down the page, a pair of gold, horizontal lines are stamped across the green cloud, though the green remains visible because the lines are split and neither the color nor the shapes are solid. The image mimes the possibilities of full visibility afforded by the book's accordion binding. If one were to separate the covers and stretch out the book, it would form a single flat surface with its entire linguistic and visual content visible at once; the layers flatten into surface, which ceases in this form to oppose depth. If the phenomenological problem of hiddenness for Berssenbrugge is that certain modes of self-representation limit perception because they disperse with the more fleeting and less tangible objects of experience, leaving "just the memory of a depth" instead of a depth itself, Tuttle's visual aesthetic responds by bringing depth to the surface and by using layers to fuse space and time.

Another flat representation of depth, the X-ray in *Hiddenness* exemplifies this mode of penetrating phenomenological vision. Significantly, the X-ray is yet another mode of looking at the body. Like Tuttle's illustrations, the X-ray's two-dimensional image implies a mode of vision capable of seeing through layers and of representing depth. Appropriately, above a row of four columns of stacked vertebrae-like forms, perhaps itself an abstracted X-ray picture, the fourth section begins:

> If one string line of a bone crosses another properly, an area of brightness
> or intensity is created, so
> that a skeleton, because it was hidden, appears to have been exposed,
> almost inadvertently

These lines describe a characteristic of X-ray photography: Bones behind other bones appear brighter on the image because the penetration of the rays through to the film is impeded by the higher density at that intersection. Significantly, this model of exposure is not quite the same as rendering visibility. A bone "appears to have been exposed"; it is not simply exposed, and it is brighter, surprisingly, because it is *more* hidden. Berssenbrugge here implies a distinction between what is literally seen and what is represented as unseen, which she casts ironically in visual terms. Phenomenological vision in this passage is not modeled on the X-ray itself as a transcendent model of vision; this is not Superman's X-ray vision. Rather, phenomenological vision foregrounds the inadvertent glimpses of our visual expectations that the technology accidentally allows. What is represented is not the hidden bone, but the fact of the bone's hiddenness. Its presence is confirmed just as its visual availability to the eye is denied. In the brightness of the bone, what we see is not the bone itself but rather its resistance to being seen, yet we treat the representation as one in which we actually see the bone. For Berssenbrugge, the revelation of the X-ray is not what it makes visible but what it reveals about vision itself. What is represented by the X-ray image is not a stable object-referent but a strange *thing* that opens questions at the very site where scientific technology seems to offer answers, the first and foremost of which asks about the possibilities of vision when not driven by the search for certainties.

By contrast, Julia Kristeva's *Powers of Horror* (1980) offers a much more limited model of seeing through X-rays, but it is one that helps elucidate the political implications of Berssenbrugge's more nuanced appropriation. An X-ray in Kristeva's lexicon has a truth value and a privileged access to ideology.[26] Kristeva appeals to the function of the X-ray—a leitmotif in her critical study—always in similar situations. In relation to the French chronicler of the abject, Louis-Ferdinand Céline: "At the doors of the feminine, at the doors of abjection, as I defined the term earlier, we are also, with Céline, given the most daring X-ray of the 'drive foundations' of fascism."[27] With regard to Céline's anti-Semitic tirades: "One has to admit that out of such logical oscillations there emerge a few striking words of truth. Such words present us with harsh X-rays of given *areas* of social and political experience."[28] Finally, in the closing pages of her book: "Would he then be capable of X-raying horror without making capital out of its power? Of displaying the abject without confusing himself for it?"[29] For Kristeva, the X-ray is a figure that encapsulates her own effort to expose the distressing and unacknowledged forces that drive abjection—the secret wishes, desires, and motivations that propel social machinery. This critical insight is then reimagined through this figure as the insuppressible "truth" of power and desire that comes out as if on its own accord. In Céline's writing, for example, we see the underlying structures of fascism. The penetrating gaze of the X-ray, which reveals the layers beneath the surface, thus becomes a metaphor for a kind of ideological exposure that takes on the force of scientific certainty. It sees a stable object, a figure of truth.

Thus, by according the penetrating gaze of the X-ray (which pierces fantasies and deliriums) a privileged access to ideology, Kristeva stabilizes ideology and underwrites a form of the same sort of symbolic knowledge that she critiques. The automated, mechanized eye of the X-ray machine draws attention away from the viewer and onto the object of the gaze, as if to equate seeing the body with seeing the truth. The act of looking at the body gives the body a materiality dissociated from the vagaries of perception and interpretation. The gaze is automatic—the flick of a switch—and the truth becomes self-evident once the object is properly viewed. Ideology in turn becomes legible, certain, and immediate, efficiently revealed by the cold eye of the X-ray. My account of Kristeva's X-rays parallels Judith Butler's critique of Kristeva's body politics in general. Butler argues that in attempting to subvert the privilege that Jacques Lacan accords to the "symbolic," Kristeva's positing of a "semiotic" dimension of language substitutes a monolithic account of signification that is based on the law of the father with an equally inflexible model that depends on a prediscursive maternal body.[30] Butler casts doubt on the multiplicity of Kristeva's model, elsewhere pointing out a moment of Orientalism in her writing as an index of the semiotic's rigidity. By positioning the maternal body prior to signification, Kristeva implicitly forecloses on its possibilities as a signifier. The body, ostensibly a field of possibility, instead becomes reduced into something more stable: an object. In looking at X-rays, insight becomes reduced to recognition.

By contrast, Berssenbrugge's X-ray does not simply expose the hidden or arbitrate truth. Rather, it implies that insight often depends on the suspension of recognition and that blindness is a consequence of concretization. The befuddling thingness of the X-rayed object is thus more of a provocation for attentive observation than it is a solved mystery. At the same time, these provocations draw inquiry toward our attraction to, and fascination for, the concrete particular. Although Berssenbrugge's treatment of actual X-rays ends with the quoted lines above, the implications for phenomenological vision continue in her treatment of color. Within this exploration of color, however, Berssenbrugge begins to sketch out a countering force and considers the limits of this phenomenological vision. On one hand, color appeals to phenomenological perception and becomes capable of an expressiveness that is fine enough to attend to that which has been hidden by representation. On the other hand, she also conveys trepidation about the universalism and abstraction that such phenomenological stances tend to take.[31] The concrete physicality emblematized by the tails, which not coincidentally are colored, turn our attention away from the perceptual possibilities of phenomenology and toward the fact of positionality.

Initially, the apprehension of color affords a privileged mode of phenomenological insight, one that is conceived in increasingly universal terms and is compatible with a female subject position:

> She can trace paths through the space of a canyon, generating a motive
> of it which to light,
> a case where there would be some way of applying the color, like some
> form of light projection,
> saturating or fusing all the particles at all levels of the insides of their
> capacities. Although
> this occurs in precisely measured lines, it is how the ghost of an image
> was made to appear in his mind.
> What she can feel about a red, and how far and how deeply are not
> matters of what feeling "a reason" causes in her.

Not attributed to an object (say, a wheelbarrow), red here is abstract and discrete. The perception of color involves an abstract appreciation of the capacities and possibilities of emotion, which is described as an encounter with light and particles. Although color at first "occurs in precisely measured lines," as if a painterly phenomenon, it dematerializes in this passage, gaining an alternative form of presence, independent of shape, figure, or weight. The "form of light projection" associated with color saturates and fuses "particles at all levels of the insides of their capacities," and color exposes the quality of unseen hiddenness, as in Berssenbrugge's X-rays. Like Tuttle's layers, color here accesses an affective depth that representation and reason cannot touch—one that registers outside of the rationalist thinking the poem has resisted from the beginning. Accordingly, the female subject in this passage dissipates into the abstractions that gather around her and becomes a subject of phenomenology coherent with its implied unpositioned universalism.

In the poem's final section, however, this universalism is pitted against positionality, which the poem figures as physical materiality. The subject of the passage thus moves in opposing directions. On one hand, this perceiving subject becomes increasingly universalized and expansive: "The human being, troubled by limits, creates a trip for herself, a honeymoon, which recreates her / as spacious." On the other hand, the limits remain troubling, and this disembodied subject seems increasingly to coincide with a material body, which becomes reimagined as a kind of art object whose central claim to objecthood is color. Like the protruding tails, color here expands into a third dimension and occupies physical space beyond the flat pictorial space of the canvas imagined in the poem. Subtly problematizing the immaterial red, which marks a subtle affective nuance that becomes perceptible in a hyperperceptive phenomenology, color here threatens to shed its hiddenness and obtain a visible physical presence:

> Now, she projects expanse onto endeavors, such as the representation of an angel,
> or the way the colors of the world would lie over the world, a pleasurable collation of objects,
> as of hues of the shadow of an emergence place.
> It passes a richness of seeing or believing back onto the impasto of the colored things,
> in which anyone else may mean anyone other than the two of us, or anyone other than you, and you will go,
> who are the color of a seam, and not a doll
> of painted bisque which makes matte protuberances or patches of invisible places across a space.
> A cloud in the morning folds over a monument on the plane, a vector like an avalanche of mist concealing it.
> She wonders what the body would reveal, if the clouds were transparent.
> It pervades the creation of a motive, like the action of a heart.

Ambiguity of vision here pervades. The body is nearly, but not quite, visible at the end of this poem, and it is unclear what relationship it bears to the female subject in the passage. It is also unclear if the subject, abstracted as "spacious," is instead *spatial*, like the "impasto of colored things," occupying a specific position. Similarly, though color becomes increasingly material throughout the passage, this materiality does not seem to accord necessarily with visibility. Concealment and invisibility thus seem to be paradoxically challenged and maintained. The physical appearance of the section reflects these tensions as well. In contrast to the sixth section, which is printed on a pair of blue pages, with a colorful illustration on the opposite page, this seventh and final section is printed alone without accompanying images, at the top left of a pair of entirely white pages. The only section of the poem printed without accompanying illustrations, this text quite literally takes the place of a material image as the central object of vision. It then asserts, by contrast, an invisible, material presence, which is shrouded by the image of clouds in the final lines, ending with an appeal to an invisible body, which, despite its hiddenness, becomes imagined in material terms. Visuality is both offered and rescinded, insisting on the presence of a materiality that we cannot see.

Color ultimately marks the limit of the poem's phenomenological aspirations, but like the hidden bone in the X-ray, it remains barely out of sight. It at once marks an imperative to attend to positionality without reducing these attentions to acts of recognition. A woman of color in a different (though not unrelated) sense, Berssenbrugge uses color to gesture toward that which is hidden and to understand it in physical, bodily terms; as an attempt to figure racial position concretely, color thus functions similarly to the plum blossoms in "Farolita." Though an obscuring cloud lingers at the end of this poem, enforcing an obscurity of vision, color seems to authorize speculation about the hidden body, insisting on the physical presence of the body that remains obscured from view. Significantly, this is a very colorful book; Tuttle's images are vibrant and rich. Nevertheless, the color to which Berssenbrugge ultimately points is one that is not so easily visible. Appropriately enough, on the only pair of blank white pages in the entire book, we end up looking for colors we cannot see. In articulating the limits of universality, seeing color operates like the Kristevan X-ray in its penetration of illusory layers to see hidden ideological stakes. Unlike the Kristevan model, the thing (and not object) of X-ray vision remains out of focus, out of view, and insistently indeterminate. This indeterminacy, however, does not challenge the existence of positionality so much as it does the ease through which it is recognized. Just because we can't see color doesn't mean it is not there. It is this subtle insistence on the materiality of color that returns us to thinking about Berssenbrugge as a woman of color in the more traditional sense. As a counterweight against phenomenological open-endedness, color is undeniably present, even though, and perhaps because, it is hidden.

Color here thus serves as a figure for race without directly referring to more conventional deployments of color metaphorics in racial discourse. In this respect, Berssenbrugge's use of color is similar to that used in Gary Ross's inventive film *Pleasantville* (1998), a film that marks the differences among characters by portraying some in full color and others in black and white. *Pleasantville* tells the story of a pair of contemporary teenagers who are magically transformed into characters from a 1950s black-and-white television show. Everything is pleasant in Pleasantville; it never rains, the basketball team never misses a shot, and life in general maintains a prelapsarian simplicity that is a function of unquestioned cultural homogeneity. When David (Tobey Maguire) and Jennifer (Reese Witherspoon) first arrive, they find that, like everyone else in town, they are literally in black-and-white, and the plot of the film develops as color is gradually introduced in the town because of the often-unintentional interventions of David and Jennifer. When, for example, certain characters have their first sexual experiences or express themselves artistically, colored objects appear in their lives (such as flowers, fruit, and bubble gum), and they themselves become colored. This transformation raises the ire of a town generally resistant to change, and the *colored* people become the object of discrimination, even on a few occasions (heavy-handedly) at the hands of a character named Whitey. As my gloss suggests, *Pleasantville* is not unaware of the racial implications of color; in fact, it constantly plays on this trope. The climactic trial scene, for example, contains an explicit homage to the courtroom scene in Robert Mulligan's *To Kill a Mockingbird* (1962), a scene in which all of the colored people are shown seated in the balcony, and all of the black-and-white people are seated below. As Benjamin Widiss argues about the film, "'colored' characters stand in for black ones, but so displace them."[32] To be clear, there are no African Americans depicted in *Pleasantville* at all, and the film is primarily concerned with their plight only as a metaphor. Instead, the film's embrace of color serves as a celebration of a universalized, liberal humanist subject, and it critiques the blinkered stasis of a static world that is unwilling to embrace individuality. To embrace color is to see the world afresh and anew; to be colored is to be yourself.

Like *Pleasantville*, *Hiddenness* uses color to invoke positionality as a provocation for alternative forms of vision, but the differences from the film are far more illustrative. Though published more than a decade before *Pleasantville* was released, Berssenbrugge's text might read as a kind of anachronistic critique of the film. In *Pleasantville*, the problem with color is that one need not look very actively to see it; it becomes a matter of immediate recognition. One either is or is not colored, and this difference, as the film expresses with evangelical zeal, is unambiguous. Because recognition involves identifying what we already know, looking at one another in human interactions becomes a form of looking at oneself; seeing color becomes akin to learning to recognize what each of us has in common: our shared, not-always-pleasant humanity. We gradually learn that the cost of Pleasantville's pleasantness is stasis, which the introduction of color interrupts. Even with the advent of color in this racially homogenous town, one form of homogeneity simply replaces another. Although universal humanist individualism supplants pre–civil rights, mock-Edenic whiteness, homogeneity remains, despite the conceit of the film, which regards this change as more epistemologically transformative. What such universalist reductions risk, Berssenbrugge-as-film-critic might complain, is an intimacy with all that we do not share—that which is not immediately recognizable—hence her emphasis on both phenomenology, in which looking and perceiving are a priori to knowing, and color, which challenges our engagements with the world, especially when conceived within universalist paradigms that deny positionality entirely. *Hiddenness* refuses the blunt metaphoric substitutions on which *Pleasantville* turns. Instead of understanding color as an insuppressible universal force whose visibility is as inevitable as it is undeniable, Berssenbrugge leaves color hidden, not to deny its existence but to make sure we have to work in order to see it; it becomes an active pursuit and not just matter of recognition. At the same time, however, Berssenbrugge is concerned that an overemphasis on positionality would constitute simply another form of reductive recognition. Because color is the locus of both the possibility for vision and the threat of another kind of blindness, she makes the power of color partly a function of its hiddenness, so it remains, on some level, invisible. Phenomenology and positionality in *Hiddenness* become mutually corrective, each marking the limits of the other's pretensions. The possibilities of perception are balanced against the physical body, which one suspects is colored.

The Body of Science

If *Hiddenness* is concerned with how the body is viewed in human interactions, *Endocrinology* is interested in one's relationship with one's own body, specifically in the context of illness. Rather than marching off in an entirely new direction, Berssenbrugge invokes illness as an analogous form of the human interactions described in *Hiddenness* and of the racial encounter recalled in "Farolita." Instead of describing it as a private struggle, Berssenbrugge imagines illness in social terms, as an encounter with otherness that is mediated by medical discourse. In this logic, when one is ill, one fights not only the illness but also a discursive battle. In this context, Berssenbrugge uses illness as an occasion to explore more fundamental issues about how we regard bodies, in terms that resonate strongly with her earlier, more explicit considerations of race.

Like its predecessor, *Endocrinology* stages a tension between phenomenology and positionality, specifically as a collision of medical and poetic discourses. A recreational reader of medical textbooks, Berssenbrugge deploys scientific language in order to explore the ways in which language can distance oneself from one's body. The endocrine system maintains homeostasis in the body through the secretion of hormones from various glands. Since these processes help regulate emotions, the science of endocrinology shadows (and threatens to overshadow) the customary terrain of poetry by offering "hard," scientific explanations for inchoate, emotional problems (such as clinical depression for sadness). Most prominent in the second section, scientific language litters *Endocrinology* in descriptions of bodily functions:

> Hormones provide a mechanism by which the body relays chemical signals through cells perfused by blood.[33]
>
> Shortly after phagocytosing material, leucocytes increase oxygen consumption and chemically produce light.[34]
>
> During pregnancy, the foetoplacental unit under the curve acts as a gland.[35]

The technical language here marks the disparity between bodily experience and the medical narrative that attempts to explain it, and the scientific terminology thus seems jarring in a poetic context. The alienating quality of technical language contrasts with the bodily wonders that these sentences describe; the transmission of chemical signals via hormones, the creation of light inside the body (an actual phenomenon), and the unique symbiosis of the mother and child's body during pregnancy all seem obscured behind the cold, hard words that block the view. Although the wonder of perception is hidden, the medical language seems to mark the point of ossification of perception into knowledge.

Endocrinology thus engages in the task of phenomenology with respect to science as expressed by Merleau-Ponty: "To return to things themselves is to return to that world which precedes knowledge, of which knowledge always *speaks*, and in relation to which every scientific schematization is an abstract and derivative sign-language, as is geography in relation to the countryside in which we have learnt beforehand what a forest, a prairie or a river is."[36] For both Berssenbrugge and Merleau-Ponty, scientific knowledge is a system of organizing perceptions that threatens to erase the very phenomena it attempts to explain. As such, the central task is to recover perception before its subsequent cooptation. *Endocrinology*, as it progresses, juxtaposes scientific language with more conventionally poetic discourse—"The bird sings on a strawberry the size of a melon. / Cells release hormones into intracellular space, where they enter local, fenestrated capillaries."—and uses medical terms to describe abstract bodily experiences—"Estrogen induces her concept of luminosity, detaching itself from his color."[37] The poem thus dissociates this terminology from the status of knowledge by repositioning medical language in an unfamiliar poetic context into whose abstractions the force of knowledge seems to dissipate.

Berssenbrugge further contextualizes this attempt to recover primordial perception of one's own body with her interest in illness. Thus, in addition to checking the alienating effect of medical knowledge, *Endocrinology* also attempts to wrest bodily experience away from the equally disaffecting effects of illness.[38] Beyond the operations of a normally functioning, healthy body, interspersed throughout the poem are descriptions of an afflicted body whose problems are often cryptic and difficult to pinpoint:

> The form of her body is important, as how she is here, though there's no evidence of her physical suffering.[39]

The thymus expends itself during stress and collapses, so an autopsy finds only a membrane.[40]

Her back bleeds.[41]

The sick, immortalized cells don't know to stop growing.[42]

Illness, like medical language, severs bodily knowledge from perception, rendering the body an objective, misunderstood other. Particularly when the illness is less obviously visible, as in the immune system disorder that Berssenbrugge suffered from during this period, one's own body becomes both the mode of perception and the object of that perception. One feels alienated from one's own body not least because there seems to be a disjunction between one's will (to heal, to feel better) and the will of the body, which is emblematized here by the unwittingly malevolent cells personified in the last line quoted above. In terms that resonate powerfully with Fanon's description of his bodily schema under the racist gaze, one's own body thus becomes alienated from oneself. This disjunction in the experience of illness renders the body itself as foreign and distant, outside the purview of perception and thus somehow unseen, even and especially when illness becomes the object of scientific knowledge.

In *Endocrinology*, Berssenbrugge's interest in the sick body intersects with Smith's interest in abject bodies. In the fourth section, Berssenbrugge references one of her collaborator's sculptures: "The woman leans on the table, forearms abnormally long. / Her milk flows and flows. She cries and cries."[43] Many of Smith's sculptures adhere to the ethos of abject art as Hal Foster describes it: "to represent the condition of abjection in order to provoke its operation—to catch abjection in the act, to make it reflexive, even repellant in its own right."[44] The sculpture to which Berssenbrugge refers, *Untitled* (1990), is the female of two human figures made of wax that hang from metal stands in slumped, corpselike postures. Her legs and shoulders are bruised, and milk secretes from her breasts. (The companion male figure has sperm running down his legs.) As Smith describes, these figures depict the frustration of procreative processes: "Her milk nurtures nothing, his seed seeds nothing. So it was about being thwarted—having life inside you, but the life isn't going anywhere, it's just falling down."[45] Visually disturbing, the damaged, corpselike figure encourages a visceral repulsion in the viewer that is associated with abjection; that is, it is not simply about abjection, but, more radically, it triggers abjection itself. The viewer's disgust and rejection of the image fulfills the sculpture's invitation for a compulsive reaction,[46] the kind of reaction that Kristeva famously describes in her treatise on abjection: "The repugnance, the retching that thrusts me to the side and turns me away from defilement, sewage, and muck. The shame of compromise, of being in the middle of treachery. The fascinated start that leads me toward and separates me from them."[47]

Berssenbrugge's lines replace this automatic compulsion, however, with a slower phenomenological mode that might dispute the narrow vision implicit in medical discourse. Rather than abjection, the final sentence of Berssenbrugge's allusion to the Smith sculpture, "She cries and cries,"[48] instead implies an empathetic identification with the female figure, a possibility made remote in the sculpture itself by its commitments to abjection, which might be described as a compulsive disidentification. If the line evokes empathy to resist compulsive abjection, it does not go so far as to reclaim an abject subjectivity or to give voice to the abject body. More measured, it functions instead to replace automatic reaction with a slower deliberation of the sort that might be associated with the other artist alluded to on the page, Richard Tuttle—Berssenbrugge's collaborator on *Hiddenness* and, by this time, her husband. Berssenbrugge refers, in particular, to Tuttle's minimalist wire sculptures, which consist of wires affixed to a wall, a pencil line drawn on the wall, and the wire's shadow, which interplays with the penciled markings: "A wire crosses in front of a line on a wall, while its shadow seems to cross behind it."[49] Whereas Smith's abject figure provokes a visceral reaction from anyone entering the room, Tuttle's lines of wire, pencil, and shadow are scarcely noticeable except from up close. Whereas Smith's sculpture immediately hails an intelligible social context, Tuttle's piece invokes a minimalist sensibility that seems to deny the very notion of context.

In Berssenbrugge's rendering, however, both art objects evoke primordial perception and call attention to the inchoate moments in which the viewer approaches the unfamiliar. Figuring the viewer himself or herself, Berssenbrugge deploys present-tense, active verbs in each case to attribute movement to otherwise static objects ("A woman leans . . . Her milk flows and flows. She cries and cries. . . . A wire crosses . . . its shadow seems to cross . . .") not to endow them with agency but to emphasize the temporality of perception as it occurs. Perception itself is imagined as an event occasioned by art objects that prevent the viewer from adopting familiar, comfortable modes of recognition. In this respect, Smith's sculpture challenges the viewer by compelling involuntary reactions, and Tuttle's by radically reducing expression to basic, nearly trivial, elements. Berssenbrugge calls attention not only to these objects themselves but also to the phenomenological acts of perception they prescribe, and she discovers in these art objects a mode of looking at one's own ill body that might challenge the reifying forces of medical discourse.

Like *Hiddenness*, *Endocrinology* uses layering, a technique that is fundamental to the construction of the book itself, as a representation of phenomenological perception. Although most books are layered and constituted by bound, stacked pages, *Endocrinology* exploits this basic material condition to transform sequence (successive pages) into simultaneity. First of all, there are many layers on each page. With the exception of the endpapers at the beginning and end of the book, all of the pages consist of two sheets of Nepalese paper glued together unevenly so pockets of air, which look like lumps of fat beneath skin, form between them. In addition, lithographs of organs are printed in various shades of a deep indigo, directly onto the outward-facing sides of the glued-together paper, and the text of the book is letter-pressed onto pieces of white, rough-cut paper, which are in turn dry-mounted onto the pages. There are also prints of handwritten words on scraps of white paper, which are similarly mounted onto Nepalese paper and supplemented with pencil-like markings that extend some of the organ images. Taken as a whole, the viewer/reader of *Endocrinology* can view the images not only on the pages but also through, behind, and beneath the pages due to the semitransparency of the paper. For example, the images, the mounted shapes, and even some of the printed words from pages three and four are visible when looking through page two (fig. 15). As in *Hiddenness*, particularly its invocation of X-rays, *Endocrinology* manifests phenomenological vision as the ability to see depth on the surface. More important, this layering strategy applies phenomenological vision to the body itself insofar as the anthropomorphic characteristics of the book—from the skinlike pages to the illustrations of organs—ask us to regard the book itself as a body. Consequently, against medical discourse, which subsumes perception with reified knowledge, and against illness, which renders

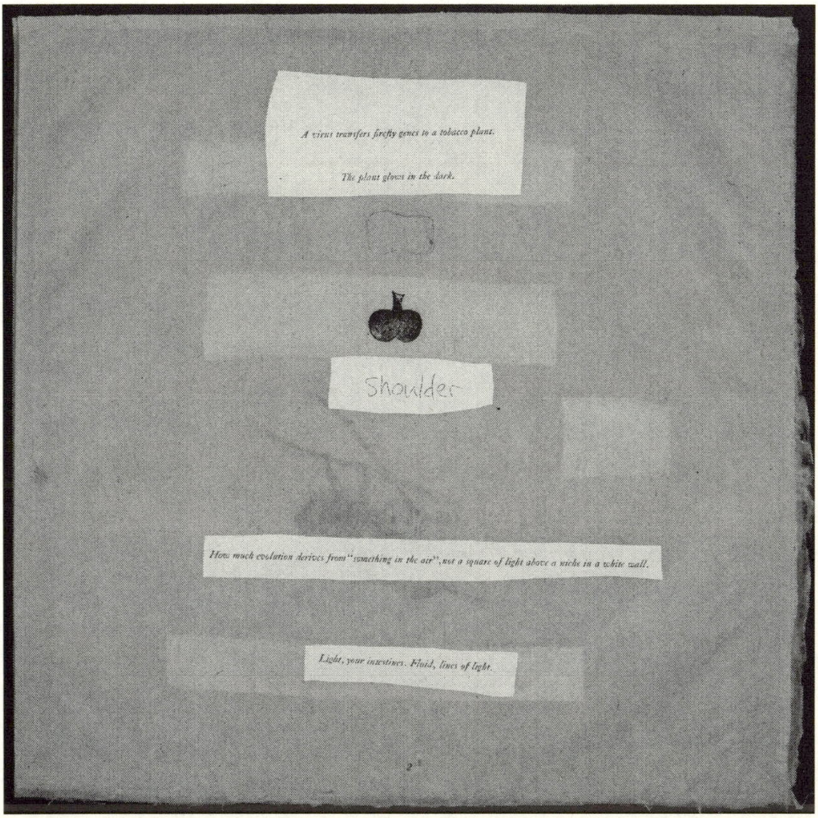

FIGURE 15. Mei-mei Berssenbrugge and Kiki Smith, *Endocrinology* (detail), 1997. Published by ULAE, Inc. © Kiki Smith, courtesy of the Pace Gallery. © Mei-mei Berssenbrugge. Courtesy of ULAE, Inc., and the artists.

the body other to oneself, phenomenological vision for Berssenbrugge allows for a renewed, undetermined reengagement with the body.

Even as she raises this possibility, however, she simultaneously announces its limits. Layering has two conflicting registers in *Endocrinology*. On one hand, it offers a model for the slow, deliberate mode of perception that the poem gathers from its contemplation of art objects. Layering imprints a temporal quality onto a static object, and the body becomes abstract. On the other hand, the layers of the book figure the contingent physicality of the body—the anatomy of a particular body—and not the universalized body of either phenomenology or medical discourse. We see this effect in the fatlike bubbles that are formed by the imperfectly glued paper; in the tanned (not white) color of the skinlike Nepalese paper; and in the rough-cut edges of the book's margins, which suggest irregularities of proportion and shape. The poetry, in fact, reflects on these clashing models of perception in its fifth and final section, which oscillates between the possibility of *the* body and *a* body:

> There is a space. / You see something at the far edge, and your eye going over this space makes a whole, like watery mass in a gourd, the feeling of old organs no longer crucial to or inside themselves, / while remembering people you loved, which flowed from the physical, about which you made decisions. / To make this whole, any object, brings into being something not in nature, an interior measurement, yourself, not yourself, bursts of growth when you sleep. / Her back bleeds. / A spray of blood on the snow. She sits on her hands physically preventing herself from scratching. / The child her sense of the world being crucial to or inside itself, of memory and specificity, like script. / B cells grow for years in a Petri dish. / The sick, immortalized cells don't know to stop growing. / Where your eye goes over space to the horizon makes a whole, but where the sky meets the earth, the fragment is not the same as a whole. / Desert ferns covered with reflecting hair may insulate the fronds. / Radiations of a state barely embodied, then dissolving in counter-reflections of light. / There's an engine. / He cannot separate from the loved person, to shed the loved body.[50]

Taken collectively, these lines juxtapose universality and contingency by counterposing reflections of abstract space and horizons against the particularities that interrupt such abstractions, as if to complicate the phenomenological view of the body. The figure of space in the opening line encapsulates a more general dematerialization of the body's internal cavities at the beginning of the passage, which is accompanied by a detached voice ("yourself, not yourself") that reinhabits the body as an unfamiliar space. The middle of this section, however, dramatizes the challenges to this reclamation project, and the phenomenological body gives way, for a few lines, to the ineluctable will imposed by the sick body. Her back bleeds, and she cannot resist the urge to scratch; the presence of a physical body refuses to give way. Similarly, the eye is drawn to the capacious horizon, but it then becomes encumbered by fragments, and the broad, wide-scope view narrows into ultraeidetic particularity; a view of the expansive sky zooms in quickly onto the hair that insulates the fronds of a desert fern. Ultimately, the person seems burdened by the body. In this manner, *Endocrinology* insistently returns its reader to a contingent physical body in which illness functions as an index of positionality posed in opposition to universality. Just as the references to bodily disorder and sickness interrupt the more abstracted experience of the body, the materiality of the book itself—all of its imperfections and marks, some of which look like actual human hairs—similarly circumscribes phenomenological possibility. The body's presence, marked here by illness, remains insistently present and material, not unlike the tails, each of which bleeds off the margin of the page.

An implicit conceit of these tails is that they threaten to become visible at any point in our experience of the book. They are visible, and they serve as indices of insuppressible visibility. In this respect, Berssenbrugge rehearses Fanon's problematic: Any conception of phenomenology for the postcolonial subject is always determined by a preexisting schema, which shapes his or her perceptions so thoroughly that one wonders if phenomenology is even available at all to the positioned subject. Similarly, *Endocrinology* is a meditation on what it means to confront one's own positionality in a phenomenological mode. Neither *Endocrinology* nor *Hiddenness* is a narrativized, quasi-allegorical treatment of minority experience. For Berssenbrugge, this would be overly limiting for her artistic enterprise; it would trade too much in precisely the kind of familiar formulations that phenomenology wishes to question.

Berssenbrugge instead translates into phenomenological terms what Donna Haraway describes as situated or rational knowledge, which Haraway argues extends not from a fictive sense of objectivity but from a partial perspective that understands its own limits. Like Berssenbrugge, Haraway conceives this sort of knowledge in relation to science, which, Haraway contends, pretends disengagement: "to be from everywhere and so nowhere, to be free from interpretation, from being represented, to be fully self-contained or fully formalizable."[51] By contrast, situated/rational knowledge replaces scientific objectivity with "positioned rationality," which formulates knowledge not as the "escape or transcendence of limits (the view from above) but the joining of partial views and halting voices into a collective subject position that promises a vision of the means of ongoing finite embodiment, of living within limits and contradictions—of views from somewhere."[52]

Always viewed from somewhere in relation to the unsituated, universalism of traditional phenomenology, Berssenbrugge's art books are open spaces of thought in which we examine the visuality of nonnormative bodies in defamiliarizing isolation, both as locations from which phenomenology extends and as the objects of perception. Even as Berssenbrugge moves away from a consideration of explicitly racialized bodies in her earlier work, these later formulations of positionality powerfully echo her earlier articulation of racial position. Both *Hiddenness* and *Endocrinology* put phenomenological inquiries in conversation on a highly abstract level with the kind of political questions that Fanon raises, using phenomenology to explore different registers of bodily materiality, particularly those that, as Butler and Foster suggest, threaten phenomenology itself. Berssenbrugge ultimately works out the impossibility of committing entirely to either a positioned subject, whose body's physicality assures its ineluctable visibility, or a universal phenomenal subject, whose conception of perception within a lived body seems otherwise ideologically unmarked. In so doing, however, she neither gives up on the task of incorporating the contingent into the universal nor indulges in any naïve disregard for the challenges to such an enterprise. Being ill is like having a tail in the sense that any access to universalist modes of perception is thwarted by the insistent contingency of the positioned body. However, Berssenbrugge implies more than just a strained analogy among different forms of abjection. By imagining one's relationship to one's sick body as a kind of human interaction with otherness, Berssenbrugge valorizes and makes imperative a certain phenomenological attitude when one regards a body, even as she acknowledges its limits. As in Ahmed's *improper* formulation, Berssenbrugge grounds phenomenology within the social and discursive and, in so doing, demonstrates that accounts of universal phenomenology are inevitably phenomenological attempts to universalize normative positions.

Scenes from a New York City Subway Car, circa 1976

Due to their bodily characteristics, which are emblematized by their tails, *Hiddenness* and *Endocrinology* imagine that the act of looking at a book is like the act of looking at a body, and it involves an encounter with otherness. So defamiliarized, reading in this regard is not unlike a human interaction, the kind of interaction that Berssenbrugge in fact explicitly thematizes in *Hiddenness*. For Berssenbrugge, viewing these books and the bodies depicted within them as art objects thus demands a balance between the appreciation of abstraction and the appreciation of physical materiality, as well as a balance between phenomenological and positional modes of viewing. In Berssenbrugge's logic, these mutually corrective balancing acts are crucial because they preserve open-ended, indeterminate acts of looking from the foreclosures of recognition. Though these books do not directly address race, they are deeply informed by its underlying dynamics and thus carry forward the interest in racial positionality that Berssenbrugge explored earlier in her career. Abstracted as a problematic about the role of the body's visuality in human interactions, seeing race becomes part of a larger contemplation of how bodies are visualized. The initial encounter with the book, for Berssenbrugge, thus serves as an apt metaphor for various encounters with otherness.

Perhaps we can speculate about one such encounter in 1976, in New York City, where Julia Kristeva penned the final lines of her afterword to the American edition of *About Chinese Women* (*Des Chinoises*). In this book, which was written after a trip to China, Chinese women occupy the same presymbolic terrain as abject bodies in *Powers of Horror* and function as living embodiments of theoretical concepts. The book begins with an infamous account of some Chinese peasants at Huxian Square; it is an encounter without interaction:

> An enormous crowd is sitting in the sun: they wait for us wordlessly, perfectly still. Calm eyes, not even curious, but slightly amused or anxious: in any case, piercing, and certain of belonging to a community with which we will never have anything to do. They don't distinguish among us man or woman, blonde or brunette, this or that feature of face or body.[53]

Lisa Lowe and Gayatri Spivak take Kristeva to task for her Orientalism. Lowe argues that this passage demonstrates that, for Kristeva, "the Chinese, and ultimately Chinese women as inheritors of a matriarchal tradition and maternal culture, are homogenized as the absolute cultural and sexual Others of the occidental tradition."[54] Similarly, Spivak argues that Kristeva's passage is a symptom of a larger tendency of narcissism in Western thought: "In spite of their occasional interest in touching the *other* of the West, of metaphysics, of capitalism, their repeated question is obsessively self-centered: if we are not what official history and philosophy say we are, who then are we (not), how are we (not)?"[55] Indeed, in this passage, Kristeva turns the physical bodies before her into evidence of her theoretical concepts. When she looks at the bodies of these Chinese women, homogenous and other, she recognizes what she already knows, and instead of seeking to overcome her experience of their difference, she renders these women as homogenous embodiments of the semiotic. Into this vacuum flows Kristeva's incipient awareness of her own estrangement, which is triggered by the eyes of the Chinese peasants. "I don't feel like a foreigner, the way I do in Baghdad or New York. I feel like an ape, a martian, an *other*."[56] Thus, recognition of the other allows Kristeva to experience herself as unrecognizable.

In 1974, the year in which Kristeva originally published *Des Chinoises* in France, Berssenbrugge, whose mother is Chinese, was not in Huxian Square but in New York City where her play "One, Two Cups" was performed at the Basement Workshop. Perhaps she walked the same streets that Kristeva would later traverse in 1976, or perhaps their time in the city overlapped. Perhaps during this time they both rode the subway—perhaps the same subway car. Perhaps this was the same subway car that Kristeva conjures a few paragraphs from the end of her afterword. Perhaps Berssenbrugge is there in the crowd:

> The New York subway mixes women of different ethnic and class backgrounds and dances transformed into bodies, or calm blocs from the North, from Africa, from the Mediterranean. . . . In life as on stage, women utter *individual* laments, which only a common destiny as slaves raises to a common *generality*. Yet in the face of a want of discourse, there is a strength that remains wordless or lacks truth when verbalized, a strength of voice, gesture, gaze sweeping over the psychological requests of speech and yet the eternal "that's not it," "that's not enough" in modern dance, music, painting.[57]

Putting aside the more obvious and plausible explanations, another reason that Kristeva does not see Berssenbrugge is that she does not really see anyone. The observation of otherness here (racial and otherwise) is blinded by its own anthropological detachment, which transforms this scene of difference into a coherent picture, viewing everyday life as if it were staged. Kristeva abstracts from the "*individual* laments" of these women to "a common *generality*," and looking at bodies seems to be a fundamentally categorical exercise. The nameless women disappear entirely, and their individual utterances give way to an aggregate, disembodied, extralinguistic voice. The wordless strength in this passage is only possible because it comes a priori to the arrival of the bodies that appear to express it. As at Huxian Square, the visual field here is predetermined by acts of recognition.

As in *Pleasantville*, Kristeva's blind spot results not from unscrupulousness but from a well-meaning commitment to progressive politics. If *Pleasantville* celebrates universal humanism in order to oppose the discursive dominance of 1990s "family values," which the film casts as a descendent of 1950s intolerance, Kristeva's semiotic targets the paternal dominance of a masculine Symbolic in order to make a case for feminism. To do so in each example, the observation of other human beings relies overly on an a priori critical apparatus that governs how people view one another. Although Berssenbrugge's attraction to abstraction is no less powerful than Kristeva's, her work, by contrast, attempts to preserve the particularity of the positioned body within her phenomenological imperatives by repeatedly insisting on the presence of an irreducible materiality, a thingness, that is at once hidden but not defined against that which is visible. At the same time, Berssenbrugge stops well short of identity politics—another well-intentioned, liberal effort—because of its foundational reliance on models of recognition.[58] The tails of *Hiddenness* and *Endocrinology* thus figure not only positionality, racial or otherwise, but also what it means to see difference, in one another and in oneself, without reductively recognizing difference as an indelible mark that, like tails extending past the page's margin, we identify without even opening the book.

CHAPTER FOUR

REFLECTIONS OF THINGS

Ekphrasis and Racial Iconology in Cathy Song and John Yau

A focus on ekphrasis, broadly defined as "verbal representation of visual representation,"[1] as a way of thinking about race might seem roundabout. Insofar as ekphrasis isolates an individual's encounter with a visual or physical object, as well as with his or her verbalization of this engagement, ekphrasis usefully provides an elemental view of how otherness is produced discursively. Because the notion of otherness is fundamental to this subgenre, these literary representations of visual phenomena allow a privileged perspective from which to dilate on how otherness is perceived and articulated. In late twentieth-century debates about ekphrasis, fueled by the rising prominence of deconstruction, critics addressed the combative relationship between the word and the image—a relationship that increasingly took on a social character.[2] Ekphrasis most typically takes the form of a poetic response to a piece of visual art, as in John Keats's iconic "Ode on a Grecian Urn," and, by now, the controversies and underlying poststructuralist assumptions should seem familiar. The image's status as the original thing to be represented—not itself a representation—is problematic, and the belief that the fundamental conceit of ekphrasis is fidelity to an original art object now seems naïve. By foregrounding the problems inherent in linguistic signification, these discussions collectively emphasize the fundamental otherness of words to images as a central representational problem. Ekphrasis as a poetic practice became an encounter not only between subject and unfamiliar object but also among ostensibly incompatible modes of signification. The Grecian urn, for example, becomes an absence that Keats, in compensation, fills with apostrophic words, which, as Barbara Johnson suggests, "allow for there to be address with no context—a shaping of the void."[3]

In this context, ekphrasis queries not only the visualized object but also the process of visualization it general, and it thus overlaps in part with the imperative implicit in the criticism of racial visuality by Anne Cheng, Peggy Phelan, and Robyn Wiegman, as laid out in the introduction to this book. Complicating prevailing notions of racial visibility, these critics suggest that racial signification has an inherent visual complexity that is missed when we treat race not as constructed but as merely recognized. Race becomes reified, and we cease to appreciate the visual possibilities and its contemporaneity—how it changes and adapts, as David Palumbo-Liu suggests, under the weight of emergent ideological pressures.[4] This chapter thus suggests that the formal questions raised in ekphrasis are useful to thinking about racial visuality because ekphrasis directly engages the question of how one visualizes and gives form to otherness. Racial form, in this respect, is not unlike a Grecian urn.

Appropriating Frederic Jameson's notion of ideologemes, W. J. T. Mitchell, in an essay entitled "Ekphrasis and the Other," broadens the political stakes of the subgenre. In Mitchell's gloss, ideologemes are "allegories of power and value disguised as a neutral metalanguage,"[5] and so, as such, ekphrasis elides the social and ideological conflict it stages in what seems to be an inert form. The reason for this capacity is what James Heffernan describes as the friction between the visual and verbal modes of representation.[6] This semiotic conflict, according to Mitchell, connects ekphrasis to broader political stakes, not necessarily through its content but rather through its form. "The 'otherness' we attribute to the image-text relationship," he suggests, "takes on the full range of possible social relations inscribed within the field of verbal and visual representation."[7] Ekphrasis thus corresponds in structure to similar relationships in which power is parsed into "the freedom to speak and see and the injunction to remain silent and available for observation."[8] Mitchell develops one of these relationships—race—in greater detail:

> Racial otherness (especially in the binarized "black/white" divisions of U.S. culture) is open to precisely this sort of visual/verbal coding. The as-

sumption is that "blackness" is a transparently readable sign of racial identity, a perfectly sutured imagetext. Race is what can be *seen* (and therefore named) in skin color, facial features, hair, etc. Whiteness, by contrast, is invisible, unmarked; it has no racial identity, but is equated with a normative subjectivity and humanity from which "race" is a visible deviation. It's not merely a question of analogy, then, between social and semiotic stereotypes of the other, but of mutual interarticulation. That is why forms of resistance to these stereotypes so often take the form of disruptions at the level of representation, perception, and semiosis: Ralph Ellison's *Invisible Man* is not "empirically" unseen; he refuses visibility as an act of insubordination.[9]

In terms that return us to Cha's exploration of ostensibly blank, white surfaces and Berssenbrugge's presentation of tails as physical marks of positional difference, Mitchell bridges the gap between aesthetic and social abstractions, suggesting that underlying both ekphrasis and racial invisibility is a connection between visibility and otherness. Mitchell's terminology bears explication: *image-text* refers to the relationship between visual and verbal; *imagetext* designates synthetic works that combine image and text.[10] Whereas the image-text relationship opens possibility for thought, the imagetext forecloses on it by producing a reified entity that elides precisely the tension that the image-text foregrounds. Since race in American culture remains one of the most powerful arenas for othering, ekphrasis becomes an appropriate means of thinking about how one conceives racial otherness in the context of how one conceives otherness in general. By contrast, blackness as the imagetext, functioning as a reification, is uninterrogated and becomes synonymous with racial visibility, so much so that the Invisible Man must reject visibility altogether.

By treating race as a relationship between image and text, Mitchell implies that the transparency of the racial sign is an effect of the suturing that produces imagetexts. Such a revelation is even more important in an Asian American context, in which, as Colleen Lye suggests, the Asian racial form, historically speaking, "has a distinctive character insofar as the sense of its deceitfulness or mystery always points to the presence of something not shown." Lye goes on to suggest, "we recognize the Asiatic as a figure for the unrepresentable."[11] If race is the insistence on suturing visual characteristics to ideological text, and one that subsequently elides this process, then how is this process complicated when the visual image is itself understood as unrepresentable? Asian racialization becomes, then, a useful site for interrogating racialization in general because racial visuality in this context is already contested and problematic.[12] By foregrounding the otherness implicit in the image-text relationship, ekphrasis, especially when it addresses race, might serve not just as an analogical form but also as a means of articulating and probing how racial form takes shape and what ideological demands it satisfies.

Mitchell's formulation of ekphrasis is part of his larger call for a critical iconology as a way to deal with the challenges of thinking about otherness. Though he is not concerned primarily with racial otherness, his critical iconology is useful in this regard. In contrast to more traditional modes of iconology or iconography, critical iconology emphasizes the ongoing conflict between the icon (image, picture, likeness) and the logos (word, discourse, science).[13] Instead of trying to formulate a hermeneutic account of how images work in general, critical iconology focuses more on the repeated and increasingly ideological encounters between words and images in order to trace the processes by which "a historical, cultural formation" can "masquerade as a universal natural code."[14] The ultimate goal then becomes "not to heal the split between words and images, but to see what interests and powers it serves."[15]

By foregrounding ekphrasis and extending Mitchell's logic, this chapter suggests that there is currently a need for a critical iconology in racial discourse, which would pay close attention to the highly contested way in which racial visibility is produced in order to serve particular ideological demands. Implicitly in conversation with the concerns of Cheng, Phelan, and Wiegman, a racial iconology would thus turn away from a conception of the racial image as a discrete, a priori object that enjoys a natural status and treat it instead with rigorous contextualization, calling attention to the way in which (to tweak Mitchell's final gloss of ekphrasis) race becomes something always made by someone at some time for some reason.[16] In the context of Asian American Studies, racial iconology provides an alternative model of politicizing representation, which responds to calls for a postidentity politics and to the increasingly antisubjective sensibilities of contemporary avant-garde poetry and art.

In order to demonstrate how such a racial iconology might operate, I will contrast the ekphrastic work of John Yau, both in *Corpse and Mirror* (1983) and in his later treatments of Hollywood icons in *Borrowed Love Poems* (2002), with Cathy Song's *Picture Bride* (1983). Both Yau and Song are highly concerned with visual images and, in particular, with visual art. *Picture Bride* juxtaposes its depictions of immigrant struggle with poetic treatments of visual images, such as the *ukiyo-e* prints by Japanese artist Kitagawa Utamaro and paintings by Georgia O'Keeffe. In a similar spirit, *Corpse and Mirror* takes its title of course from Jasper Johns's 1974 painting, one of the best examples of Johns's signature cross-hatch style. Not surprisingly, given Yau's background as an art critic, ekphrasis in various forms occupies a central position in his poetic practice. Although Song and Yau share an interest in visual art, however, the difference in their choice of metaphor—picturing and mirroring, respectively—implies different attitudes toward the function of ekphrasis, not only in representing the visual in verbal terms but also in terms of racial form. Whereas Song's picturing ultimately stabilizes and contains the visual image, Yau's mirroring treats images as nascent and in shifting conversation with their historical antecedents, modeling thus a kind of racial iconology.

Picturing and mirroring thus become modes of seeing race, but, of the two, only Yau's mirroring is capable of attending to its complex, ever-changing visuality. In the relationship between poetry and visual art objects, Song's ekphrastic poems probe and redress the depths of loss that one associates with otherness, but her implied mode of seeing ultimately expresses its own limits.[17] By contrast, Yau's ekphrastic practice worries less about the dilemma of capturing visual form in verbal terms, and it accepts the impossibility of such an enterprise as an initial premise, a concession reflected by the failed mirrors in the poems. Instead, Yau responds to the kind of plight that burdens the Invisible Man, who is, Mitchell reminds, not empirically invisible but, rather, unable to control the ways in which he is seen and in which racist assumptions reduce his visibility into a woefully inadequate, transparently readable sign. Accordingly, Yau makes race visible, not as a reified imagetext but as a protracted operation of diffusion, entropy, and flux. Seeing race in Yau becomes a matter of charting the trajectory of images as they change in time, and his exemplary figure becomes the classic Hollywood icon, particularly white actors such as Peter Lorre and Boris Karloff who played Asian roles. Especially in these later treatments of film icons, Yau traces racial visuality as a series of wandering images—mutable, contested figures that morph and adapt to the ideological context in which they arise. By employing such a racial iconology, Yau awakes these stereotypical images from their dormancy, challenging these reified images by calling attention to their construction.

Because of the presence of such resistant challenges in his work, critics have argued that the political crux of Yau's poetics is the destabilization of identity, which, according to Priscilla Wald, "calls attention to certain inherent contradictions in all subjectivity"[18] and, in Timothy Yu's account, shows "that all identities, all selves are 'false' in some way."[19] Rather than foreground *identity* as a central term, I suggest that, for Yau, *iconicity* instead becomes the primary mode of thinking about race. Such a shift allows us to move beyond the impasses of identity politics without disregarding the activist values that gave rise to it in the first place and to call attention to the historically contingent production of racial form, which never disappears, even in contemporary fantasies of a postracial society. By thinking of race as iconicity, Yau tracks changes and modulations in racial form as a complex history, thus enacting a racial iconology as a supplement to identity politics where what is fought over is not the fact of visibility but the coding of visual representations.

Picturing Pictures

A quintessential figure of the powerless immigrant struggling with cultural and familial dislocation, the picture bride has been an important historical figure in Asian American Studies. Cathy Song's work suggests that an underexamined aspect of this figure is the relationship to images implicit in it.[20] For Song, picturing is an act of recovery that attempts to redress loss; it is one in which words take on the impossible task of restoring presence. The picture in "Picture Bride" appears only briefly about halfway through the poem, which represents a grandmother's difficult travels halfway around the world to fulfill the responsibilities of a picture bride.

> a man waited
> turning her photograph
> to the light when the lanterns
> in the camp outside
> Waialua Sugar Mill were lit

and the inside of his room
grew luminous
from the wings of moths
migrating out of the cane stalks?[21]

The barely mentioned picture here becomes visible only when the lights of the camp illuminate it—before the focus immediately shifts to the room and then the landscape around the camp. Both the grandmother's subjectivity and her image in the picture, apparently, are difficult to see. As recompense, the poem struggles to depict the grandmother's thoughts and feelings, which seem permanently lost. Unable to picture the original figure, the picture stages a double estrangement: The picture for the waiting husband is that of a stranger who becomes in turn a stranger to the poem's speaker. Picturing thus ironically implies a certain failure of vision; though the poem claims a lyric agency by taking on the task of depiction, it ironically remains unable to picture the absent central figure.

Though not a typical example of the genre, "Picture Bride" is ekphrastic in its desire to speak on behalf of a mute picture. Unable to ascertain the grandmother's thoughts and feelings during this life-changing event, the poem instead considers a series of speculative visual images of suggestive gestures that offer only subjective traces:

And when
she arrived to look
into the face of the stranger
who was her husband,
thirteen years older than she,
did she politely untie
the silk bow of her jacket,
her tent-shaped dress
filling with the dry wind
that blew from the surrounding fields
where the men were burning the cane?[22]

Central to the play of images here is the way in which foreground gives way to background. One's attention shifts away from the grandmother herself to her clothing to the surrounding landscape. The project of the poem—to imagine the speaker's connection to the grandmother—thus remains frustrated by an inability to focus the depiction. The final image of the grandmother's dress billowing in the smoke-filled winds from the cane fields marks an arrested moment that cannot be completed and doubles the picture of her as viewed by the grandfather. In both cases, the relationship to the image is not just estranged, it is irreparably so, and the grandmother comes to function not unlike the face of the other in the work of Emmanuel Levinas, which is not a specific, contingent face but a more abstract representation of alterity in general—not a particular other but Otherness writ large.[23] In short, "Picture Bride" bespeaks the limits of the picture.[24]

The second half of Song's volume turns to more conventional examples of ekphrasis. The third section of the volume begins with a series of poems that address the life and work of eighteenth-century Japanese ukiyo-e artist Kitagawa Utamaro, who was known for his stylized, woodblock prints that depicted women (often in erotic poses). Song's poem, "Beauty and Sadness," which is dedicated to Utamaro, focuses less on his art and more on the artist's biography, as is typical of Song's ekphrasis in *Picture Bride*. In this context, the prints themselves become traces of the artist's hand, which are ambivalent to the women they depict. Though a feminist critique in the mode of Laura Mulvey might seem appropriate, given the awareness of gender demonstrated in "Picture Bride"—that the capturing of the female image guarantees the mastery of the male artist—such a critique is absent from the poem, which celebrates Utamaro as an "invisible presence," which "one feels in these prints / is as delicate / as the skinlike paper / he used to transfer / and retain their fleeting loveliness."[25] The women, by contrast, become aestheticized through a series of similes that secure the evacuation of subjectivity and transformation that guarantees their image/commodity status: "Crouching like cats," "Or poised like porcelain vases," "They resembled beautiful iridescent insects, creatures from a floating world."[26] Fully art objects, these women, like the geisha who were sometimes Utamaro's subjects, become property: "Utamaro graced these women with immortality / in the thousand sheaves of prints / fluttering into the reverent hands of keepers."[27]

Unlike "Beauty and Sadness," "Girl Powdering Her Neck" focuses on a specific print (from which the poem takes its title), but the overall effect is similar. The poem alternates between representing the woman in the print as an autonomous subject and as an objectified image, but the latter clearly prevails:

> The eyes narrow
> in a moment of self-scrutiny.
> The mouth parts
> as if desiring to disturb
> the placid plum face;
> break the symmetry of silence.
> But the berry-stained lips,
> stenciled into the mask of beauty,
> do not speak.[28]

Although the mouth and lips suggest an attempt at articulation, the poem concludes by imagining these lips as aestheticized, metaphorically and visually: "Two chrysanthemums / touch in the middle of the lake / and drift apart."[29] Disappearing into their own metaphoric registers, the slightly parted lips reflected in a mirror described earlier in the poem as "a winter pond" become flowers—objects intended to be appreciated by the eye and not heard. Like the picture bride, the woman in Utamaro's print is a silent figure whose subjectivity becomes the object of speculation, for which speculation takes the form of narrative biography that attempts to redress the failure of the image to speak for itself. Rather than giving voice to the abject women or rendering their silence articulate, the poems leave them inert.[30]

At the center of Song's volume is her engagement with Georgia O'Keeffe, and "Blue and White Lines after O'Keeffe"—whose section titles, named after O'Keeffe paintings, are the same as the titles of the sections of the entire book—seems to occupy a privileged place therein. Although the poem names specific paintings, Song uses these references to mark various moments in the painter's biography. The poem takes on the form of ekphrasis, but Song's primary referent is O'Keeffe's eponymous 1976 autobiography,[31] which is a retrospective of O'Keeffe's oeuvre, cataloged in full-page color prints and accompanied by a self-penned narrative that recounts the painter's development from childhood. Each of the five sections of the poem corresponds to a painting, and four of them are associated with locations where O'Keeffe spent some time (New York; Taos, New Mexico; Makena Beach, Maui, Hawaii; and Sun Prairie, Wisconsin).

In this autobiographical mode, "Blue and White Lines after O'Keeffe" takes the voice of O'Keeffe herself, and the trajectory of the poem is not unlike that of a Bildungsroman, from youthful uncertainty toward artistic maturity. The poem begins in New York where O'Keeffe began her career; accordingly, the "Black Iris" section offers a portrait of the artist as a young woman in New York, alienated by her surroundings and the people around her. This alienated stance continues through the poem, modulating, for example, into an orientalizing treatment of the locals at Makena Beach in Maui (she references "island children" whose "eyes are the eyes of old fishermen" and the "bird language" of the Filipina on the beach).[32] As we learn in the final section, the trope of alienation originates from the painter's estranged relationship with her mother, the primal other in the poem. Though the poem expresses some dissatisfaction with the mother, it ultimately imagines a reconciliation through the act of painting: "When I stretch a canvas / to paint the clouds, / it is your spine that declares itself: / arching, / your arms stemming out like tender shoots / to hang sheets in the sky."[33] Given that all of the paintings alluded to in the poem are paintings of flowers, the rendering of the mother as a flower that grows through the conduit of the daughter's painting is particularly striking. In this figure, Song reprises the picture bride who is at once mute and expressively suggestive. The enterprise of art in both cases, be it poetry or painting, endeavors to recover the subjectivity of the ancestor and redress the pains caused by repressive social and historical conditions in the hope of reconnecting with the estranged stranger, for whom the anonymous New York neighbors and Hawaiian natives are both metaphoric substitutions. The fundamental characteristic of Song's ekphrasis, picturing, functions to compensate for the otherness of the other by turning pictures into words. However, in capturing the image with language, Song seems only able to rehearse the terms in which these figures are captured.

Interested in the relationship of poetics to Asian American politics, both Stephen Sumida and Shirley Lim conspicuously use the word *danger* in their commentaries on *Picture Bride.* Sumida locates it in the Makena Beach section of "Blue and White Lines after O'Keeffe," which might be misconstrued, he suggests, as perpetuating a noble-savage exoticization of the Asian American figures on the beach. Sumida quells this danger by arguing that the poem acknowledges the limitations of the point of view expressed—that of the painter—and thus implicitly critiques it.[34] Similarly, Lim takes Song to task for using clichéd Asian American images throughout her volume and senses the "danger of falling into predictable mannerisms": "One almost sees the creative writing instructor breathing over the poet's shoulder, urging her to write concretely about the particulars of her ethnic background, and although one can also imagine that it may be possible to write about jade, tofu and buddhas so that they illuminate Asian-American experiences, Song's repeated use of these Asian cultural fragments is strained, mechanical, and unconvincing."[35] Part of the danger here is that ekphrasis in Song implies a tendency toward containment—that the frame of the picture implies a boundary as well. Neither Sumida nor Lim attributes the danger entirely to Song herself; instead, they describe it as if it were a land mine on which Song is unwittingly encroaching. The danger here is that of accidental compliance—that race itself might be unwittingly determined by Song's reliance on its visible markers.[36] Sumida and Lim thus express a version of Phelan's critique (see introduction), in which certain images associated with race, because naturalized and reified, automatically trigger certain, predetermined reactions. The danger of ekphrasis in Song is the reduction of the possibilities in the visual field into subjectivism, that picturing inevitably involves an act of framing in which the subject is secured at the cost of containing the other. *Picture Bride* seems aware of the precariousness of the situation and thus works to repair estrangement, but in so doing, it reinforces precisely the enclosures that it laments.

Despite the efforts to picture the bride, women, or mother, Song's acts of depictive visualization fail to visualize the other in a field of difference and instead reproduce the kind of static visualization, the mode of seeing and coding, that has long been the hallmark of racialization in the United States. Despite the dangers, Sumida and Lim ultimately refrain from more vehement denouncement; whatever is malevolent in Song's poetics does not seem actively wielded by her own hand, but rather lurks from within the form itself. Song nevertheless leaves visibility entirely uncontested, and the ekphrastic frame of her poems seems to reify the strangeness of strangers by reinforcing the otherness of images and leaving their visibility unchallenged.

Mirroring Mirrors

Aware of the dangers of framing, containment, and reification within ekphrasis —which are precisely the dangers of the imagetext—Yau develops a racial iconology over the course of his career in order to treat images as deeply implicated in ongoing ideological struggles, handling images as if they had a life of their own that was not already predetermined and stabilized. In contrast to Song's picturing, in which the lyric subject attempts to redress the loss of the pictured object, Yau's mirroring reimagines the poetic act of ekphrasis as an extended visual engagement with the strangeness of the art object. The *Corpse and Mirror* poems, for example, take their title from and explore a Jasper Johns painting. Taking their cue also from John Ashbery's ekphrastic poem, "Self-Portrait in a Convex Mirror" (1975), which was inspired by a Francesco Parmigianino painting, Yau's poems enact the logic of Johns's visual aesthetics and appropriate Johns's painterly ethos by interpreting the diptych's divided, unevenly mirrored structure as an occasion to explore the implications of such rampant, proliferating divisions. Two, for Yau, is something of a magic number. *Corpse and Mirror* contains, for example, two sections of poems that explicitly reference Johns: "Corpse and Mirror" and "Variations on Corpse and Mirror." Within each section, all six poems are further divided into two sections. Furthermore, the volume concludes with a section entitled "Carp and Goldfish," a distorted double of the original title, and it is littered with poems that appropriate Johns's divided structure (such as "Two Mediations on Guanajuato," "Two Dreams of Life of a Coffin Factory in Lynn, Massachusetts," and "Two Kinds of Story-Telling"). As with Ashbery's rendering of Parmigianino's flawed mirror, Yau's acts of mirroring refuse accuracy and instead deteriorate the original. His choice of a highly abstract point of departure, a painting that entirely rejects mimetic representation, further complicates the question. What would ekphrastic fidelity to a visual abstraction look like, given the image's implicit rejection of mimetic conventions? More than holding the proverbial mirror up to the world, reflection in Yau multiplies such that the binary relationships between objects and their reflections diffuse and complicate the act of looking at and interpreting an already complicated art object.

Intimate with postmodern idioms, Yau's poetics thus reproduces, without explicitly naming, a trope that is often associated with postmodern art: the house of mirrors. The term is typically used to characterize the dizzying replication of multiplying images that replaces the "real" in postmodern thought, as well as the crisis of reference that arises in such a milieu.[37] In Yau's hands, the house of mirrors modulates away from a flattened, synchronic figure that signals undifferentiated postmodern distortion and toward a more a diachronic figure that situates diffusion and flux within time. The fact of distortion yields to an interest in a protracted process of mirroring mirrors, a process in which mutations become traceable. Yau's house of mirrors thus figures critical iconology, a series of complex images that exposes traces of the ideological conflicts and ambivalences that produced them. Yau's ekphrastic mirroring thus finds inspiration in Johns's promiscuous complexity, which becomes more inhabitable and less disorienting in Yau's hands. Deriving from Johns a decided aversion to stasis, a primary mode in Yau's poems is the interruption of repetitive patterns. His mirror is thus one with a proclivity for refraction.

A diptych, Jasper Johns's *Corpse and Mirror* consists of a left panel composed in oil and a mirror-reversed right half in encaustic (fig. 16). As the difference in material might suggest, the mirroring between the two sides of the painting is imperfect, not least because the cross-hatched patterns are clearly done with an obstinately imperfect hand. In addition, the colors on the left panel are more vivid than those on the right, which seem to have been the subject of a half-hearted attempt at erasure. Although these patterns offer a provisional nod to system and repetition, they ultimately reject the machine-like precision that characterizes some pop art and minimalist forms. Three other details of the right side of the panel should be noted: an imprint of an iron about halfway down the side, a long slashlike mark on the far border, and an *X* centered at the top. Together, these details give the impression that the right half of the piece has been vandalized. In a catalog for a 1974 exhibition at the Philadelphia Museum of Art, Mark Rosenthal describes the painting as a study in difference: "In contrast to the left half, the right side of *Corpse and Mirror* is an arena of exaggerated action and interruption."[38] If the divided

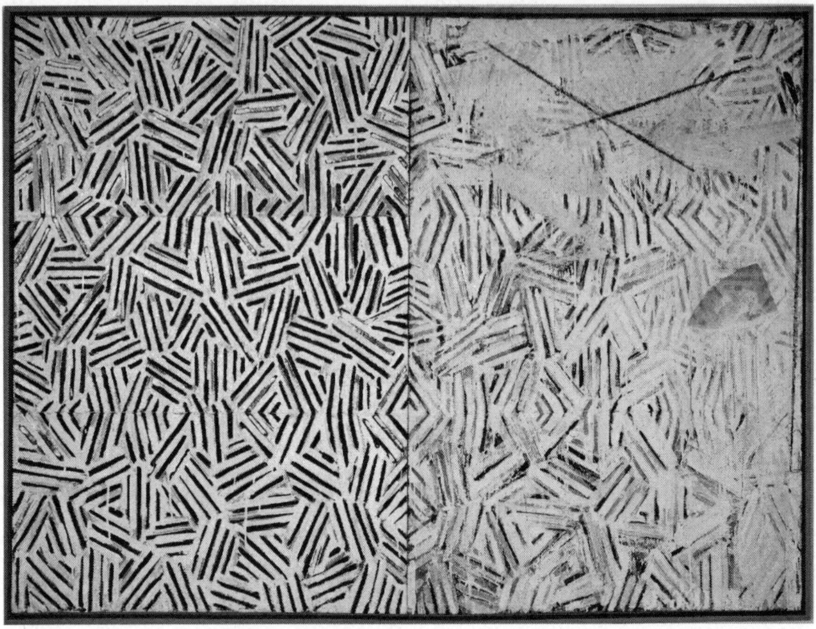

FIGURE 16. Jasper Johns, *Corpse and Mirror* (1974). Art © Jasper Johns/Licensed by VAGA, New York, New York. David Geffen Collection. Courtesy of the artist.

nature of the diptych invites the viewer to regard the painting as an instance of mirroring, it is one that distorts the referent image even more radically than that of Parmigianino. Furthermore, the distortions in Johns are not a purely optical effect, as in the case of Ashbery's inspiration; they are an implicitly social one as well—a result of the image as if left in irresponsible or malevolent hands, reflecting the life of the image in the world that might receive it.

Yau finds in Johns's aesthetics what Priscilla Wald locates in Yau's poetics: a demonstration of "not only a critical dimension of aesthetic experimentation, but also an aesthetics of critique."[39] More specifically, Yau's *Corpse and Mirror* and Johns's painting both perform a disingenuous commitment to system, ritual, and form. In both cases, orderly systemization inevitably veers off from its plotted course, and the aspiration toward repetitive structure is always undone by entropy. Perhaps because of these shared aesthetics, Yau's art criticism on Johns in his *The United States of Jasper Johns* (1996) reads as if it were a statement of his own poetics. For Yau, the heart of Johns's work is "his recognition not only that the individual lives in a world of uninterrupted change but that society, which is the collective expression of individuals, repeatedly denies this fact."[40] In his more recent writing on Johns, a book entitled *A Thing Among Things* (2008), Yau extends and nuances this argument: "The increasing visual complexity of Johns' art is the result of his gaining a farther, more powerful understanding of his primary fixation: What does it mean to be a thing caught in, and carried along by, time?"[41] In this model, patterns, systems, and other figures of stasis subtend a fundamental repression of the world's constant flux and of the inevitability of time. According to Yau, Johns puts patterns into motion and watches them dissolve, as if the agent of dissolution were not the painter himself but rather the flawed initial conceit, the arrogance of the pattern that remains ignorantly comfortable in stasis. In this passage, Yau specifically refers to Johns's flag and map paintings, familiar symbols that imply "deep-seated deceptions," but the question that they give voice to for Yau seems equally important with respect to *Corpse and Mirror*: "If time doesn't stand still, what does it mean to use a flag and a map, two social representations that don't register the passage of time, as ways to examine the individual's relationship to change?"[42] To remain committed to inert and static images, in both Johns and Yau, represents a failure to live in an ineluctably changing world in favor of the comforts of familiar symbols that encourage us not to interrogate further.

Quite cognizant of change, and equally suspicious of stasis, each section of the first three *Corpse and Mirror* prose poems explores the idea of decorum in a social setting or network. Each begins with a subordinate clause that locates in time the action of the sentence, which invariably has to do with a corpse. Each considers a spectacle and the ways in which these spectacles provoke attempts to produce social meaning out of them. "Corpse and Mirror (I)" begins, for example, "When one of our citizens dies, his corpse is placed in his chariot."[43] "Corpse and Mirror (II)" begins, "When a comet passes over the town, whoever sees it knows a corpse will soon be discovered at the edge of the forest shortly after dawn."[44] "Corpse and Mirror (III)" begins, "When the movie ends and the lights come on, the audience is puzzled by the sight of a corpse reclining on a velvet sofa in clothes of human hair."[45] Typically in this series, opening lines such as these employ a quasi-anthropological point of view in order to establish a fairly ridiculous premise, which the remainder of each poem plays out in wildly inventive detail. They all have in common an interest in ritual and decorum, which the poems take pains to map out in wonderfully silly particulars. The first poem deals with absurd burial rituals; the second with strange, arbitrary superstitions; and the third, very loosely, with the experience of going to the movies.

Yau refigures Johns's cross-hatchings by rigorously imposing orderly rules that fail to keep order; aesthetic patterns become reenvisioned as social conventions.[46] Keeping in mind the conceit of the poems—that the objects of the mirroring are corpses, which are figures of otherness—these rules then always fail to reify into stasis; like corpses, patterns in Yau decompose. The burial ritual in the second section of the poem, for example, in which the deceased's head is buried in a box separately from its body, ends mired in contingencies that spill messily about:

> One night, after the box has been buried or burned, you will hear something outside your window, inside your dream. The words may not be words at all but the fluttering of a bird caught in a snare. A broken pot. A bucket falling into a well. Listen carefully. He may need to speak to you again.[47]

The boundary between outside and inside here seems permeable. Various containers and restraints—pots, buckets, snares, dreams, and even words—have trouble with their primary appointed functions. Doubling the trouble, syntax breaks down into short, clipped sentence fragments as the prose poem sputters into a paratactic conclusion, ultimately departing from the previously intoned, self-assured certainty and turning toward contingency and speculation: "The words *may* not be words at all. . . . He *may* need to speak to you again."

Because Yau's ekphrastic poems shed identity, lyric or otherwise, as a normalizing force and validate John Cage's famous gloss of Johns's work as having "structures, not subjects,"[48] the extent to which Yau's early work engages questions of race and ethnicity has thus been the subject of some critical attention. Dorothy Wang argues that *Corpse and Mirror* "maintains a balance between pieces that address autobiography and questions of ethnicity directly and those that treat Yau's experiences as an Asian American subject in more transmuted form."[49] Wang suggests that Yau's contribution to Asian American discourse has less to do with the explicit Asian American markers in the poem and more to do with the ways in which hybridity and variation explore modes of social engagement that offer alternatives to official and dominant histories.[50] She thus reads Yau's treatment of the diptych as a material embodiment of minority double consciousness. Timothy Yu suggests that Yau's work self-reflexively ponders its own status as an Asian American text. By reducing Asian American markers in the text to ambiguous signs, Yu argues, Yau begs the question: "What marks a piece of Asian American writing if not its explicitly ethnic signifiers, beginning with the Asian name of the author—a marker that is all too easily essentialized into some notion of Asian American identity or consciousness?"[51] This antiessentialist turn foregrounded in Yu's account then calls into question the authenticity of all identities; the emptiness of "Chinese American" as a category calls attention to falsity of identity in general.[52] Both Wang and Yu thus conceive of Yau's departure from traditional minority writing as itself a political gesture that critiques less flexible models of racial thought. Both also imply that formal difference in Yau becomes a way of exploring racial difference.

Justifying such readings, *Corpse and Mirror* repeatedly dramatizes how the imposition of formal structure and order onto visual, material, and social phenomena always fails to hold. By toying with entropy, negation, and erasure, Yau elevates formal tinkering into social critique. Stylistic variation, Wang argues, subtly becomes a mode of suggesting ideological variation. Appropriately, ethnic/racial markers in the volume of poetry, Yu suggests, function as catalysts for accreting ambiguity rather than as indexes of authenticity. "Chinese Villanelle," for example, implicitly asks what must be done to an Italian form to make it Chinese. The poem offers no obvious answers. Potentially stereotypical "Asian" images in the poem—a lute filling the room and a pelican on a dam—are mobilized within a kind of silly, playful context that counters their stereotypical effect, but in so doing makes them seem less Asian. Instead, what makes the poem different from the original model—or, in other words, to bite on the title's invitation, what makes it Chinese—is its formal divergence, its tendency to wander from the villanelle, the most stylized of poetic forms. The poem has five tercets followed by a quatrain. The first and third lines of the opening tercet repeat, culminating in the final couplet of the last stanza, according to the traditional form. However, instead of the customary repetition that characterizes the villanelle, the repeated lines change subtly each time they appear. The third line of the poem, for example, begins as a simile, "I was like a lute filling the room with description," which later gets divided with a forced caesura and turned into questions ("Why am I like a lute? left only with description"). The poem then drops the simile entirely and introduces the memory of a second-person interlocutor ("I remember you looking at me without description") before finally reproducing the original simile with a difference in the poem's final line ("Now I am like a lute filled with this wandering description").[53] Crucially, the adjective *wandering* marks the difference from the past and the present *Now* as well as the poem's divergence from the traditional villanelle. With no other reliable indicators of Chineseness in the poem, the ethnic qualifier thus seems linked to its propensity for formal wandering, its playful decline of the traditional strictures, and its unwillingness to accede to any prescribed patterns of repetition. The poem tweaks its repetitions, and part of the task of reading is to chart difference within repetition.

Similarly, in "Two Kinds of Story-Telling" and "Two Kinds of Language," two poems from the volume's final section, the feeling of not fitting in, particularly strong for immigrant children, is reimagined as occasions to toy with imposed orderly patterns. The bifurcations named in the titles of these poems imply a distance from an unfamiliar language, but it is one that allows a space of playfulness. Yau's vision seems always to respond to an imposition by holding out for the prospect of wild possibility, as if to reappropriate and celebrate the nonnormative status associated with race. That which is foreign becomes imbued with the pleasure of wandering; divergence becomes diversion, which challenges stasis and repetition not as intervention but as inevitability.

Placed within this context, the many corpses in the *Corpse and Mirror* poems may be read as figures of Asian Americaness (not because they somehow morbidly embody deceased Asian American subjects). Rather, they figure the various forces of entropy that undermine and dissipate the desire for orderliness. Identity position becomes a less important question than the failure of the normative to hold its privilege. The penultimate poem in the series, "Third Variation on Corpse and Mirror," veers from the established pattern of longer prose poems and opts instead for a short, first-person lyric. Two sentences divided among twelve lines replete with heavy enjambment, this poem repeatedly thematizes breaches, cuts, and divisions of both the literal variety ("I crossed the street" and "two further choices") as well as the figurative ("the knife poised along the moment's throat").[54] These depictions in turn yield to breaches of decorum ("two dogs playing catch with someone's head") and of possibility ("a hand waved good-bye to the body it once carried"), as if standards of order and stability were being slowly debauched by an odd cosmic mitosis.[55] Variation in this poem, and in this series of poems in general, implies a kind of perpetual wandering—formal or otherwise—that subjects the desire for order and stasis (originally implied in Johns's cross-hatch patterns) to the slow and steady ravages of entropic time in small but ineluctable increments. The corpse in the poem, far from a racialized melancholic figure, becomes a part of, as well as an emblem of, this gradual dissipation and diaspora. In the larger context of Yau's work as it develops from these early iterations, the failure of normative order represented here become part of a larger critique of racial politics, which is less a critique of the wrongness of the racial status quo and more a conviction of how impossible it is to sustain.

It is no surprise that, when Yau decided to write criticism about Jasper Johns, he chose to begin with the most political works of Johns's oeuvre: his flag and map paintings. In this overtly political context, it becomes much easier to see how the inevitable instability of a static object (such as an American flag) resonates with racial politics. Though he does it in subtler strokes, Yau similarly politicizes Johns's *Corpse and Mirror* while avoiding the language of American racial discourse. He focuses instead on the more abstract question of how social meaning is produced and imposed as a normative standard in relation to visual phenomena. Toward the top of the right panel of Johns's *Corpse and Mirror*, one notices an *X* that spans the majority of the panel's width. Rosenthal reads the *X* as a symbol of negation, related to its use in printmaking to signify cancellation.[56] Beyond negation and cancellation, it is ironically a visible symbol; it is a presence that stands in for its opposite, erasure. Similarly, the pink zigzagging paint that partially covers the lower-left portion of the *X* and extends downward from it, as well as the slash near the right border, also seem to function as impediments to visibility: visible evidence of half-hearted attempts at marring the coherence of the cross-hatching. Distinct from the way in which Ellison's Invisible Man refuses visibility as an act of insubordination, the *X* and other marks of erasure do not so much refuse visibility as they make visible the figure of erasure without having to concede visuality entirely. They function, in fact, like the *X* that Malcolm X and others in the Nation of Islam during the 1950s and 1960s took as a surname in order to reject the slave name and allude to the *X* that was sometimes branded onto a slave's body. As in the case of Malcolm X (though in a much different context), the *X* in Johns is a visible figure of negation; it is an ironically visible figure of invisibility that emblematizes the various impediments to static order to which Yau's poetry constantly calls attention. Unlike Malcolm X, for whom the negation becomes the basis of a racial identity, Yau's ekphrasis avoids such coherences and instead abstractly locates race at highly visible moments of interruption, points of elision, and junctures where form wanders from its normative patterns. Latent in his early work, this dynamic is more fully explored in his later writing.

I Am Your Density!

Nowhere are Yau's ekphrastic treatments more suffused with racial questions than in his handling of Hollywood icons, especially Peter Lorre and Boris Karloff.[57] For Yau, these icons are racial things. Though they lack the materiality of physical objects, such as Cha's sculptures or Berssenbrugge's tails, these icons are understood as entities distinct from the people from whom they derive, and they have an entirely independent life of their own. Yau selects these figures partially because they were white actors who portrayed stereotypical Asian characters with some degree of regularity, particularly during the 1930s, but more important for Yau is the relationship between these Asian portrayals and the larger iconography of the creepy roles for which these actors were famous: monsters, miscreants, and murderers. Infamous for his role as a child killer in Fritz Lang's *M* (1931), Lorre brought some of his trademark shiftiness to the sly Mr. Moto. Having already played the monster in James Whale's *Frankenstein* (1931) as well as a more traditionally monstrous Asian character in the title role of *The Mask of Fu Manchu* (1932), Karloff's four restrained portrayals of Detective James Lee Wong between 1938 and 1940—during which period he reprised his most iconic role in *Son of Frankenstein* (1939)—subtly borrowed a distinctively mysterious aura from his previous roles. In both cases, the otherness of their Asian characters is informed by associations carried over from other more sinister portrayals.

These films roughly coincided with the Second Sino-Japanese War and the years prior to World War II and Japanese internment in the United States, a period in which the discourse of yellow peril shifted. David Palumbo-Liu suggests that portrayals of Asianness in this period became less concerned with population, the encroaching masses of Asian bodies, and more concerned with Asia as an emerging political and economic threat; the figure of the Asian thus became both admired and feared for embodying efficiency and resourcefulness. In contrast to the exclusionist logic of yellow peril before this period, the American imaginary began to move toward a "more complex notion of how Asia would be part of America,"[58] and so political, economic, and cultural intercourse with Asia became "increasingly unavoidable and unpredictable."[59] Lorre's Moto and Karloff's Wong become legible in this context, detective heroes who nonetheless are often regarded with suspicion and unease. Yau's interest in these portrayals, roles that were more complicated than unproblematic negative stereotypes, is telling.

Concerned with more than just debunking racist typologies, Yau takes these Asian portrayals as occasions to examine the processes of racialization. Focusing on the iconicity of these filmic figures, Yau subtly explores how visual signs become understood discursively as racial signs. Particularly in his treatments of Lorre and Karloff, iconicity becomes a way of thinking about race, foregrounding the ideological and discursive implications of being seen and reorienting racial discourse so that it becomes more finely attuned to the complex density of racial signs, which Yau refuses to leave reified. Hence, Yau's Hollywood icons rehearse their long litany of roles compulsively, as if it were a long series of identities provisionally assumed and immediately discarded. Though such performances lend themselves to a Butlerian view of identity as a performed, false construct, the primary effort of these Hollywood poems, I argue, is not simply to destabilize racial identity but to expose and archive the modes through which images accrete ideological associations. In this manner, Yau enacts a racial iconology, mobilizing the perpetual conflict between visual and verbal in ekphrasis as a way to stage the complex interactions that conspire to form iconicity, foregrounding flux, distortion, and imbalance. In Yau's hands, this visual/verbal conflict becomes an index of the furious fray in which conflicting ideological forces collectively produce visions of race.

Like a religious icon, a film icon becomes an entity unto itself, imbued with an energy and aura somehow independent of the person from which it derives. In this context, identity and iconicity also have a good deal in common. Both attempt to codify contingencies into a coherence that focalizes reception and carves out a niche. Karloff's identity as horror-film actor (monster, villain), for example, helps determine how he will be marketed to the viewing public and placed within film history. Similarly, conceiving of Karloff's iconicity requires a broad view of how the myriad concrete images from his films produce a sense of a collective abstract image, an admittedly inchoate sense of his overall cultural significance. Despite these similarities, identity and iconicity have an important difference. Whereas identity relies more on a differentiated symbolic system in order to produce its coherence, iconicity relies more on a system with a much greater degree of density. These terms are borrowed from Nelson Goodman's distinction between text and image, which he describes as the difference between a graduated and ungraduated thermometer. In the former, there are a finite number of marks by which one can gauge temperature; all other increments are rounded off to the closest mark. In the latter, everything is, as Mitchell glosses, "relational and approximate."[60] Since there are no marks to organize difference, there are an infinite number of possibilities. In a dense system, as Mitchell suggests, "every difference would make a difference."[61]

A sloppily written letter *a* does not change it qualitatively because its symbol system only requires that one differentiates the letter from other letters. By contrast, a sloppily drawn picture of a face is extremely different from a neat, more mechanical picture because its symbol system foregrounds finer distinctions that go beyond recognition. Similarly, though one might have a sense of mixed identity, the range of possible identities is finite, ultimately having to do with the various categorical possibilities. By contrast, though iconicity is also an aggregation of a figure, there are infinitely more possibilities for difference beyond the categorical. The lighting of the scene when the monster makes an appearance, the scene's set design, or costume design make less difference to Karloff's identity (a monster is a monster, just as an *a* is an *a*) than they might to his iconicity. As in the thermometer example, the difference between the two models is a matter of degree. However complex identity might be, iconicity is exponentially more so.

The difference between iconicity and identity in Yau's poems about Lorre and Karloff is measurable as the difference between these Hollywood icons and the Whitmanian subject invoked in them. In this context, "Peter Lorre Records His Favorite Walt Whitman Poem for Posterity" performs in two distinct ekphrastic registers, in which Yau's handling of Lorre is doubled by Lorre's imaginary treatment of Whitman, setting up a chain of representation that, like the *Corpse and Mirror* poems, degrades as it progresses. Referring to *Leaves of Grass*, the opening couplet of the poem (the first below) faintly echoes a line from Whitman's "I Sing the Body Electric" (the second below) and erodes its romantic vision:

> I am an indigestible vapor rising from the dictionary
> you sweep under your embroidered pillow[62]

> I am drawn by its breath as if I were no more than a helpless vapor—
>   all falls aside but myself and it[63]

In the second passage, Whitman imagines a physical intimacy between the speaking subject, depicted demurely as a "helpless vapor," and its other. The vaporized subject is absorbed sensually and intimately into the other's breath. By contrast, Yau's version fashions Lorre as an "indigestible vapor" that is marginalized from the sensual stage, rejected and rendered inassimilable. Accordingly, the poem supplants the idealized Whitmanian identity with fragmentary images of Lorre's numerous roles, degrading the singularity of the lyric *I* as well as the power of Whitman's signature, anaphoric utterance: *I am*.[64] As Yau's poem progresses, would-be declarations of identity become undone just as the idealized, unified subject becomes reduced to a transient interloper. As in "Chinese Villanelle," one can chart the formal wandering; the *I am* of the opening couplet becomes a possessive adjective ("*My* only offer . . .") before giving way to an object pronoun used improperly as the grammatical subject in a kind of caveman English ("*Me* criminal . . . / *Me* signaled") before finally settling into obscurity (*Me* modulates into "*Mere* . . .").[65]

The poem denies the possibility of Whitmanian unification and replaces it with entropy. Lorre is a thus a serial shape-shifter: "Call me Zanzibar Sam, Bulging Pharaoh, Narcoleptic Swill."[66] Appropriately for this "indigestible vapor," Yau resists the decidedly digestive poetics of Whitman, supplanting it with an amalgamation of Lorre's filmic roles.[67] Instead of a capacious subject that absorbs and thus erases difference, the Lorre figure in the poem becomes an archive that preserves it: a messy collection of fragmented roles that is compressed into a dense aggregate but fails to cohere into an identity. Concluding with an image ("gnawed leaves") that chews up the central metaphor of *Leaves of Grass*, the poem presents the figure of Lorre as an entity that cannot be assimilated into the Whitmanian subject and instead parades around as a parodic substitution that is superficial and trivial—"all pomade and fancy."[68] The iconicity of the central figure bursts at the seams with a hodge-podge of disguises and roles. In contrast to Whitman, Lorre is a failed container, too porous or transient to aggregate into anything unified except a dense amalgam of affective fragments associated with a lifetime of roles.

The title of this section comes from Robert Zemeckis's film *Back to the Future* (1985), in which a nervous George McFly (Crispin Glover) attempts to woo Lorraine Baines (Lea Thompson), the woman whom he will eventually marry, and accidentally declares "I am your density" before correcting himself with "I mean your destiny." This is a time travel narrative, or what Catherine Gallagher terms an "undoing plot."[69] Such narratives are characterized by a protagonist who tries to repair a future that he or she has compromised; *destiny* is thus the primary term, whereas *density* is a slip of the tongue. George is suggesting to Lorraine that, although she might feel ambivalent toward him in the present, she will feel differently in the future, and they somehow belong together. Another consequence of time travel, however, that develops as the film and its sequels play out, is the density of possible outcomes, which Gallagher describes in terms that resonate with Yau's reading of Johns: "The multiple time-track, parallel universe theory, in short, produces, paradoxically, not only an entropic dynamic, in which the constant forking divides the narrative energy, but also universes in which all effort seems unavailing precisely because all possibilities become realities."[70] There is no end to the different changes and outcomes that become possible once the past becomes malleable. *Destiny*, it seems, then, has a *density*; difference over time depends on moments that make a difference, opening one possible outcome while closing another. As the film franchise continues to play out in sequels, the possibilities of the future are infinite because even small changes in the past have dramatic, unforeseen effects. The time travel narrative has the potential to open up a Pandora's Box of density.

In "Peter Lorre Records His Favorite Walt Whitman Poem for Posterity," the spatial and temporal coordinates of density and destiny offer a way of thinking of iconicity that does not lapse into a postmodern vision of flat images heaped in an undifferentiated scrap yard. Yau reconstructs Lorre's iconicity as a dense network of images and associations, but instead of sweeping this loose collection of disjointed fragments under the rug of postmodern meaninglessness, the poem aggregates them—though fragmentary and incoherent as an identity—into a sense of destiny; the images themselves have a history and a future. The title, "Peter Lorre Records His Favorite Walt Whitman Poem for Posterity," makes this suggestion somewhat glibly, but the question of posterity—the lasting power of iconicity—remains an important question in the poem.[71] In the Goodman sense, the poem begins to accrete density, as if the language in it were itself behaving more like images. Scraps derived from Lorre's roles are squeezed together, in some cases two or three to a line. Although the poem cannot escape its intrinsically linguistic limits, it also seems intent on exhausting the dictionary, which is mentioned in the opening line, before it will surrender to the finitude of language. In linguistic terminology, *lexical density* signifies the difficulty and complexity of language—the higher the lexical density the more complicated the language. A Dr. Seuss book, for example, with its repetitions and backward-circling sing-song, would have a lower lexical density than, say, a legal brief. When read in this context, "Peter Lorre Records His Favorite Walt Whitman Poem for Posterity" seems to aspire to some kind of lexical density record, so much so that it seems willing to sacrifice the most fundamental forms of clarity:

> Me criminal puss no longer muzzled and mugged by snoring camera
> Me signaled pasty or patsy, but donned smooth glacial twitches
>
> Mere slip in a sequined slapper, lolling whimper of purring grape,
> Not just smoothed flotsam bulk and hankering moss[72]

Aside from the pronouns *me* and *your*, not a single noun, verb, adjective, or adverb repeats in the poem, a feat that is more remarkable given Yau's propensity for stuffing his lines full of animated, often frivolous language. Dismissing the burdens of semantic intelligibility and even grammar, the passage above furthermore seeks smaller increments of lexical difference (muzzled/mugged, pasty/patsy, me/mere, lolling/purring, smooth/smoothed). As if there were no such thing as a synonym, proliferations of language seem to accelerate as the poem attempts to represent Lorre as an icon.

The density of Lorre's iconicity does not, however, lapse into mere postmodern indeterminacy. Instead, the poem aggregates the disjointed collection of fragments into a sense of destiny; the images themselves have a history as well as a future. Contextualizing Lorre with respect to Whitman's legacy, the poem attempts to represent somehow the collective energy of a lifetime of roles. It presents not only an actor but also a career, and it considers how this career might be remembered. The poem thus serves not only as a record of Lorre as icon (so iconic that he was even cartooned in the 1946 Bugs Bunny short "Hair-Raising Hare," among others) but also as an archive of the various associations that have become a part of Lorre's iconicity in a parade of lovely, idiosyncratic words. More specifically, Yau considers what Lorre's iconicity tells us about twentieth-century American conceptions of liminality. Interrogating Lorre's myriad portrayals of fringe figures, Yau queries liminality itself and the place of Asian racial form within this dense nexus. Lorre functions as a figure of Asianness not because his portrayals were sufficiently authentic but because his inauthenticity provides clues to how race as a construct is made.

The parallel between race and iconicity in the poem is not, however, merely structural. Lorre's iconicity is also quite specifically in conversation with American mid-century conceptions of Asianness. Lorre is mysterious and inscrutable ("a gravedigger counting shoes in a candlelit saloon," "the outer me, the bun you tufted, was heavy-lipped"). He is unscrupulous ("Me criminal puss no longer muzzled"). He is an afterthought ("an indigestible vapor . . . swept under your embroidered pillow"). Finally, he is foreign ("Call me Zanzibar Sam, Bulging Pharaoh"). Even when they do not directly refer to portrayals of Asian characters, the constitutive fragments of Lorre's iconicity seem associated with Asian stereotypes. In envisioning Lorre, Yau suggests that we experience the process through which we see race—specifically Asianness. An attention to density helps us recognize the diachronous multiplicity and complexity involved in ordinary acts of seeing. For Yau, race is a dense construct, more discursive than authentic, and one can see Asianness in someone who is not in fact Asian. A series of codes compiled over time, race, without such scrutiny, might lose its density and become reified when reduced to acts of recognition. Yau's poetics resists this simplification and preserves the density it so painstakingly excavates. In calling attention to the construction of racial representations, this vigilance also implicitly leaves the destiny of these representations open-ended. How racial visuality has been produced leads to the question of how it will be done in the future. Appropriately, the poem refuses to reproduce a Whitmanian subject and instead preserves a sense of what Lorre means as an icon not by offering any iconic role in particular but by proffering a dense series of images from his career, whose progress requires a rigorous racial iconology to query the destiny of density.

"I Was a Poet in the House of Frankenstein" is not as dense as "Peter Lorre Records His Favorite Walt Whitman Poem for Posterity," but it similarly builds an archive that ultimately ties iconicity to posterity. More so than the Lorre poem, however, "I Was a Poet in the House of Frankenstein" toys with autobiography, not to retrieve a sense of Karloff-the-person from underneath his roles but to examine the relationship between the self and the overdetermined images that seem to supplant it. Much longer and more protracted, the poem is equally in conversation with Whitmanian poetics, particularly, in this case, with Whitman's catalogs, and it rehearses a similar poetic strategy through which Boris Karloff becomes an iconic/racial figure. More specifically, the poem consists of Karloff, the poem's first-person speaker, cataloging without much embellishment the long list of the roles he has played over the course of his career, and the repetition of the construction *I am* —which the Karloff figure uses to recount his various roles—strongly resonates with the appropriation of the Whitmanian subject in "Peter Lorre Records His Favorite Walt Whitman Poem for Posterity." The first-person voice in the poem is not so much a representation of Karloff himself, however, as it is a representation of his iconicity speaking as if on its own behalf. Like Lorre's, Karloff's *I am* differs from the Whitmanian utterance; instead of working to connect the speaker with various others across boundary lines of difference and build a collective unified identity, the *I am* in "I Was a Poet in the House of Frankenstein" instead works to serialize images, rendering them transient parts of a proliferating sequence that moves from one to the next too quickly to allow for any sustained self-reflection.

Karloff's ability to play Asian characters, however determined by Hollywood's ambivalence toward racial authenticity (or its confidence in its make-up artists), particularly fascinates Yau, and much of the middle of the poem addresses these roles (Dr. Fu Manchu, the Chinese bandit Fang, detective James Lee Wong). Surprisingly, the poem does not seem to be an indictment against inauthenticity; rather, it is more interested in the operations of iconic signification. After all, to be a poet in the House of Frankenstein is to be able to exist as an image, rendering the question of authenticity irrelevant. Potentially offensive comments about "the Chinese" in this poem (such as referring to a blow dart as "a weapon / well known to the Chinese / and those familiar with their ways") are thus diffused and passed off as citations of silly Hollywood clichés, voiced with a knowing irony.[73] In Karloff, Asianness becomes a series of signifiers that is neither more nor less ridiculous than any other he took on throughout the course of his career. The line "This is the fourth time I am Mr. Wong, but the sixth time I am Chinese"[74] speaks to the fact that Asianness itself is part of a vocabulary of easily accessible stereotypes, but the ease with which one can slip into the stereotype, in this poem, seems to blunt its offending edge.

The poem instead becomes a semi-rigorous effort to catalog iconicity through the use of an actor known for his highly stylized roles, and it ends, significantly, not with a famous image of Karloff as a monster but with an image of the actor in one of his most forgettable roles, which ironically was also his most autobiographical. In *Targets* (1968), one of his final films, Karloff plays Byron Orlock, a version of Karloff himself: an aging iconic actor who is tired of playing in the same old horror films and so decides to retire. It was Peter Bogdanovich's first credited film, and the opportunity was offered to the writer/director by studio executive Roger Corman, partially because Karloff owed the studio exactly two days' work, and there is certainly a perfunctory quality in Karloff's performance. Using footage from two of Karloff's more significant earlier films—*The Terror* (1963), which costarred a young Jack Nicholson, and *The Criminal Code* (1931), directed by Howard Hawkes—*Targets* is partially homage. In this vein, it laments the passing of the old horror film, a genre that Karloff helped define but is no longer considered terrifying by contemporary audiences who now confront senseless violence in their everyday lives. As such, *Targets* is in many ways a film about Karloff's iconicity. At one point, Orlock declares, "I couldn't even play a straight part decently anymore. I've been doing the other thing too long. And even that isn't the point. You know what they call my films today? Camp.

High camp. . . . My kind of horror isn't horror anymore. . . . No one's afraid of a painted monster."

Like "I Was a Poet in the House of Frankenstein," *Targets* considers the relationship between iconicity and self-regard, implicitly asking if the target of the film's camera suffers the same tragic fate as that of the gunman's rifle. The plot involves the lives of Orlock, who gives a final promotional appearance at a drive-in movie theater before retiring, and Tim O'Kelly, an average, white, clean-cut, young man who inexplicably decides to kill his wife and mother before going on a shooting spree. The film climaxes at the drive-in theater, where O'Kelly takes shots at the audience from a hole in the movie screen before he confronts Orlock in two forms. Yau ends his poem with this scene:

> I am Byron Orlock, an aging actor
> who became famous for his horror roles.
> I want to retire.
> A young married man
> with an obsession for guns
> decides to kill me.
> He sees me once,
> through a telescopic lens,
> and then in two places.
> I am on the screen of a drive-in movie,
> where he has come with his rifle,
> to kill more innocent bystanders,
> and I am walking toward him,
> an aged but determined man with a cane.[75]

The poem refers to two encounters between Orlock and O'Kelly. In the beginning of the film, when the young man coincidentally sees Orlock in the sight of the rifle that he is thinking about buying, and at the end of the film when Orlock, using his cane to walk, bravely approaches the still armed O'Kelly. In this final scene, O'Kelly becomes implausibly confused (it is not the greatest of films) and shoots until he runs out of bullets—adhering to the laws of forced symbolism—at both the Orlock walking toward him and the similarly dressed image of Orlock/Karloff in *The Terror*, which happens to be projected on the screen at the time. Orlock knocks the gun out of O'Kelly's hand with his cane and proceeds to slap him with both sides of his free hand, which (again, implausibly) is enough to cause the boyish gunman to cower in a corner until the police arrive. The ending of "I Was a Poet in the House of Frankenstein" thus imagines self-awareness as the kind of understanding of one's relationship to images that *Targets* stages so heavy-handedly in its climax. By placing this scene at the end of a long rehearsal of a lifetime of roles, Yau implies that self-awareness involves the ability to see oneself as an image. *Targets* begins with Orlock screening the final cut of one of his earlier films, watching himself and dismissing it as terrible when the lights come on. The film reprises this scenario of Orlock watching himself on film in the finale, which Yau re-creates at the end of his poem. Yau's choice here is important because it is the most authentic role of Karloff's career; he plays a version of himself: "an aging actor / who became famous for his horror roles." In this final moment of the poem, when there is an opportunity to reunite image with an authentic sense of self, the iconic speaker of the poem instead confronts his own iconicity as an inassimilable, larger-than-life image that negates the possibility of authentic selfhood.

In so doing, the poem offers a figure for the racial images explored earlier in the poem and presents an alternative mode of racial visuality that unmoors race from its reified associations. Instead, race becomes iconicity, a matter of one's relationship to images, and imagined here is a mode of double consciousness in which looking at oneself through the eyes of others does not privilege the external perspective that confers judgments and determinations, a mode that acknowledges the fact of corporeal visibility without complying with corporeal inscription. Yau thus uses iconicity to present a mode of contextualized, historicized vision in which the act of looking itself becomes the object of critique. In this context, self-knowledge does not defer to a prescriptive authority; it depends instead on the realization that such knowledge is mediated by a history of images that are ideologically imposed and governed. When looking at Byron Orlock, the Karloff figure in the poem confronts not himself, despite the strong autobiographical elements of the role, but rather the contours of his own iconicity—what he means as an image as constructed by his roles throughout the years. The problem for the poet in the House of Frankenstein is how to regard one's own image and how to understand oneself when these images depend on their public circulation, a process in which their affective meanings may become overdetermined by forces outside of one's control. To regard one's visage in such a milieu is not to peer proverbially into the mirror but, more radically, to wander into an unsettling house of mirrors where the original point of reference gets lost in a dense shuffle. Rather than dissolving entirely into postmodern unease, the iconological approach to the icon in the poem treats the confusion not as a reason to surrender but as a challenge to continue; densities provoke questions, not resignations.

The images that Karloff catalogs throughout "I Was a Poet in the House of Frankenstein" thus provocatively suggest ways in which notions of Asianness in American culture coincide and interact with figures of monstrosity through the iconic figure who encompasses both. Yau's point, however, is not to model a more complex figure of yellow peril but to use these icons to track how visual images within a particular social discourse become legible on particular bodies and to demonstrate how these bodies can become freighted with affective associations. At the same time, the wandering quality of the icon, which resists aggregation of the affective associations it accumulates, reminds us that racialization is as much contested as it is imposed. Yau thus avoids the essentializing reductions of identity politics or the free-for-all of performative destabilization by understanding racialization within a discursive history that might be combated by a racial iconology that fights not over the products of these visual codes—namely identities—but over the process of coding itself. In this respect, this mode of seeing is similar to spying in Jasper Johns's famous distinction between the watchman and the spy as figures of two modes of perception.[76] As Yau glosses, both are "engaged with and by the material world," but in contrast to the watchman, the spy requires "certain interrogative techniques to what has been looked at."[77] Whereas the watchman, to cite the same quotation that Yau cites from Johns, "leaves his job & takes away no information," the spy "must remember & remember himself & his remembering."[78] Similarly, racial iconology tracks not only how race is visualized but also how these visualizations relate to past visualizations. Both Lorre and Karloff, in Yau's reflective poems, remember themselves and their remembering. Following an imperative not only to remember but also to do so with an awareness of how memory itself can be unreliable, they see themselves both in the context that their previous portrayals created and, more abstractly, as part of a dense history of signification.

For this reason, though it might seem odd for Yau to select non-Asians such as Lorre and Karloff as quintessentially Asian American figures, their inauthenticity calls attention to the powerful forces that dictate these visual codes. Yiman Wang suggests that the appeal of yellow face and other forms of racial masquerade during this period is "the *in*transitive relationship between the star body and the character's body."[79] The appeal, in other words, is not the mimetic accuracy of the portrayal but the falseness of the representation and, hence, it is the experience of otherness between the portrayer and portrayed that is coherent with the modernist taste for antimimetic art as it filters into popular culture. Though Lorre and Karloff, in Yau's hands, are indeed fraudulent as representations of Asians and satisfy the kind of appetites that Wang describes, they are accurate as embodiments of Asianness in twentieth-century American racial discourse, precisely because their portrayals embody and anatomize the falseness of the portrayal that Wang locates in yellow face. For Yau, racial iconology is a kind of rigorous relativism that not just includes a debunking gesture that challenges reified constructions of race but also, more importantly, can function as an archival tool, capable of tracing and investigating how these constructs came to be and how previously determined destinies are unraveled by their densities.

Knowing Racial Things

In an earlier poem, "Eleven Things We Need to Know about Ourselves" (1998), Yau brings this critical iconology to bear on Asian American self-knowledge. The prose poem plays with stereotypes, some more absurd and invented than others, which it presents as an enumerated list. Specifically, the poem imagines a relationship between knowledge about oneself and misperceptions that shape this knowledge. As he/she runs through the list, the speaker of the poem takes on a tone of amused detachment:

> 5.
>
> Since we have never been classified, and none of us have ever been informed as to how long we would have to inhabit this shifting purgatory, we have stayed strange, even to ourselves.

> 6.
> We are the men who eat pigeons, turtles, ducks, dogs, and cats, whatever runs through the park at night. Squirrel is high on our list, as are the feet and ears of certain small animals. . . .
>
> 9.
> No one knows how to address us because our names—single syllables strung together like pearls—sound like a cross between a puppy's growl and a cat's yelp. Maybe that's why we began sneaking into the park at night, a dozen nylon bags folded neatly in our freshly laundered knapsacks. We wanted to get closer to our ancestors, the ones who walk on all fours or fly short distances in the dark.[80]

Misinformed yet exceedingly detailed, the opinions expressed in this poem are absurdly humorous and voiced by a supposed cultural insider, presumably capable of confirming the veracity of these "facts." The point of this list is to suggest how the Asian American subject's self-understanding is challenged and complicated by a set of predetermined assumptions that have no factual basis. The problem of the Asian American subject also mirrors the problem of the film icon, as embodied by both Lorre and Karloff. In both cases, self-conception is mediated by the public circulation of preconceptions that become increasingly dominant through a series of proliferating associations. By combing through each stereotypical proposition with a feigned seriousness and by cataloging them along with others in a kind of iconological critique, they become intelligible as part of a history of signification rather than as self-evident derivations that one sees written on the body.

One of the most powerful elements in the poem is its treatment of Asian invisibility as a trope, ironically rendering it iconic. The second item in the poem as list, for example, speaks about learning "to wear masks that resembled our memories of our faces."[81] The third describes a street artist who refuses to depict the Asian American form, telling "us to come back after the news of our status had been widely broadcast over the airwaves."[82] The fourth describes a strategy of self examination: "In each group one of us is assigned to scrutinize magazines, movies, and television—the repository of faces—to learn whether any of them has finally become a mirror we might examine, so as to discover something more about ourselves."[83] In each of these cases, the visible is marked not merely as invisible, but visibly invisible. Like the *X* on Johns's canvas, the Asian American face and body are marked as figures of negation that figure invisibility itself.

The eleventh and final piece of self-knowledge in the poem, which has to do with pictures, seems a metacommentary on the act of depiction, and it responds to the kind of limited ekphrasis that I earlier located in Song. Here, the failure of the pictures to offer knowledge implies a broader distrust of pictures in general: "We learn almost nothing from pictures of our relatives that we managed to smuggle across the border. They spoke another language, they lived in a different time."[84] The reason for distrust is not an implicit question about the authenticity of the pictures. Instead, justifying the provocation toward critical racial iconology, the problem with these pictures is our inability to read them in context. Therefore, the problem is not with the pictures themselves but rather with the way they have become divorced from the context in which they become intelligible and expressive. We learn "almost nothing" from pictures because, out of context, they become static objects that lack any dynamic visuality. The alternative form of knowledge (*things* and not *facts* that we know about ourselves) that the poem offers, however, comes not from any one of the eleven items on the list but from the way in which the density of these aggregated images collectively offer an iconological look at the way in which Asianness is visualized in the United States. Though we learn very little about ourselves from these pictures, we gain a valuable sense of how they might function as mirrors, however cloudy or distorted, for how we continue to see and be seen.

CODA

HATING YOKO ONO AND THE NEW YELLOW PERIL

While I was doing research on Theresa Hak Kyung Cha at the Berkeley Art Museum in the spring of 2007, I happened to speak with Yoko Ono. Stephanie Cannizzo, the wonderful curator whose unenviable task it was to sit with me as I sifted through the Cha material, had also organized the Yoko Ono exhibit that was showing at the museum. The exhibit included an unmarked telephone mounted on a wall, which Ono would occasionally call in order to speak with curious visitors. It was one of the final days of the exhibit. When the phone rang, we ran into the hallway and stared at it until she finally suggested that I answer. I did, and it was indeed Yoko Ono. We spoke about the weather in New York and made small talk about the exhibit until I handed off the phone to an eager undergraduate. Only after it was too late did it occur to me how much Yoko Ono and Cha had in common as Asian American artists working in an avant-garde style, and I began to regret that I did not have a more substantial conversation. Indeed, Cha's piece, *Surplus Novel*, with which this book begins, references Ono (though it responds more to the appropriation of her name as a racial slur). Of course, there is a good reason that the connection did not occur to me right away. Although her entrance into the national imaginary coincided with the emergence of Asian American politics, Ono remained a discrete figure. Because she neither claimed any kind of Asian American identity nor engaged race in any explicit or sustained way in her work,[1] Ono might seem an unlikely culminating figure for a study of Asian American racial form; she is rarely discussed in Asian American Studies.

As a highly visible Asian woman who inspired such virulent enmity, however, she is useful for examining the visual coding of Asianness in contemporary America and for deploying the kind of racial iconology that I developed in chapter 4. In this critical mode, Leslie Bow presents Ono as an exemplary figure and suggests that "Ono's public reception revealed that their coupling [with John Lennon] had been taken another way; it was the West's corruption by the East abetted by the distaff's controlling influence, a perception later reinforced by her feminist phase."[2] Bow goes on to sketch out the distinctiveness of this case: "Reaction to Ono reveals more than the fact that women often take the blame for men's choices, including infidelity; it demonstrates the powerful mythmaking surrounding an Asian female public figure whose notoriety lay in an imagined seductive power. Ono's 'foreignness' was an intrinsic part of that notoriety although explicit references to her outsider status might often remain veiled."[3]

This notoriety was often greeted with hatred, and even today, remnants of this hatred persist. At the moment I am writing this, there are numerous groups on Facebook (to take one measure of popular opinion) dedicated to hating Yoko Ono, including "Yoko should have died instead of John Lennon," "Everyone knows a Yoko Ono" (note the fairly common usage of Ono's name to signify a woman that breaks up male friendships), "Damn you Yoko Ono, you broke up the Beatles. . . . How do you sleep at night?," "Fuck Yoko Ono," "Me No Like-o Yoko Ono," and a few in Spanish, such as "Yo también odio a Yoko Ono . . . La destructora de los Beatles." I list these somewhat at length because the sentiments these groups represent are a holdover from popular sentiment in the 1960s and 1970s, for which the manifestations in the popular press are only the tip of the iceberg. By 1969, as Jerry Hopkins, one of Ono's unauthorized biographers, suggests in a chapter entitled "Enter: the Dragon Lady," "it seemed that virtually everyone in the Christian World hated her, and that she was well on her way to becoming the most vilified woman on earth."[4]

Hate Object

Hatred and antipathy in popular culture are somewhat difficult to recover after the fact. Although anyone who remembers the late 1960s and 1970s can testify to the prevalence of anti-Ono sentiments and to the virulence of these feelings, hard evidence of this past vitriol is more difficult to recover. Certainly, the label "Dragon Lady" was common—Lennon himself acknowledged this characterization in interviews[5]—but what one might say in private company may not find itself in print. Outright displays of hostility, such as Charles McCarry's December 1970 piece in *Esquire*, entitled "John Rennon's Excrusive Gloupie: On the load to briss with the Yoko nobody Onos," which was accompanied by a full-page David Levine caricature of Ono towering over a cowering Lennon as a beetle (the bug) she holds on a taut leash, were more the exception than the rule.[6] The attitude implicit in McCarry's title, which makes fun of an Asian accent, was typical of Ono's reception during the period. Ono acknowledged as much in a 1973 *New York Times* Op-Ed piece: "People say that for the last five years I have been a hate object of the world. It was sort of fashionable to put me down."[7] Appearing a few short paragraphs after a discussion of her perceived Oriental foreignness, Ono's phrasing here—including the term *hate object*—is revealing for the way in which it subtly imbricates racial and avant-garde discourse, particularly for an artist whose own work focused so intently on the strangeness of things.

After my brief conversation with Yoko Ono, it occurred to me that the form of the hatred directed toward her helps to elaborate the political stakes of what are often regarded as apolitical avant-garde abstractions and to foresee the contours of future racial discourse in an increasingly globalized era. Bow suggests that the "hatred leveled at her was not so much due to her association with the avant-garde."[8] True enough. There were certainly other much more important issues for her detractors, but in many cases, the hatred of Ono was often expressed as an aesthetic distaste for her avant-garde art, and denigrating this art, I would argue, became a mode of objectifying Ono in racial terms, of reaffirming her foreignness. This is precisely the dynamic that the writers and artists in this study have attempted to invert. One of the overarching arguments of *Racial Things, Racial Forms* has been the utility of the avant-garde emphasis on things for interrogating the trope of the Asian as perpetual foreigner. Avant-garde Asian American art often mobilizes the strangeness of the thing as a means of investigating overlapping structures of reification and racialization, and the avant-garde poets I examine bring this focus on thingness to a poetry and literature that is otherwise dominated by narratives of Asian American subjective identities. The implicit connection between racialization and avant-garde aesthetics in Ono's iconicity notably anticipates the various modes in which the artists examined in *Racial Things, Racial Forms* have recalibrated race by politicizing avant-garde aesthetics. Though these aesthetics were a point of denigration for Ono's detractors, this negative appraisal of these aesthetics ironically indicates their positive political possibilities—that a large proportion of the American public found the avant-garde in Ono so threatening confirms rather than denies its potential.

Ono's iconicity joins avant-garde aesthetics and social discourse, epitomizing what it means to be a racial thing. Not only does her visual art foreground thingness in order to defamiliarize and resituate familiar and mundane objects and actions, but she also functions as an iconic nodal point, perhaps indeed a hate object, at which antipathy for the inscrutable nature of avant-garde art intersects with anxieties about emergent Asian (specifically Japanese) capitalist power, particularly during the 1970s and 1980s. Both as a producer of avant-garde art that seemed to many diametrically opposed to John Lennon's popular art and as a pop-culture figure that did not assimilate smoothly into narratives of celebrity commoditization (at least not until well after Lennon's death), Ono, like Yau's Hollywood icons, functions as a figure in which one may witness the inner workings of the recombinant ideological forces that compose her iconicity.

In this coda, I wish to place this hatred of Ono at the beginning of a speculative genealogy of a new yellow peril that is emerging in the current era of globalization. I do this in order to suggest new directions for future inquiry. Specifically, I argue that the common aversion to Ono updates versions of older models of yellow peril, anticipating a new manifestation of this antipathy in contemporary American discourse. Complicating narratives of assimilative advancement, recent studies point out the continuity between the yellow peril discourse in the United States of the late nineteenth and early twentieth centuries and the model minority discourse of the second half of the twentieth century.[9] Rather than signaling progress toward a more equitable society, the myth of the model minority in these accounts instead becomes a more insidious and covert form of its less subtle ancestor, reformulated for contemporary ideological demands. This change does not also mean, however, the end of more explicit displays of anti-Asian antipathies. That Ono was frequently called "Dragon Lady" over the years certainly proves the point.

Of greater interest here is the hatred directed toward Ono that refers to her Asianness only indirectly. The expressions of this hatred in popular culture often focused instead on her avant-garde aesthetics and particularly on its unaccountably bewitching effect on John Lennon.[10] In her musical forays, Ono's dissonant screaming and wailing seem aberrant and foreign—particularly to those invested in Lennon's more mainstream sensibilities—and her general avant-garde aesthetics and politics, manifested earlier in their relationship in various forms of public nudity, seemed to have changed Lennon from mainstream pop star to something decidedly different and marginal. As if from worried relatives expressing concern for Lennon, and underscored by an anxiety about interracial marriage, the popular sentiments asked of him were: Can't you see how weird she is? Can't you see what she is doing to you? Denied any complexity or subtlety, avant-garde aesthetics in this manifestation comes to oppose common sense. What seemed obvious to Ono's detractors, they believed, somehow escaped Lennon's notice.

Talking about Ono's avant-gardism, I argue, became a way of circumscribing Asianness, particularly in the shadow of an emergent anxiety about Japan's rapidly burgeoning economic power and a mounting frustration with U.S. military efforts in Southeast Asia. In this multitextured context, constructed by the ongoing war in Vietnam, the entrance of Asian communism into the discussion of Cold War politics, Nixon's historic trip to China in 1972, and Asian economic expansion, U.S.–Asia relations increasingly became a central preoccupation of public consciousness. Ono was an iconic figure who resonated with at least some of these issues, so hatred of Yoko Ono encompassed more than simply personal dislike. Perhaps even more radically than in many of the texts discussed in *Racial Things, Racial Forms*, avant-garde aesthetics and racialization in the case of Ono become nearly indistinguishable. Accordingly, expressions of hatred for her during this period, which often fetishize her art, parallel emerging frustrations with globalization and simultaneously give voice to a newly emerging strand of yellow peril in which anxiety about Asia in general becomes an anxiety about Asian influence in particular. Bow mentions Ono's perceived talent at both sexual and psychological seduction,[11] but the hatred directed toward Yoko Ono, whose appeal was lost on these detractors, often imagines Ono's power as something more unaccountable. The influence in turn becomes reimagined as radically unseeable and thus supplants earlier nervousness about the coming hordes of Asian bodies. Hatred of Yoko Ono resonates, I suggest, with recent anxieties about the invisible baggage that accompanies global trade with Asia (such as SARS, avian influenza, lead paint on toys, and outsourcing) in that both displace an older nervousness about the traffic of Asian bodies with one that worries about a much more inchoate, even more abstract, sense of Asian influence—more perfidious because it is more difficult to see.

Although a complete genealogy of this trajectory is beyond the scope of this coda, I sketch out here its parameters and unpack how the hatred directed toward Ono epitomizes this contemporary form of yellow peril, which befits a new globalized economy. In the older model, the invisibility of the Asian body was part-and-parcel of its objecthood (the Asian body's invisibility was an index of its subaltern anonymity), but invisibility of this newer Asian influence becomes more literal. Yoko Ono is a protofigure in this discourse insofar as much of the hatred directed toward her had to do with her mysterious and unaccountable influence over her beloved husband, an influence that is often recoded in capitalist terms. Hatred of Ono can thus be read as an example of Lacanian "paranoic alienation" expressed by the subject of Western capitalism who projects outward his or her sense of alienation onto various threatening figurations of otherness.[12] The paranoiac's own sense of instability becomes displaced onto an other that externalizes the threat and makes it more visible. The epicenter for this anxiety in Ono's case became, strangely, her avant-garde ethos. What, then, did it really mean to hate Yoko Ono?

Peter Occhiogrosso's 1980 interview begins plainly: "I always hated Yoko Ono." To be fair, the interview attempts to repair popular misconceptions of Ono and ultimately treats her kindly. Occhiogrosso simply expresses up-front a common attitude toward Ono that was prevalent since the late 1960s, when she graduated from art-scene figure to pop-culture icon through her association with Lennon. Occhiogrosso goes on to specify his dislike, which in his case was not based on a deep love of The Beatles: "No, what I really hated about Yoko was what she appeared to be doing to John Lennon. What was the guy who wrote stories like 'No Flies on Frank' doing with someone who wrote things like 'Tunafish Sandwich Piece'?"[13] Specifically, Occhiogrosso dislikes Ono's instrumentality—her inchoate influential power—which he associates specifically with her avant-garde sensibilities. Occhiogrosso laments

Ono's role in changing Lennon's aesthetic values, the way in which she led him toward avant-garde indulgences such as poems about sandwiches. This would be harmless enough if this turn were not a precursor to a more insidious power grab:

> Now, in 1980, here was an even more palpable reason to distrust her. After having gotten John to trade in his guitar for an apron, Yoko was reported running his business affairs, investing in apartments in the Dakota, secluded estates, and quarter-of-a-million-dollar cows.
>
> She had exercised an unfathomable power over her husband at some crucial point in his life, turned him around from what he was then to what he is now, and consequently had come to call all, or almost all, of the shots. John calls Yoko "Mother."
>
> All things considered. I really didn't expect to like Yoko Ono.[14]

The inscrutability that Occhiogrosso earlier associated with Ono's art here modulates into an "unfathomable power," which manifests itself as aggressiveness in business. This power also infantilizes Lennon, who seems to be both bystander and victim. The mere silliness of Ono's avant-garde poems about tuna fish sandwiches thus magnifies into the kind of capitalistic accumulation, fiduciary irresponsibility, and whimsical excess that one associates with only the most delusional of the wealthy. Occhiogrosso later goes so far as to link financial aggressiveness with artistic inclination: "Yoko's real estate projects and business deals are an extension of her performance art."[15] Remarkably, the claim here is not merely that she approaches art and business with the same tenacity; it is that they are somehow part-and-parcel of the same activity, that Ono's avant-garde artistic practice is not just *like* capitalist aggression, it somehow fundamentally *is* capitalist aggression. In both art and business, then, Ono is represented abstractly as an enigmatic but highly effective force; this is in contrast to Lennon, who seems oblivious and helpless. Furthermore, rather than conceiving it in terms of recognizable, even desirable, human traits (such as ability, acumen, and diligence), this force seems instead defined by its unaccountability. Occhiogrosso ultimately yokes avant-garde aesthetics to a capitalist power play that casts Lennon as an innocent bystander to Ono's aggressions.

This anxiety over her enigmatic influence is thus linked to the accumulation of capital. Even before Ono took the lead role in her family's financial affairs, her relationship with Lennon was imagined in the popular press in financial terms. A 1969 *Look* article makes this point abundantly clear in its title: "Top Pop Merger: Lennon/Ono Inc." As in Occhiogrosso's article, rather than portraying Ono in more conventionally unseemly terms (such as a gold digger), the *Look* article eschews such clichés and instead represents her as more radically unrecognizable, as enigmatic in intention and mysteriously effectual in gaining power. Throughout the article, author Betty Rollin expresses a dislike, but, unlike Occhiogrosso, she has no interest in recuperating Ono, whom she describes at one point, invoking Lady Macbeth, as standing "as if deserted by the other two witches . . . stirring a pot."[16] Coincidentally, Rollin, Ono, and the photographer for the piece had all attended Sarah Lawrence College, though this fact seems to have effected little good will between the women.[17] The interview for the article took place at the couple's home just a day after Ono had suffered a miscarriage, a fact that is not revealed until the article's third page. Surprisingly, this mitigating circumstance fails to inspire any sympathy in Rollin, who insists on using the moment to reiterate her thesis: "But today, at any rate, it's business as usual."[18]

Rollin's article demonstrates how disliking Yoko Ono, and specifically her art, also implies an exercise in drawing borders. In contrast to her fawning over Lennon, to whom she clearly takes an immediate liking, Rollin struggles to articulate why she doesn't like Ono. "Yoko is giving me a pain," she states definitively before searching for the terms to elaborate: "Not for moral reasons. And not that I don't respect her art. I do. Maybe it's not art. But whatever it is, it's creative; she has integrity about it; and, generally, I think far-out art or non-art stretches our awareness and, if nothing else, gives us a better perspective on what's far-in. Beside, it's great just to be silly sometimes, don't you think so?"[19] Although Rollin uses the colloquialism *far out* to express a measured enthusiasm for Ono's art, the term also seems to mark another implicit boundary that Rollin draws throughout the course of the essay between foreign and familiar, between aberrant and normative. Ono is *far out*, whereas Rollin, the readers to whom she directly appeals in an aside, and even Lennon are presumably *far in*. Rollin attempts to build such a consensus, and if the mostly negative letters to the editor that appeared a few weeks later are any indication, she achieves it. One reader from Glendora, California writes in supernatural terms about what marks otherness: "Our all-American 'Apple-Pie' family just isn't interested in people who resemble warlocks and witches." Another reader from Brooklyn, New York, attempts humor by registering Ono as a foreign object: "What is a Yoko Ono?"[20] Rollin immediately turns this as-yet-unconfirmed consensus against Ono in order to denigrate her art, which she clearly disfavors, despite claims to the contrary: "But the thing about Yoko is that when she's being silly, she doesn't think it's silly."[21] Ono's resistance to silliness marks her difference from Rollin's imagined coalition; silliness has a universal transparency that Ono somehow misses. Ono is ultimately unlikeable for Rollin because of her foreignness, which Rollin enfolds into distaste for her avant-garde sensibilities and recodes as silly and far out.

These aesthetic judgments about Ono's art lead Rollin directly to money, which is the crucial subtext for her: "Actually, Yoko is pushy—ambitious is a nicer word—the way 20-year old actresses are. But she is 34. John, by the way, is 28. Yoko is bossy too. She is bossy with the people in the Beatles' Apple office, and they resent it. And she is bossy with us."[22] The nod toward niceness here is disingenuous, and Rollin none-too-subtly makes inferences about Ono's motivations for her relationship with Lennon, which, she suggests, have ultimately to do with wealth, self-promotion, and power. As in Occhiogrosso's article, being avant-garde for Ono oddly subtends a kind of financial imperialism that is strangely dispositional and based on an unaccountable, self-perpetuating need for power, against which Lennon needs to be protected. More in the mode of a hostile corporate takeover than an abuse of romance, Ono is thus much more insidious than the typical gold digger who blinds her target with the requisite feminine wiles.

At least Rollin refrains from the kind of the cheap shots taken in McCarry's *Esquire* piece. Although antipathy directed toward Ono is rarely formulated in such starkly racial terms (at least in print), it is striking how closely these negative feelings mirror American anxieties about the much-heralded Japanese challenges to U.S. economic dominance during the period. What Americans worried that Japan was doing to the United States was precisely what Yoko Ono was supposedly doing to John Lennon, usurping its (his) financial independence by buying up property and other assets while exercising an unfathomable power over its (her) weakening adversary. Far more than the occasional derisive taunts of "Dragon Lady," the implicit analogizing of

Ono's degenerative influence on Lennon with Japan's economic forays into the United States suggests how hatred of Yoko Ono was subtly coded in racial terms. When Ono's detractors speak about her avant-gardism, they seem implicitly to speak about her Asianness as well. That is, they mobilize the obtuseness of the avant-garde as a way to reify her strangeness and delineate between far out and far in; hence, the inscrutability of the avant-garde stands in for the inscrutable Asian.

These expressions of dislike perpetuate the discursive tradition of yellow peril in the United States by imagining an insidious, hidden Asian influence abstracted into an unseen force that has a degenerative effect on nation and home. Unlike in traditional models of yellow peril, racial judgments are here recoded and deflected away from the realm of race, allaying post-multicultural sensitivities while preserving a powerful sense of inassimilable Asianness. This work of abstraction thereby obviates any overt engagement with race itself and reinscribes the old problem of the inscrutable Asian. I am not suggesting that it is fundamentally racist to dislike Yoko Ono's music; likewise, there is nothing wrong with wanting to keep harmful toys that were made in China away from your children. It is important to register, however, how the particular manifestation of these fears and antipathies in public discourse often performs other cultural work. Ono's avant-gardism becomes central because it becomes the mark of the inassimilable. Her art seemed generally inconsumable by the general American public who regarded it as "hokum" (to cite the infamous description of Ono's 1971 Everson Museum of Art exhibition).[23]

Displaced onto the avant-garde, Asian influence becomes reduced into abstracted instrumentality or force, particularly in the context of modern and global capitalism. Lye argues that earlier models of yellow peril share with more recent conceptions of the model minority "a trope of economic efficiency." Specifically, she argues that the Asiatic is a monstrous presence—a "mechanical abstraction"—in naturalist literature, a presence whose dehumanization becomes insidiously appropriate for the emerging modern capitalist economy that demands cheap, mindless labor.[24] This anxiety undergirds exclusionist fears, which defend American labor by abstracting the Asian figure into a malicious force that acts invisibly: "Asiatics can look just like friends, and enemy aliens have already taken up residence within. As in the threat of degenerationism, the 'yellow peril's' alien danger implies internal decay."[25] Lye's model emphasizes how yellow peril becomes difficult to recognize because the Asiatic registers as both compliant and adversarial, a figure of internal decay with illegible intentions. Regarding more recent incarnations of the phenomenon, David Palumbo-Liu suggests that this conception of the Asian as a mechanical abstraction modulates, in the late twentieth-century American imaginary, into envy: "The abstract 'Asian' psyche might well be better equipped for an age of 'post-industrial,' transnational economies, such that 'America' might do well to learn from Asia."[26] In both cases, an abstracted sense of Asianness becomes the locus of anxiety regarding U.S. economic health. As we have seen, for her detractors, Yoko Ono seems to embody abstraction itself as if it were pure instrumentality and unfathomable force, a disembodied viral agent that plays out the etymological connection between influence and influenza. My invocation of the microbial here is less an attempt to establish a dominant trope and more a way to articulate a particularly contemporary mode of visualizing race. The visuality of race in this model becomes, to invoke Berssenbrugge's term, a kind of hiddenness; it is like a virus, both visible in a microscopic sense and invisible in plain sight. It obtains an insistent material presence that one perceives despite the lack of any obvious empirical evidence, at least in the realm of everyday life.

Fictions of Globalization

As such, this new yellow peril also participates in the construction of a particularly American fantasy—that of infinite and infinitely reproducible innocence. It indulges this vision of American innocence by constructing the United States as a victim of globalization rather than as its protagonist or an enthusiastic participant. A recurring trope in U.S. history, American innocence seems infinitely reproducible if only to serve as the precursor for its subsequent loss. The tag line, "the end of innocence," in U.S. history and literature has been promiscuously attached to World War I, *The Great Gatsby*, the quiz show scandals of the 1950s, the McCarthy hearings, the assassination of JFK, the war in Vietnam, the Watergate hearings, and September 11th, to name a few. In antipathetic accounts of Yoko Ono, John Lennon fills the role of the boyish upstart from humble origins who, impressionable and naïve, falls prey to the ambitious, malicious predator that leads him astray. Lennon was English of course, but his status as an American icon is justified, not only by the enormous popularity of The Beatles and Lennon himself in the United States, not only because he was the only member of The Beatles to permanently reside in the United States, and not only because he played a quintessentially American form of music but also because the connection of Lennon to the United States became itself such an explicit public question during the mid 1970s and the protracted period in which the U.S. government sought to deport him. In the case of the new yellow peril, the borders of the United States now need to be protected not only from immigrants but also from dangerous contact with the unregulated products of a globalized era.

This construction of innocence, however, requires a massive forgetting project. Elided here is the specter of imperialism that Fredric Jameson suggests looms behind contemporary globalization.[27] Particularly with respect to Asia, the United States comes to think of itself first as a discrete economic entity and then as the victim (rather than the catalyst) of globalism, and it forgets how heavily its own corporate interests are invested in precisely the models of flexible accumulation that propel, for example, Chinese manufacturing. This innocence thus reprises Fried's critique of imperialist subjectivity in chapter 1. Like the Conradian obsession with blank pages that reimagine imperialist aggression as the passive reception of experience in an ahistorical drama of individualism, this innocence allows for a mode of imperialism, to borrow Victor Bascara's formulation, that wishes to be seen as not imperialistic at all.[28] To put it in the even stronger terms of R. Radhakrishnan, this construction of innocence perpetuates the "lie of globalization" that insists the West is "virtuous and immaculate" and demands that the rest of the world "follow the Western lead," since non-Western people are "flawed and roguish in their repetition of our deeds."[29] The foregrounding of the viral threat posed by Asian influence deflects attention from the threat posed by neoimperialist aggression.

Sara Bongiorni's seemingly benign book, *A Year Without "Made in China": One Family's True Life Adventure in the Global Economy* (2007), epitomizes how this new yellow peril reconstructs American innocence and participates in the fantasy of globalization. The book is an autobiographical account of a woman who decides not to purchase products made in China for an entire calendar year. What is striking about Bongiorni's book is that she and her family seem like nice, tolerant people with liberal values and prolabor politics.[30] They are not xenophobic or jingoistic. In fact, when she reads a letter to the editor in her local newspaper by a man who advocates that Americans do exactly what she is already doing—boycott Chinese products—she recoils. Uncomfortable that her actions accord to the beliefs of someone who "starts name-dropping Jesus" while "tossing around the word 'enemy,'" she becomes introspective:

> Jim A. and I seem to have little in common. I don't consider the Chinese to be my enemies. . . . We're even boycotting China for different reasons. With him, it's personal. Red China offends Jim A.'s sensibilities, whereas I like to tell myself that our family boycott is an experiment in globalization. Sure, I have my China-is-taking-over-the-world panic attacks, especially in the toy aisle, especially before Christmas, but at heart our boycott isn't personal. Why, I like to think it's practically *scientific*. And yet . . . I'm probably as close to a model citizen as Jim A. is going to get.
>
> I don't like that one bit.[31]

In such moments of crisis, Bongiorni begins to consider the central question of her enterprise. Why is she doing this? For someone like Jim A., the answer is quite clear, but for Borgiorni, the answer is far less so. In fact, she has a great deal of difficulty explaining the boycott to her children and at one point worries that her daughter is becoming a xenophobe.[32] In the passage above, she tries out a few formulations that might distinguish her from Jim A., but none are ultimately satisfying. Though she frequently restates that her enterprise is experimental in nature—to see if it can be done—she nonetheless articulates her frustration with the new global economy and attempts to formulate a vague answer, to her own dissatisfaction, about fairness. She even acknowledges old-time yellow peril discourse at one point: "*Inscrutable*, they would have said in the old days, and they would not be far off the mark today."[33] Though Bongiorni endeavors to keep things civil, avoiding the more explicit racism that characterized yellow peril in years past and rechanneling the anxiety about Asian influence once directed at Asian people toward an abstract notion of Asian influence, she never, however, really resolves the *why* question.

Bongiorni thus abstracts a notion of an invasive Chineseness that is largely invisible, except on the small print of product labels, mere traces of a larger global illness. An interesting element of Bongiorni's experience is that she has a trace of Chinese blood in her ancestry. Though she does not describe the visible traces of this ancestry as viral per se, they are nonetheless represented in similar terms as unwanted, aberrant marks—specifically, black hairs—that appear on her body against her will: "As a child, black hairs occasionally sprouted on my pale head. . . . China was reclaiming me three centuries and an ocean away from the motherland."[34] The same Chinese hairs also appear on her daughter's head, causing much consternation. This conception of China as abstraction, which returns from the repressed as an unwanted mark on an otherwise un-Chinese and unracialized body, allows her to imagine her own home as an occupied terrain that must be defended against this silent invasion: "And yet we are not cogs in a China wheel, at least not yet. We can stop bringing China through the front door. We can hold up our hands and say no, thank you, we have had enough."[35] An anthropomorphized abstraction, China intrudes not just at the cash register but also in the home, and the book seems very anxious when China appears where it is not supposed to be. The whole enterprise begins, for example, when Bongiorni realizes that China has subsumed Christmas, which she fears has become a "Chinese holiday." This leads her to evict China from her house: "Suddenly I want China out."[36] In short, China becomes an unwelcome houseguest.

For Bongiorni, this abstract figuration of China ultimately functions as a way to boil down the complexities of globalization, creating a fiction of discrete economies and aligning the polarities of victim and aggressor along national lines. The underlying frustration she experiences is with her inability to dictate how her consumer activities contribute to the flow of global capital. However, absent here is a consideration of how global capital in the age of flexible accumulation radically transcends national boundaries. There is little consideration of how the need for cheap manufacturing on the part of U.S. companies helped create the made-in-China phenomenon. There is no mention, for example, of whether the family owns mutual funds, or if they own stock in American investment banks with financial interests in China or, for that matter, Mattel or Hasbro (toy companies headquartered in the United States who recalled defective toys manufactured in China). Clearly, in her account of Jim A.'s letter, Bongiorni has a vague sense that she is using China as a kind of straw man, but her investigation into consumer products never goes beyond country of origin. Of course, it is impossible to trace exactly where one's money goes every time one spends it, but the abstraction of China in this case acts as a dangerous supplement that occludes the complex workings of global economics and creates a stable enemy that one can more easily target. Fetishizing the made-in-China label becomes a way of parsing various interests anachronistically along national lines. In so doing, it imagines an ahistorical vision of the United States as removed from precisely the capitalist mechanisms that she most abhors.

Bongiorni and her family are not somehow bad people; they seem quite the opposite. Indeed, the new yellow peril lacks the venomous edge of its earlier incarnations. Because it seems to offer stability and comfort in disconcerting times while also seeming to minimize the specter of racism, perhaps the new yellow peril is even more perilous. Just as the anti-avant-garde sentiment toward Yoko Ono stabilizes the transgressiveness of the avant-garde and reaffirms borders, yet elides any racial implications, Bongiorni alleviates the transgressiveness of globalization and reaffirms borders through a kind of vague anti-Chinese position, reimagined as one that is not anti-China. What both have in common is an unwillingness to acknowledge the complexities (of avant-garde provocations and of global commerce), and thus they both implicitly seek simple solutions for difficult problems. Both become complicit in a reification project that re-demarcates foreign from familiar and ignores how inseparable those categories have become. The new yellow peril repackages the older version into a kinder, gentler model that nonetheless preserves the abstraction of invisible (indeed, inscrutable) Asian influence in addition to the ideological work of reaffirming the boundaries that globalization troubles.

Yes Yoko Ono

The affirming title of Ono's 2000 retrospective, which was organized by the Japan Society, is not only a reference to one of her most well-known pieces, entitled *Ceiling Painting (YES Painting)* (1966),[37] but also a rejoinder to a long history of rejection by detractors who categorically dismiss her art, such as the Syracuse *Post-Standard*, which conspicuously used scare quotes when referring to Ono as an "artist" and to her work as "art." Perhaps in this case, scare quotes really do imply fear, however muted by the pretense of aesthetic judgment. By marking the avant-garde as foreign and refusing to engage its provocations, these respondents decline the invitations of the art for experience and thought. These refusals are particularly cutting because so much of Ono's art invites participation. Often framed as instructions to activities that straddle the border between quirky and banal—such as taking a bite out of an apple, hammering a nail, and lighting a match—Ono's Fluxus aesthetic is antielitist and suffused with populist sensibilities. In an interview promoting her Everson Museum of Art exhibition, she explained that her art demonstrated you do not need talent to be an artist.[38] *Yes Yoko Ono* thus legitimates Ono as an artist simply by offering a belated attention to her art, which perhaps was not possible two decades earlier when the invitation apparently seemed much more nefarious. Saying *yes* to Yoko Ono implies accepting these invitations.

Shin Yu Pai's ekphrastic poem, also entitled "Yes Yoko Ono" (2003), does so by enacting engagement and interest and by affirming Ono's work entirely independently of her life with Lennon. Itself reprinted in a gorgeous art book,[39] Pai's poem paces through a series of Ono's art works as if walking through the exhibit itself. It dwells within the logic of each piece, using Ono's original "instructions" as an occasion for imaginative branching. A series of these instructions, Pai's poem is both copy and interpretation. Though mostly based directly on Ono's artwork, it also includes two pieces at the tail end of the series that do not belong to Ono, but which extend one's sensibilities. By dwelling within Ono's art, Pai implicitly responds to the degradation of Ono by reading her art as legible instead of inscrutable. Pai expresses a fondness for Ono's work that counters the reifying/racializing discourse that I have been elaborating, and she also reflects the work's own sense of transparency, taking seriously the kind of participatory populism to which it aspires.

Furthermore, Pai extends and expands the instruction into the realm of sensory experience and consequence. Whereas Ono's instructions are literal and functional, Pai's version brings Ono's art more fully out into the world, into the open air, and into the hands of people, realizing the populist enterprise in the work itself. Pai's version of *Painting to Hammer a Nail*, for example, veers from the specifics of Ono's instructions, but it expresses the spirit of the enterprise with fidelity.[40] Ono instructs the viewer to:

> Hammer a nail into a mirror, a piece of
> glass, a canvas, wood or metal every

> morning. Also, pick up a hair that came
> off when you combed in the morning and
> tie it around the hammered nail. The
> painting ends when the surface is covered
> with nails.[41]

The conceit of this piece is the expansion of the artistic activity to the realm of the viewer who not only participates in its construction but also becomes a literal part of the art object produced. By aestheticizing manual labor, the piece redresses alienation by resituating human experience (as well as the human body) as newly intimate with the object world. By shattering a mirror, one's attention shifts from one's own visage to the mirror itself as a thing. As more and more nails are driven into the painting and its surface becomes covered, the reflection in the mirror becomes completely obscured. Instead of selves, viewers see things. Pai's version retains this participatory logic, but it removes the exercise from the gallery space:

> Hammer a nail into a mirror.
> Place the pieces
> in an abandoned lot
> with an unobstructed view of
> the sky.[42]

Whereas Ono's piece retains a sense of temporality (the "painting ends . . .") that accords with the time of artistic making, Pai's depiction of the experience of the work claims a quiet permanence not for the art object itself but for the experience it prescribes. Befitting Bill Brown's formulation, the fragments of the art object—here the viewer instead of the viewed—survive to live the secret life of things beyond the gallery space that usually gives them animus. If, in Ono's original piece, things become more visible in inverse proportion to selves, then, in Pai's interpretation, things seem to gain the power of vision.

Taken as a whole, the series of Ono-inspired instructions in Pai's "Yes Yoko Ono" trace a dispersal of the energies originally located in Ono's artwork, as attitudes toward art objects become attitudes toward the world. Though they depart from direct engagements with Ono's art, Pai's final two sets of instructions —"Sheep Piece" and "Housecleaning Piece"—expand on Ono's playful aesthetics. Referring to a poetry project by Valerie Laws, "Sheep Piece" finds in Laws not only a kindred spirit to Ono but also a distillation of the kind of possibility Pai sees in Ono's work.[43] The project involved painting words on the backs of sheep. The sheep were then sent to wander around and, in so doing, arrange words that formed random poems. The agents of the self-arranging poems are the sheep whose whims produce accidents of meaning. That these poems occur in open space reflects Pai's effort to widen the experiential realm in which one can engage art objects. Paralleling to a degree the logic of Cha's *Surplus Novel*, "Painting for the Wind" recommends that, after writing down one's favorite words on scraps of paper, one should "Leave the paper where there is wind."[44]

Appropriately, then, the final section, "Housecleaning Piece," a poem that reflects on the poet's move from Dallas to Boston,[45] reimagines the private and personal as a space of artistic experience. A reflection on moving, Pai ends her poem on Ono with a depiction of packing one's things:

> Remove all the light
> bulbs from the fixtures.
> When night has fallen
> organize your things
> into boxes.[46]

In contrast to many of the other instruction sets in "Yes Yoko Ono," this final section ends not with dispersive possibility but enclosure, and, contrary to the illumination of the art object in "Painting to Let the Evening Light Come Through," "Housecleaning Piece" ends with encroaching darkness. The poem's ending, however, coincides with a new beginning that is implied in the act of moving. In this seventh poem, marked by the Chinese character for the number seven (the only nod toward Asianness in the poem), putting things into boxes is decidedly different than, say, putting a corpse into a coffin. This is a cyclical rather than linear ending—not a death but a renewal.

Like the sheep in the previous section, Pai's things can no longer be regarded as inert, even though they are stored away here in boxes. Indeed, things throughout this study and *racial things* in particular, such as the fragmentary poems in Cha's *Surplus Novel*, have transcended such enclosures. Through a greater attention to the visual and physical complexity of avant-garde things, we have gained a metacritical perspective from which to critique the complicit operations of racialization and reification. Although Pai's poem does not explicitly address questions of racialization, it does implicitly redress the treatment of Ono's art as inassimilable and foreign. In the simple act of acknowledgment, of saying *yes* to Yoko Ono, Pai acknowledges the thingness of the art objects and treats them as expressive, engaged, and dynamic rather than as inert, silly, and illegible. Pai's poem ultimately remains removed from the visualizations of contemporary race that *Racial Things, Racial Forms* examines, but it shares with this other work one important characteristic: Engagement with things in Pai counteracts the foreign objecthood usually ascribed to both the avant-garde art object in particular and Asianness in general.

The act of putting things in boxes is less about enclosure and more like putting the fragments of a poem in a bowl; it is an activity meant not only to hide the contents but also to invite us to question our relationship to them. It is to regard how the container informs and precludes our knowledge of what is inside and limits our intimacy and engagement with it. It has become customary in the United States to think of race as a trajectory of progress—that the labels on the boxes will matter less when old prejudices have faded and globalization makes insularity an increasingly remote possibility. As I write these final lines, we have a president who is often described as a postracial figure. Although the election itself bespoke the prematurity of such statements (indeed, race was a crucial issue in the campaign), such a time still seems near because of the progress that appears to have been made in the wake of civil rights. One of the possibilities explored in *Racial Things, Racial Forms* is that of the contemporaneity of race—that race is not only a legacy but also a response to new, emergent ideological forces. If, for example, Asian economic power continues its meteoric rise and Asian political and cultural influence follow suit, then the collisions and collusions between East and West, American and Asian will intensify and shift according to new demands. In this context, race becomes a more pressing issue. The examination of avant-garde treatments of these problems ultimately calls attention to the ways in which we engage these new forms, these new things in new bowls and boxes. The best way to visualize them, I suggest, is ironically not unlike the reaction of the frustrated viewer—What is this thing?—who has difficulty understanding what it is he or she is supposed to see when looking at avant-garde art. Rather than standing as a statement of resignation, I would recharacterize the inquiry as a self-reflexive mode of attention to how we experience distance from a thing, how we register its foreignness, and what we then make of it all.

NOTES

Introduction

1. For the sake of convenience, I will refer to the two *Surplus Novel* pieces collectively hereafter.

2. Constance M. Lewallen, ed., *The Dream of the Audience: Theresa Hak Kyung Cha (1951–1982)* (Berkeley: University of California Press, 2001), 100.

3. Julia Goldman, "The Two Women Who Broke Up the Beatles," *McCall's*, July 1971, 72–73.

4. *Knots* (Laing 1970) was a mass-market psychology book in poetic form that addressed problems in human relationships.

5. See William Carlos Williams, *The Collected Poems: Volume II, 1939–1962*, ed. Christopher MacGowan (New York: New Directions, 1991), 55 and Edmund Husserl, *Ideas: General Introduction to Pure Phenomenology* (New York: Routledge, 2010).

6. There are of course notable exceptions, the foremost of which is the work of Adrian Piper.

7. Lucy R. Lippard, *Six Years: The Dematerialization of the Art Object from 1966 to 1972* (Berkeley: University of California Press, 1973), xiii.

8. See Georg Lukács, *History and Class Consciousness; Studies in Marxist Dialectics*, trans. Rodney Livingstone (Cambridge, MA: MIT Press, 1970).

9. See Arjun Appadurai, ed., *The Social Life of Things: Commodities in Cultural Perspective* (New York: Cambridge University Press, 1986).

10. Bill Brown, *A Sense of Things: The Object Matter of American Literature* (Chicago: University of Chicago Press, 2003), 4.

11. Bill Brown, "How to Do Things with Things (A Toy Story)," *Critical Inquiry* 24, no. 4 (1998): 954.

12. Ibid., 960.

13. David R. Roediger, *The Wages of Whiteness: Race and the Making of the American Working Class* (New York: Verso, 1991), 133–64.

14. Christopher Bush, "The Ethnicity of Things in America's Lacquered Age," *Representations* 99 (2007): 85. By his term *ethnic thing*, Bush refers to Japanese commodities imported to the United States that served a particular function in the emerging national imaginary. I am less interested in the material culture of the commodity

as such, though it would be naïve to argue that avant-garde art objects are not commodities. Whereas Bush foregrounds things that are unproblematically commodities —imports from Japan meant for American consumption—my argument focuses on things that fundamentally problematize this commodity status. By *things*, I thus refer to things in decontextualized moments of irregularity in which they become, however fleetingly, metacritical abstractions. Following Bill Brown, for whom to call a thing a commodity is to defer to an already articulated history of commodities, my term *racial things* thus seeks to locate what makes the thing different from a reified object.

15. Bill Brown, "Reification, Reanimation, and the American Uncanny," *Critical Inquiry* 32, no. 2 (2006): 197–99.

16. See Brown, "How to Do Things with Things," 958. Brown makes a similar claim about Wong's *Homebase*: "If literary texts possess a material unconscious—whereby the history in things, however unacknowledged by the text, seems to overdetermine their textual presence—then we might say that lurking within the cultural transaction in *Homebase* is some other motivating transaction that lies somewhere in the history of the object."

17. Bill Brown, "Reification, Reanimation, and the American Uncanny," 204.

18. See Colleen Lye, *America's Asia: Racial Form and American Literature, 1893–1945* (Princeton, NJ: Princeton University Press, 2005), 7. The point here parallels Colleen Lye's warning against anthropomorphizing Asiatic racial form, which prevents us from asking crucial and fundamental questions about the visuality of race.

19. Tina Chen, *Double Agency: Acts of Impersonation in Asian American Literature and Culture* (Stanford, CA: Stanford University Press, 2005), 17–18.

20. Bill Brown, "How to Do Things with Things," 962.

21. See Juliana Chang, "Reading Asian American Poetry" *MELUS* 21, no. 1 (1996): 81–98; Sunn Shelley Wong, "Sizing Up Asian American Poetry." In *A Resource Guide to Asian American Literature*, Sau-ling Cynthia Wong and Stephen H. Sumida, eds. (New York: Modern Language Association, 2001), 285–308; George Uba, "Coordinates of Asian American Poetry: A Survey of the History and a Guide to Teaching." In *A Resource Guide to Asian American Literature*, Sau-ling Cynthia Wong and Stephen H. Sumida, eds. (New York: Modern Language Association, 2001), 309–31.

22. Josephine Nock-Hee Park, *Apparitions of Asia: Modernist Form and Asian American Poetics* (New York: Oxford University Press, 2008), 95. For another study of Asian American poetry relative to modernist forms, see Yunte Huang, *Transpacific Displacement: Ethnography, Translation, and Intertextual Travel in Twentieth-Century American Literature* (Berkeley: University of California Press, 2002).

23. Harryette Mullen, "Poetry and Identity." In *Telling It Slant: Avant-Garde Poetics in the 1990s*, Mark Wallace and Steven Marks, eds. (Tuscaloosa: University of Alabama Press, 2002), 27.

24. Jinqi Ling, *Narrating Nationalisms: Ideology and Form in Asian American Literature* (New York: Oxford University Press, 1995), 9. See also Colleen Lye, "Form and History in Asian American Literary Studies," *American Literary History* 20, no. 3 (2008): 548–55. As Colleen Lye's recent article points out, Ling's text is underappreciated in Asian American Studies, and I share Lye's valuation of the book. What I take issue with is how Ling's argumentative frame needlessly limits the possibilities of avant-garde forms.

See also Viet Nguyen, *Race and Resistance: Literature and Politics in Asian America* (New York: Oxford University Press, 2002), 145. Nguyen links the equation of complexity and greater political sophistication critiqued by Ling with an overinvestment in complex resistance against a simplistic accommodationism in Asian American literary criticism that limits its political possibilities. Nguyen is particularly insightful about how this practice in Asian American Studies trades long-term blindness to the political contradictions of such practices for short-term political mobilization.

25. See also Susan Koshy, "The Fictions of Asian American Literature," *Yale Journal of Criticism* 9 (1996): 316: "Much of the scholarship in the field has either continued to rely on paradigms of ethnicity produced in the inaugural moment of the field, or has sought to incorporate the changes through the fashionable but derivative vocabulary of post-modernism, post-colonialism or post-structuralism; formulaic invocations of 'multiculturalism,' 'hybridity,' 'plural identities,' or 'border-crossing' are used promiscuously without any effort to link them to the material, cultural or historical specificities of the various Asian American experiences."

26. In fact, Ling's point about avant-garde texts seems more about Cha's *DICTEE* in particular. Cha's *DICTEE* and Jessica Hagedorn's *Dogeaters* have, until recently, been the only avant-garde texts examined in studies of Asian American literature with any frequency. With the exception of Cha criticism, the explosion of Asian American Studies in the past two decades has paid surprisingly little attention to the relationship between avant-garde art and racial politics or to poetry in general, which has remained on the margins of an Asian American political discourse that tends to privilege the novel for its more traditionally social inclinations.

27. For versions of this genealogy, see George Uba, "Versions of Identity in Post-Activist Asian American Poetry." In *Reading the Literatures of Asian America*, Shirley Geok-lin Lim and Amy Ling, eds. (Philadelphia: Temple University Press, 1992), 33–48 and Timothy Yu, *Race and the Avant-Garde: Experimental and Asian American Poetry Since 1965* (Stanford: Stanford University Press, 2009).

28. Sunn Shelley Wong, "Sizing Up Asian American Poetry," in *A Resource Guide to Asian American Literature*, ed. Sau-ling Cynthia Wong and Stephen H. Sumida (New York: Modern Language Association, 2001), 291.

29. For commentary about the relationship between avant-garde art and theory,

see Tyrus Miller, "Avant-garde and Theory: A Misunderstood Relation," *Poetics Today* 20, no. 4 (1999): 549–79.

30. Timothy Yu, *Race and the Avant-Garde: Experimental and Asian American Poetry Since 1965* (Stanford: Stanford University Press, 2009), 73–74, 98–99.

31. Ibid., 73.

32. Ibid., 122. See also 137.

33. Ibid., 139.

34. Steven G. Yao, *Foreign Accents: Chinese American Verse from Exclusion to Postethnicity* (New York: Oxford University Press, 2010), 15.

35. Colleen Lye, "Racial Form," *Representations* 104 (2008): 99.

36. Michael Omi and Howard Winant, *Racial Formation in the United States: From the 1960s to the 1990s*, 2nd ed. (New York: Routledge, 1994), 55.

37. Colleen Lye, "Racial Form," 99.

38. Colleen Lye, "Introduction: In Dialogue with Asian American Studies," *Representations* 99 (2007): 2.

39. See Susan Koshy, "The Fictions of Asian American Literature," 326 and Viet Nguyen, *Race and Resistance*, 145.

40. Anne Anlin Cheng, "Passing, Natural Selection, and Love's Failure: Ethics of Survival from Chang-rae Lee to Jacques Lacan," *American Literary History* 17, no. 3 (2005): 553–54.

41. A danger here is that this attention would comply with recent appropriations of "color-blindness" to justify status-quo inequalities by rendering race arbitrary and unrecognizable. By characterizing racial visibility as negotiated through a complex visual field, I am not also implying that there is no such thing as race, as history can plainly attest.

42. W. J. T. Mitchell, *Picture Theory: Essays on Verbal and Visual Representation* (Chicago: University of Chicago Press, 1994), 5.

43. Mitchell, *Picture Theory*, 24 and Mitchell, *Iconology: Image, Text, Ideology* (Chicago: University of Chicago Press, 1986), 44.

44. So much so that Linda Martín Alcoff suggests that "identity politics has become the shibboleth of cultural studies and social theory, and denouncing it has become the litmus test of academic responsibility, political acceptability, and even a necessity for the very right to be heard." See Linda Martín Alcoff, "Who's Afraid of Identity Politics?" In *Reclaiming Identity: Realist Theory and the Predicament of Postmodernism*, Paul Moya and Michael Hames-Garcia, eds. (Berkeley: University of California Press, 2000), 313. Alcoff, like the other critics who appear in *Reclaiming Identity*, attempts to recuperate the term and its politics: "A realistic identity politics, then, is one that recognizes the dynamic, variable, and negotiated character of identity. It is one that acknowledges the variability in an identity's felt significance and cultural meaning. Yet it is also one that recognizes that social categories of identity are often helpfully engaged in, among other things, political judgment" (341).

45. Peggy Phelan, *Unmarked: The Politics of Performance* (New York: Routledge, 1993), 10.

46. Robyn Wiegman, *American Anatomies: Theorizing Race and Gender* (Durham, NC: Duke University Press, 1995), 4.

47. Ibid.

48. Ibid., 6.

49. Susan Koshy, "Morphing Race into Ethnicity: Asian Americans and Critical Transformations of Whiteness," *boundary 2* 28, no. 1 (2001): 158–63.

50. Colleen Lye, *America's Asia*, 7.

51. Ibid., 9.

52. David Palumbo-Liu, *Asian/American: Historical Crossings of a Racial Frontier* (Stanford: Stanford University Press), 171.

53. For commentary, see Dorothy J. Wang, "Undercover Asian: John Yau and the Politics of Self-Identification." In *Asian American Literature in the International Context: Readings on Fiction, Poetry, and Performance*, Rocío G. Davis and Sämi Ludwig, eds. (Hamburg: LIT Verlag, 2002), 138–40.

54. In addition, I would argue that this kind of critique represents the legacy of a foundational New Critical value, namely the belief that texts should be understood as unified, self-contained, and interpreted as discrete from the world from which they emerge, a value that arose as a reaction against coarse historicism and myopic biographical criticism. The New Critics made a case for the textual unity in order to show how the text could operate independently of such determinisms, but as this justifiable value reified into critical dogma, a new imbalance emerged. It remains undesirable to return to deterministic reading practices, but it is also objectionable to ignore context entirely. By their very nature, analogies are often extratextual and require the importing of disparate contexts. The work of the analogy often parallels that of avant-garde artistic practices, which often employ defamiliarizing strategies to encourage the viewer to engage the art object in alternative terms.

55. See Lisa Lowe, *Immigrant Acts: On Asian American Cultural Politics* (Durham, NC: Duke University Press, 1996), 152–53; Viet Nguyen, *Race and Resistance*, 145–46; and Kandice Chuh, *Imagine Otherwise: On Asian Americanist Critique* (Durham, NC: Duke University Press, 2003), 4–6.

56. See Walter Benn Michaels, *The Shape of the Signifier: 1967 to the End of History* (Princeton, NJ: Princeton University Press, 2004), 4–10.

One. Black Things, White Things

1. Frantz Fanon, *Black Skin, White Masks*, trans. by Charles Lam Markman (New York: Grove Press, 1967), 109.

2. Michael Fried, "Art and Objecthood," in *Art and Objecthood: Essays and Reviews* (Chicago: University of Chicago Press, 1998), 160.

3. Cf. Aimé Césaire, *Discourse on Colonialism*, trans. Joan Pinkham (New York: Monthly Review Press, 1972), 42. "My turn to state an equation: colonization = 'thingification.'"

4. See *Absorption and Theatricality: Painting and Beholder in the Age of Diderot* (Berkeley: University of California Press, 1980).

5. Bill Brown, "Thing Theory," in *Things*, ed. Bill Brown (Chicago: University of Chicago Press, 2004), 4.

6. Ibid., 5.

7. See Tina Chen, *Double Agency*, 17–18 and Colleen Lye, *America's Asia*, 7.

8. W. E. B. Du Bois, *The Souls of Black Folk* (1903; New York: Penguin, 1989), 5.

9. Fanon, *Black Skin, White Masks*, 110–11.

10. Ibid., 110.

11. Ibid.

12. Homi K. Bhabha, "The Other Question: Stereotype, Discrimination, and the Discourse of Colonialism," in *The Location of Culture* (New York: Routledge, 1994), 76.

13. Sara Ahmed, *Queer Phenomenology: Orientations, Objects, Others* (Durham, NC: Duke University Press, 2006), 132.

14. James Meyer, *Minimalism: Art and Polemics in the Sixties* (New Haven, CT: Yale University Press, 2001), 229.

15. Michael Fried, "Almayer's Face: On 'Impressionism' in Conrad, Crane, and Norris," *Critical Inquiry* 17, no. 1 (1990): 198. Here, Fried cites from his own *Realism, Writing, Disfiguration: On Thomas Eakins and Stephen Crane* (Chicago: University of Chicago Press, 1987), xiv. Fried's logic parallels and is informed by that of Walter Benn Michaels, whose work has been concerned with the difference between a word and mark since the "Against Theory" debates of the 1980s. For a full view of the "Against Theory" debates, see W. J. T. Mitchell, ed., *Against Theory: Literary Studies and the New Pragmatism* (Chicago: University of Chicago Press, 1985). See also Walter Benn Michaels, *The Shape of the Signifier: 1967 to the End of History* (Princeton, NJ: Princeton University Press, 2004).

16. Fried, "Almayer's Face," 202.

17. Ibid., 227.

18. Ibid., 233.

19. Ibid., 235–36.

20. Richard Dyer, *White* (New York: Routledge, 1996), 4.

21. Trinh T. Minh-Ha, "White Spring," in *The Dream of the Audience: Theresa Hak Kyung Cha (1951–1982)*, Constance M. Lewallen, ed. (Berkeley: University of California Press, 2001), 35: "Indeed the remainder of the piece plays with variations on the theme. There are pairs of black pages, pairs of white pages framed by a black border, pairs of full page photographs of a brick wall in grey tones that draw a parallel, perhaps, between the act of looking at a blank screen and the act of looking at a blank

wall." See also Josephine Nock-Hee Park, "'What of the Partition': *Dictée*'s Boundaries and the American Epic," *Contemporary Literature* 46 (2005): 234.

22. Theresa Hak Kyung Cha, Preface, in *Apparatus: Cinematographic Apparatus: Selected Writings*, Theresa Hak Kyung Cha, ed. (New York: Tanam Press, 1980).

23. Ibid.

24. Cf. Hiroshi Sugimoto's "Theatres" series, in which he photographs film screens and movie theatre interiors, using extended exposure to produce the effect of an illuminated, white screen.

25. For an account of how the medium in *Commentaire* invokes race, see Sue J. Kim, "Apparatus: Theresa Hak Kyung Cha and the Politics of Form," *Journal of Asian American Studies* 8, no. 2 (2005): 143–69. Kim's article is particularly useful because of the way it extends Jinqi Ling's skepticism toward the politics of avant-garde form. Kim is careful "not to reject wholly the potential of avant-garde art forms," but at the same time she "questions the notion that formal innovations and the particular strategies employed to read them necessarily constitute political resistance" (162–63). Like Ling, Kim argues that the mere fact of indeterminacy that is often associated with avant-garde forms is not a sufficient political stance.

26. Toni Morrison, *Playing in the Dark: Whiteness and the Literary Imagination* (Cambridge, MA: Harvard University Press, 1992), 33.

27. Samuel Otter, *Melville's Anatomies* (Berkeley: University of California Press, 1999), 139. See Herman Melville, *Moby Dick* (New York: Norton, 1967), 169: "But not yet have we solved the incantation of this whiteness, and learned why it appeals with such power to the soul; and more strange and far more portentous—why, as we have seen, it is at once the most meaning symbol of spiritual things, nay, the very veil of the Christian's Deity; and yet should be as it is, the intensifying agent in things the most appalling to mankind.

"Is it that by its indefiniteness it shadows forth the heartless voids and immensities of the universe, and thus stabs us from behind with the thought of annihilation, when beholding the white depths of the milky way? Or is it, that as in essence whiteness is not so much a color as the visible absence of color, and at the same time the concrete of all colors; is it for these reasons that there is such a dumb blankness, full of meaning, in a wide landscape of snows—a colorless, all-color of atheism from which we shrink?"

28. This point is made by Sue J. Kim. See "Apparatus: Theresa Hak Kyung Cha and the Politics of Form," *Journal of Asian American Studies* 8 (2005): 160–61. Kim quotes from James Monaco, *The New Wave: Truffaut, Godard, Chabrol, Rohmer, Rivette* (New York: Oxford University Press, 1976), 238.

29. Quoted in Trinh T. Minh-Ha, "White Spring," in *The Dream of the Audience: Theresa Hak Kyung Cha (1951–1982)*, Constance M. Lewallen, ed. (Berkeley: University of California Press, 2001), 33.

30. Cf. Peter Brooks, *Body Work: Objects of Desire in Modern Narrative* (Cambridge, MA: Harvard University Press, 1993), 3. Brooks discusses the scene in which Homer's Odysseus is recognized through a scar on his body: "It is as if identity, and its recognition, depended on the body having been marked with a special sign, which looks suspiciously like a linguistic signifier. The sign imprints the body, making it part of the signifying process. Signing or marking the body signifies its passage into writing, its becoming a literary body, and generally also a narrative body, in that the inscription of the sign depends on and produces a story. The signing of the body is an allegory of the body become a subject for literary narrative—a body entered into writing." Unlike Brooks's example, the bodily sign as linguistic sign in *Markings* halts along this trajectory before moving fully toward narrative. Rather, the bodily sign and linguistic sign seem to remain frozen and confined by their own materiality, and part of the effort of the text is to refuse the bruise a broader discursive context, narrative or otherwise.

31. Elaine H. Kim, "Poised on the In-between: A Korean American's Reflections on Theresa Hak Kyung Cha's *Dictée*," in *Writing Self, Writing Nation: A Collection of Essays on Dictée by Theresa Hak Kyung Cha*, ed. Hyun Yi Kang, et al. (Berkeley, CA: Third Woman Press, 1994), 8.

32. As Viet Nguyen argues, this imperative toward pointing out resistance stems from a much broader imperative in Asian American Studies. See *Race and Resistance*, 3–32. This is also Jinqi Ling's resistance to avant-garde texts. See *Narrating Nationalisms*, 9.

33. Mayumi Takada, "Annihilating Possibilities: Witnessing and Testimony through Cinematic Love in Theresa Hak Kyung Cha's *DICTEE*," *Literature Interpretation Theory* 17 (2006): 23–24.

34. Takada, "Annihilating Possibilities," 45.

35. Ibid., 31.

36. Ibid., 26.

37. Theresa Hak Kyung Cha, "Paths," M.F.A. thesis, 1978, 1.

38. Ibid.

39. Johanna Drucker, *The Visible Word: Experimental Typography and Modern Art, 1909–1923* (Chicago: University of Chicago Press), 55, 59.

40. Theresa Hak Kyung Cha, *Earth* (1976). Berkeley Art Museum.

41. Marc Vernet, "Blinking, Flickering, and Flashing of the Black-and-White Film," in *Apparatus*, Theresa Hak Kyung Cha, ed. (New York: Tanam Press, 1980), 365, 368.

42. Ibid., 366.

43. Ibid., 368.

44. Ibid.

45. Omi and Winant, *Racial Formation in the United States*, 55–56.

46. Theresa Hak Kyung Cha, "Paths," 2.

47. Elaine H. Kim, "Poised on the In-between," 8, and Theresa Hak Kyung Cha, *DICTEE* (New York: Tanam Press, 1982), 20.

48. For commentary on the politics of illegibility, see Craig Dworkin, *Reading the Illegible* (Evanston: Northwestern University Press, 2003).

49. See Garret Stewart, "*Cinécriture*: Modernism's Flicker Effect," *New Literary History* 24 (1998): 731.

50. Roger Ebert, "*The Ninth Gate*," *Chicago Sun-Times*, March 10, 2000. http://rogerebert.suntimes.com

51. Fanon, *Black Skin, White Masks*, 140.

Two. Speaking in Tongues

1. Myung Mi Kim, "Into Such Assembly," *Under Flag* (Berkeley, CA: Kelsey Street Press, 1991), 13.

2. Paul de Man, "Phenomenality and Materiality in Kant," *Aesthetic Ideology*, ed. Andrzej Warminski (Minneapolis: University of Minnesota Press, 1996), 88–90.

3. Cf. Lynn Keller, *Thinking Poetry: Readings in Contemporary Women's Exploratory Poetics* (Iowa City: University of Iowa Press, 2010), 153–54: "Kim is interested in both how defamiliarized attention to visual phenomena may support resistance to dominant ideologies and in how space and other visual information in the pages she produces may enhance her poetry's complex communication."

4. Marjorie Perloff, *Poetic License: Essays on Modernist and Postmodernist Lyric* (Evanston, IL: Northwestern University Press, 1990), 12. See also Jeannie Chiu, "Identities in Process: The Experimental Poetry of Mei-mei Berssenbrugge and Myung Mi Kim," in *Asian North American Identities: Beyond the Hyphen*, ed. Eleanor Ty and Donald C. Goellnicht (Bloomington: Indiana University Press, 2004), 85: "[Berssenbrugge and Kim] challenge not only essentialist notions of ethnic and racial identity, but also the transcendent 'I' of conventional lyric poetry."

5. See Rosina Lippi-Green, *English with an Accent: Language, Ideology, and Discrimination in the United States* (London: Routledge, 1997), 228.

6. David Palumbo-Liu, *Asian/American: Historical Crossings of a Racial Frontier* (Stanford: Stanford University Press, 1999), 98–99. Palumbo-Liu cites D. Ralph Millard, "Oriental Peregrinations," *Plastic and Reconstructive Surgery* 16 (1955): 331.

7. Palumbo-Liu, *Asian/American*, 100–101.

8. Ibid., 85. The immediate context here is a discussion of a 1911 immigration report, but the description is more broadly applicable.

9. Walter Benjamin, "The Task of the Translator," in *Illuminations*, trans. Harry Zohn, ed. Hannah Arendt (New York: Schocken Books, 1969), 72–73.

10. Benjamin, "The Task of the Translator," 80–81. Benjamin quotes from Pannwitz's *Die Krisis der eurpäischen Kulture* (1917).

11. See Steven G. Yao, *Translation and the Languages of Modernism: Gender, Politics, Language* (New York: Palgrave Macmillan, 2002), 2.

12. De Man has of course commented on this Benjamin essay. See Paul de Man, "'Conclusions' Walter Benjamin's 'The Task of the Translator' Messenger Lecture, Cornell University, March 4, 1983," *Yale French Studies* 69 (1985): 25–46. Rather than tease out the combinatory possibilities of translation, de Man instead re-creates Benjamin in his own image: "Benjamin, who is talking about the inability of trope to be adequate to the meaning, constantly uses the very tropes which seem to postulate the adequation between meaning and trope; but he prevents them in a way, displaces them in such a way as to put the original in motion, to de-canonize the original, giving it a movement which is a movement of disintegration, of fragmentation. This movement of the original is a wandering, an *errance*, a kind of permanent exile if you wish, but it is not really an exile, for there is no homeland, nothing from which one has been exiled" (44). For commentary on translation in de Man and Benjamin, see Niranjana Tejaswini, *Sitting Translation: History, Post-structuralism, and the Colonial Context* (Berkeley: University of California Press, 1992), 110–40.

13. Patricia P. Chu, *Assimilating Asians: Gendered Strategies of Authorship in Asian America* (Durham, NC: Duke University Press, 2000), 4. Another way of asserting the problem is addressed in David Palumbo-Liu, "Universalisms and Minority Culture," *Differences: A Journal of Feminist Cultural Studies* 7, no. 1 (1995): 188–208. The essay takes up the question of how the minor might problematize models of universality that are policed by dominant culture.

14. For a useful account of Kim's poetics in relation to Theresa Hak Kyung Cha, see Josephine Nock-Hee Park, "'Composed of Many Lengths of Bone': Myung Mi Kim's Reimagination of Image and Epic," in *Transnational Asian American Literature: Sites and Transits*, ed. Shirley Geok-lin Lim, John Blair Gamber, Stephen Hong Sohn, and Gina Valentino (Philadelphia: Temple University Press, 2006), 242–43.

15. See Myung Mi Kim, interview by James Kyung-Jin Lee, in *Words Matter: Conversations with Asian American Writers*, ed. King-Kok Cheung (Honolulu: University of Hawai'i Press, 2000).

16. Myung Mi Kim, *Under Flag*, 13.

17. Ibid.

18. For an account of Kim's use of the physical page as a metaphoric space in *Commons*, see Lyn Keller, *Thinking Poetry*, 164–65.

19. I thank Youngmin Choe for both this connection and the translations that appear in this chapter. When necessary, I will Romanize parenthetically using the McCune-Reischauer system for the sake of convenience, though this notion, as I will discuss later, is not unproblematic with respect to Kim's work.

20. Myung Mi Kim, *Under Flag*, 13.

21. For an account of the relationship between sonic, thematic, and metaphoric ele-

ments of this passage, see Josephine Nock-Hee Park, "'Composed of Many Lengths of Bone': Myung Mi Kim's Reimagination of Image and Epic," in *Transnational Asian American Literature: Sites and Transits*, ed. Shirley Geok-lin Lim, John Blair Gamber, Stephen Hong Sohn, and Gina Valentino (Philadelphia: Temple University Press, 2006), 236.

22. Myung Mi Kim, *Under Flag*, 14.

23. This ontological playfulness is, for example, reminiscent of Darl Bundren's existential contemplation of *is* and *was* in William Faulkner's *As I Lay Dying*.

24. Myung Mi Kim, *Dura* (Los Angeles: Sun and Moon Press, 1998), 49.

25. Myung Mi Kim, *The Bounty* (Minneapolis: Chax Press, 1996), 11.

26. See Young-Key Kim-Renaud, introduction to *The Korean Alphabet: Its History and Structure* (Honolulu: University of Hawai'i Press, 1997), 1.

27. Kim, *The Bounty*, 18.

28. Lisa Lowe, "Unfaithful to the Original: The Subject of *Dictée*," in *Writing Self, Writing Nation: Essays on Theresa Hak Kyung Cha's* Dictée, ed. Elaine H. Kim and Norma Alarcón (Berkeley, CA: Third Woman Press, 1994), 39.

29. Lowe, "Unfaithful to the Original," 39.

30. For a related account of translation and transliteration in Kim, see Xiaojing Zhou, *The Ethics and Poetics of Alterity in Asian American Poetry* (Iowa City: University of Iowa Press, 2006), 272.

31. Myung Mi Kim, *Under Flag*, 13.

32. Ibid., 15.

33. Sang Oak Lee, "The Second Best Compromise: The National Academy of Sciences' Proposal on Romanization of Korean," *Korea Journal* 22, no. 8 (1982): 9.

34. Hyun Bok Lee, "Romanization of Korean: In Defence of the MOE System," *Korea Journal* 22, no. 8 (1982): 63.

35. Edward F. Klein, "Romanization of Korean: Do Armchair Linguists Have the Answer?" *Korea Journal* 22, no. 8 (1982): 17.

36. Lee, "The Second Best Compromise," 13.

37. The poem and, indeed, the entire final section of *Commons*, entitled "Pollen Fossil Record," function as a kind of reader's guide to her initially enigmatic poetry. For an excellent reading of this section as well as an account of how it broaches the larger problematics of elision and negation in *Commons*, see Warren Liu, "Making Common the Commons: Myung Mi Kim's Ideal Subject," in *American Poets of the 21st Century*, ed. Claudia Rankin and Lisa Sewell (Middletown, CT: Wesleyan University Press, 2007), 252–66.

38. Myung Mi Kim, *Commons* (Berkeley: University of California Press, 2002), 110.

39. Kim, *Commons*, 76.

40. The five sections translate as follows: (1) to the people of the world; (2) listen to these words of mine; (3) when it is daytime, the water is clear; (4) when it is nighttime,

the light is bright; (5) this time what time does it happen to be. Note that these statements are given in a form that would be adopted by an older or more respected person to someone with whom that speaker feels familiar, as if they were words of a protective and gentle older sister. As an address to "the people," these might, for example, be the words of a benevolent king. In addition, "time" in the final translation is not literal time but time in the sense of juncture—time that is momentous in some way.

41. Cf. Xiaojing Zhou, *The Ethics and Poetics of Alterity in Asian American Poetry*, 272. Zhou reads the poem differently: "These variations of transcription and transliteration of Korean challenge the dominance of English, while illustrating the plurality and contingency of meaning, and enacting resistance of Korean to assimilation." Though I agree with her account as descriptive of Kim's larger poetic project involving issues of translation and transliteration, I would argue that the interest in "Siege Document" is more specific.

42. Kim, *Commons*, 110.

43. Chu, *Assimilating Asians*, 4.

44. Kim, *Commons*, 110.

45. Myung Mi Kim, *Under Flag*, 15.

46. Benjamin, "Task of the Translator," 74.

47. Ibid., 75.

48. Myung Mi Kim, *Under Flag*, 15.

49. Ibid.

50. Ibid.

51. Chang-rae Lee, *Native Speaker* (New York: Riverhead Books, 1995), 233–34.

52. Bill Brown, "The Secret Life of Things (Virginia Woolf and the Matter of Modernism)," *Modernism/Modernity* 6, no. 2 (1999): 3.

53. Myung Mi Kim, *Under Flag*, 29.

54. Benjamin, "Task of the Translator," 76–77.

55. For commentary on *River Antes*, see Lynn Keller, *Thinking Poetry*, 170–80. Though more concerned about the presentation of space in the text, Keller makes a similar point to mine with respect to the sociopolitical interventions of the volume: "One point of the attention in *River Antes* to 'root' knowledge of what has gone before is that it enables a clearer view of the social structures and structures of knowledge we have seen Kim critique in *Commons*" (176–77).

Three. The Body of the Book

1. I have seen two copies of *Hiddenness*—one at the Johns Hopkins University's Milton S. Eisenhower Library and the other in the 2005 San Francisco Museum of Modern Art Richard Tuttle retrospective. They have tails of different shapes and size, though it is impossible to tell if either has been damaged at all. I have also managed to see two copies of *Endocrinology*, the first at Rice University's Fondren Library and

the second in images that were sent to me from the Universal Limited Art Editions archives. The former has the tail, but the latter lacks it, seemingly because of the particular shape of the paper at the edge of the page. In a personal correspondence with Berssenbrugge, she points out that the tail also implies for her "intimacy, vulnerability, aliveness and visual playfulness." I am deeply grateful to her for taking the time to read this chapter.

2. See Richard Tuttle, *Perceived Obstacles* (Köln: Verlag der Buchhandlung Walther König, 2000). Measuring 31 by 91 centimeters, this book is difficult to view without placing on the floor or, at very least, on a long table. Page turning is thus laborious, and I have yet to make it through the book without breaking a sweat.

3. For an account of artist books as auratic objects, see Johanna Drucker, *The Century of Artists' Books* (New York: Granary Books, 2004), 93–120.

4. Mei-Mei Berssenbrugge, "Three Conversations with Mei-mei Berssenbrugge," interview by Laura Hinton, *Jacket* 27 (April 2005), http://jacketmagazine.com/27/hint-bers.html

5. Maurice Merleau-Ponty, *Phenomenology of Perception*, trans. Colin Smith (New York: The Humanities Press, 1962); originally published as *Phénoménologie de la Perception* (Paris: Gallimard, 1945), 206.

6. Judith Butler, "Sexual Ideology and Phenomenological Description: A Feminist Critique of Merleau-Ponty's *Phenomenology of Perception*," in *The Thinking Muse: Feminism and Modern French Philosophy*, ed. Jennifer Allen and Iris Marion Young (Bloomington: Indiana University Press, 1989), 95.

7. See also Shannon Sullivan, "Domination and Dialogue in Merleau-Ponty's *Phenomenology of Perception*," *Hypatia* 12, no. 1 (1997): 1.

8. Hal Foster, *Return of the Real: The Avant-Garde at the End of the Century* (Cambridge, MA: MIT Press, 1996), 43.

9. Fanon, *Black Skin, White Masks*, 110–11.

10. Linda Martín Alcoff, *Visible Identities: Race, Gender, and the Self* (New York: Oxford University Press, 2006), 184, 185.

11. Ibid., 188.

12. Ibid., 78.

13. Sara Ahmed, *Queer Phenomenology*, 27.

14. Mei-mei Berssenbrugge, "Blurring the Borders between Formal and Social Aesthetics: An Interview with Mei-mei Berssenbrugge," interview by Xiaojing Zhou, *MELUS* 27, no. 1 (2002): 208–9.

15. Mei-mei Berssenbrugge, *The Heat Bird* (Providence: Burning Deck, 1983), 39.

16. Mei-mei Berssenbrugge, "One, Two Cups," in *Summits Move with the Tide* (New York: Greenfield Review Press, 1974), 68.

17. Miguel Fernández-Cid, "Words on Images," in *Richard Tuttle: Field of Stars: A Book on the Books* (Galicia: Centro Galego de Arte Contemporánea, 2002), 8.

18. Mei-Mei Berssenbrugge, "Three Conversations," http://jacketmagazine.com/27/hint-bers.hitml

19. Johanna Drucker, *The Visible Word: Experimental Typography and Modern Art, 1909–1923* (Chicago: University of Chicago Press, 1994), 238.

20. Mei-Mei Berssenbrugge, *Hiddenness* (New York: Library Fellows of the Whitney Museum, 1987), unpaginated.

21. Charles Altieri, "Intimacy and Experiment in Mei-Mei Berssenbrugge's *Empathy*," in *We Who Love to Be Astonished: Experimental Women's Writing and Performance Poetics*, ed. Laura Hinton and Cynthia Hogue (Tuscaloosa: University of Alabama Press, 2002), 59.

22. Altieri, "Intimacy and Experiment," 59.

23. Merleau-Ponty, *Phenomenology of Perception*, 176.

24. For other phenomenological readings of Berssenbrugge, see Linda Voris, "A 'Sensitive Empiricism': Berssenbrugge's Phenomenological Investigations," in *American Women Poets in the 21st Century: Where Lyric Meets Language*, ed. Claudia Rankine and Juliana Spahr (Middletown, CT: Wesleyan University Press, 2002), 68–69 and Megan Simpson, *Poetic Epistemologies: Gender and Knowing in Women's Language-Oriented Writing* (Albany: State University of New York Press, 2000), 140–41. Linda Voris locates a sensitivity to the complexities of phenomenological experience in Berssenbrugge's experimental poetics, which "continually disrupts narrative and rhetorical representation that simplify experience by insistently tracing the myriad and minute ways in which the phenomenal world enters experience." Similarly, Megan Simpson calls attention to Berssenbrugge's phenomenological approach to language itself: "She never lets her readers lose sight of the act of perception itself or the material activity of language in perceptual acts, even in her most abstract and discursive philosophical passages." Simpson calls attention to the capacity of Berssenbrugge's work to instill in its reader an adventurous taste for the exploration of possibility.

25. For accounts of the politics of palimpsests in literature, see Deborah Kelly Kloepfer, "Fishing the Murex up: Sense and Resonance in H. D.'s 'Palimpsest.'" *Contemporary Literature* 27, no. 4 (1986), 553 and Susan Stanford Friedman, *Penelope's Web: Gender, Modernity, H. D.'s Fiction* (New York: Cambridge University Press, 1990), 91–95.

26. For a visual culture history of the X-ray, see Lisa Cartwright, *Screening the Body: Tracing Medicine's Visual Culture* (Minneapolis: University of Minnesota Press, 1996), 107–42. For an account of the racial implications of X-rays, see Maureen F. Curtin, "Materializing Invisibility as X-Ray Technology: Skin Matters in Ralph Ellison's *Invisible Man*," *LIT* 9 (1999): 281–311. Both pieces might contextualize Kristeva's usage in their discussion of the X-ray as a visual technology that seems to offer a privileged access to knowledge.

27. Julia Kristeva, *Powers of Horror: An Essay of Abjection*, trans. Leon S. Roudiez (New York: Columbia University Press, 1982), 155.

28. Ibid., 177.

29. Ibid., 210.

30. Judith Butler, *Gender Trouble: Feminism and the Subversion of Identity* (New York: Routledge, 1990), 90. "Here Kristeva reifies maternity and then promotes this reification as the disruptive potential of the semiotic. As a result, the paternal law, understood as the ground of univocal signification, is displaced by an equally univocal signifier."

31. In an interview, Berssenbrugge states that her introduction to philosophy was Wittgenstein's *Remarks on Colour*, which was given to her by a friend. Interestingly, in the opening proposition in that book, the color of the body is put in conversation with a more abstract vision of color. See Ludwig Wittgenstein, *Remarks on Colour*, ed. G.E.M. Anscombe, trans. Linda L. McAlister and Margarete Schättle (Berkeley: University of California Press, 1977), 2e: "1. A language-game: Report whether a certain body is lighter or darker than another.—But now there's a related one: State the relation between the lightness of certain shades of colour."

32. Benjamin Widiss, "Exchanging Pleasantries for History: Pleasantville's Escalating Appropriations" (paper presented at the International Narrative Conference, Burlington, VT, April 22–25, 2004). I thank Professor Widiss for sharing his paper with me.

33. For this text, I will cite from the mass-produced edition. Mei-mei Berssenbrugge and Kiki Smith, *Endocrinology* (Berkeley, CA: Kelsey Street Press, 1997), 5. The limited edition version was published in 1997 by Universal Limited Art Editions (ULAE) in Bay Shore, New York.

34. Berssenbrugge, *Endocrinology*, 8.

35. Ibid.

36. Merleau-Ponty, *Phenomenology of Perception*, ix.

37. Berssenbrugge, *Endocrinology*, 12.

38. See Megan Adams, "Mei-mei Berssenbrugge and the Uses of Scientific Language," *HOW(ever)* 1, no. 3 (1984), http://scc.Rutgers.edu/however/print_archive/alerts0284. Adams makes a similar point about Berssenbrugge: "Her manner subverts the authoritarian pretensions of the language it employs. She incorporates scientific language while remaining completely free of its traditionally loaded implications—i.e., that nature is the brute observed and human consciousness is alienated." Although I generally agree with Adams's suggestion, I question the limits to this subversion and freedom, as does, I suggest, Berssenbrugge's own poetics.

39. Berssenbrugge, *Endocrinology*, 4.

40. Ibid., 19.

41. Ibid., 24.

42. Ibid., 26.

43. Ibid., 17.

44. Hal Foster, "Obscene, Abject, Traumatic," *October* 78 (1996): 115–16.

45. Kiki Smith, "In Her Own Words: Interview with David Frankel," in *Kiki Smith*, ed. Helaine Posner (Boston: Bulfinch, 1998), 38–39.

46. See Hal Foster, "Obscene, Abject, Traumatic," 116. As Foster notes, this kind of artistic gesture is problematic: "The danger of course is that this mimesis may confirm a given abjection. Just as the old transgressive Surrealist once called out for the priestly police, so an abstract artist (like Andres Serrano) may call out for an evangelical senator (like Jesse Helms), who then completes the work, as it were, negatively." Foster here refers to the 1989 exhibition of Serrano's *Piss Christ*, a photograph that depicts a plastic figure of Christ on the crucifix suspended in a glass of urine. Helms, among others, called the piece heresy and criticized the National Endowment for the Arts for its partial sponsorship of the work. According to Foster's logic, however, Helms's outraged reaction to the piece is on one level entirely appropriate, insofar as abject art asks for at least Helms's initial, instinctive rejection if not also for a subsequent sanction.

47. Kristeva, *Powers of Horror*, 2.

48. Berssenbrugge, *Endocrinology*, 17.

49. Ibid.

50. Ibid., 23–28. I have extracted and compiled this text for the sake of convenience. It should not be forgotten, however, that these lines occur over several pages and are interspersed among numerous illustrations.

51. Donna Haraway, "Situated Knowledges: The Science Question in Feminism and the Privilege of Partial Perspective," *Feminist Studies* 14, no. 3 (1988): 590.

52. Ibid.

53. Julia Kristeva, *About Chinese Women*, trans. Anita Barrows (New York: Urizen Books, 1977), 11. For commentary on this text and on Kristeva's interest in China in general, see Eric Hayot, *Chinese Dreams: Pound, Brecht, Tel quel* (Ann Arbor: University of Michigan Press, 2004), 103–12.

54. Lisa Lowe, *Critical Terrains: French and British Orientalisms* (Ithaca, NY: Cornell University Press, 1991), 187.

55. Gayatri Chakravorty Spivak, "French Feminism in an International Frame," in *In Other Worlds: Essays in Cultural Politics* (New York: Routledge, 1987), 137.

56. Kristeva, *About Chinese Women*, 12.

57. Ibid., 208.

58. See Nancy Fraser, "Rethinking Recognition," *New Left Review* 3 (2000): 107–20. For a critical response to Fraser, see Linda Martín Alcoff, *Visible Identities*, 28–36.

Four. Reflections of Things

1. James Heffernan, *Museum of Words: The Poetics of Ekphrasis from Homer to Ashbery* (Chicago: University of Chicago Press, 1993), 3.

2. See Wendy Steiner, *The Colors of Rhetoric: Problems in the Relation between Modern Literature and Painting* (Chicago: University of Chicago Press, 1982); Steiner, *Pictures of Romance: Form against Context in Painting and Literature* (Chicago: University of Chicago Press, 1988); Murray Krieger, *Ekphrasis: The Illusion of the Natural Sign* (Baltimore, MD: Johns Hopkins University Press, 1992); James Heffernan, *Museum of Words: The Poetics of Ekphrasis from Homer to Ashbery* (Chicago: University of Chicago Press, 1993); and W. J. T. Mitchell, *Iconology: Image, Text, Ideology* (Chicago: University of Chicago Press, 1986).

3. Barbara Johnson, *Persons and Things* (Cambridge, MA; Harvard University Press, 2008), 65.

4. David Palumbo-Liu, *Asian/American: Historical Crossings of a Racial Frontier* (Stanford, CA: Stanford University Press), 171. See also David L. Eng, "The End(s) of Race," *PMLA* 123, no. 5 (2008): 1479–80. Eng examines a particular example of these reformulations in the current discourse of racial color-blindness.

5. W. J. T. Mitchell, *Picture Theory: Essays on Verbal and Visual Representation* (Chicago: University of Chicago Press, 1994), 157. Mitchell cites Fredric Jameson, *The Political Unconscious* (Ithaca, NY: Cornell University Press, 1987), 87.

6. Heffernan, *Museum of Words*, 4.

7. Mitchell, *Picture Theory*, 162.

8. Ibid.

9. Ibid., 162–63

10. Ibid., 89. A third term, *image/text*, designates ruptured or otherwise problematic relationships between the visual and verbal in representation.

11. Colleen Lye, *America's Asia*, 7.

12. For an account of Asian American racialization in relation to African Americans, see Claire Jean Kim, "The Racial Triangulation of Asian Americans," *Politics and Society* 27, no. 1 (1999): 105–38.

13. Mitchell, *Iconology*, 1 and *Picture Theory*, 28.

14. Mitchell, *Picture Theory*, 31. Mitchell is talking specifically about Panofsky's notion of perspective here, but the revelation of perspective as ideological and the stakes of that revelation apply to his broader notion of critical iconology.

15. Mitchell, *Iconology*, 44.

16. Mitchell, *Picture Theory*, 180.

17. Song's model of race resonates with Anne Cheng's conception of racial melancholia. See *The Melancholy of Race: Psychoanalysis, Assimilation, and Hidden Grief* (New York: Oxford University Press, 2000), 3–29.

18. Priscilla Wald, "'Chaos Goes Uncourted': John Yau's Dis-orienting Poetics," in *Cohesion and Dissent in America*, ed. Joseph Alkana and Carol Colatrella (SUNY Press, 1994), 134.

19. Timothy Yu, "Form and Identity in Language Poetry and Asian American Poetry," *Contemporary Literature* 41, no. 3 (2000): 450.

20. See Stephen H. Sumida, "Pictures of Art and Life," *Contact II* 7 (1986): 52 and Gayle Fujita-Sato, "'Third World' as Place and Paradigm in Cathy Song's *Picture Bride*," *MELUS* 15, no. 1 (1988): 50.

21. Cathy Song, *Picture Bride* (New Haven, CT: Yale University Press, 1983), 3.

22. Ibid., 3–4.

23. See Emmanuel Levinas, *Totality and Infinity: An Essay in Exteriority*, trans. by Alphonso Lingis (Pittsburg: Duquesne University Press, 1961), 48–52. For a reading of Levinas in the context of Asian American poetry, see Xiaojing Zhou, *The Ethics and Poetics of Alterity in Asian American Poetry* (Iowa City: University of Iowa Press, 2006).

24. In this respect, Song's depiction of the picture bride resonates with Mitchell's reading of Keats's representation of the urn as a "still unravish'd bride" in "Ode on a Grecian Urn." Mitchell speculates that "the scholarly controversy over the boundary between what the urn says and what Keats says reflects a kind of ekphrastic disappointment. If the poet is going to make the mute, feminized art object speak, he could at least give her something interesting to say." Mitchell, *Picture Theory*, 170–71.

25. Cathy Song, *Picture Bride*, 37. See also Fu-Jen Chen, "Body and Female Subjectivity in Cathy Song's *Picture Bride*," *Women's Studies* 33 (2004): 602–4. Chen cites Laura Mulvey and the male gaze but ultimately ends up recuperating Song: "Song attempts to present, re-present, and thereby subjectify certain *real* bodies that have never been symbolized and represented in Utamaro's portraits of women. By disclosing the previously unsubjectified imaginary body, Song de-fetishizes and de-naturalizes the female body" (604). Though I see the attempt to subjectify the objectified bodies in the poem as a possibility, it seems that is ultimately closed down in the poem. What is odd about the poem is that it seems to perpetuate rather than deflate the Mulvian dynamic.

26. Cathy Song, *Picture Bride*, 37.

27. Ibid., 38.

28. Ibid., 40.

29. Ibid.

30. See King-Kok Cheung, *Articulate Silences: Hisaye Yamamoto, Maxine Hong Kingston, Joy Kogawa* (Ithaca, NY: Cornell University Press, 1993), 126–67.

31. See Fujita-Sato, "Third World," 55.

32. Cathy Song, *Picture Bride*, 45.

33. Ibid., 48.

34. Sumida, "Pictures," 53. The argument is plausible, but the poem does not really provide any reason to be critical about the painter figure whom Song clearly admires and in fact emulates in some ways.

35. Shirley Lim, Review of *Picture Bride, MELUS* 10, no. 3 (1983): 98–99.

36. In fairness, Yau's first book of poems, *Crossing Canal Street* (1976) has engendered similar critiques. Dorothy J. Wang, "Undercover Asian: John Yau and the Politics of Ethnic Self-Identification," in *Asian American Literature in the International Context: Readings on Fiction, Poetry, and Performance*, ed. Rocío G. Davis (Hamburg: Lit Verlag, 2002), 142: "What is discomfiting in *Crossing Canal Street* is the distance and disdain—at moments, disgust—with which Yau observes the inhabitants of Chinatown. In his portrayals, Chinese men and women and their body parts are likened to animals and objects."

37. See Fredric Jameson, "Hans Haacke and the Cultural Logic of Postmodernism," in Brian Wallis, ed., *Hans Haacke: Unfinished Business* (Cambridge, MA: MIT Press, 1986–1987), 42: "A whole new house of mirrors of visual replication and of textual reproduction has replaced the older stable reality of reference and of the noncultural 'real.'"

38. Mark Rosenthal, *Jasper Johns: Work Since 1974* (Philadelphia: Thames and Hudson, 1989), 25.

39. Wald, "Chaos Goes Uncourted," 135.

40. John Yau, *The United States of Jasper Johns* (Cambridge, MA: Zoland Books, 1996), 5.

41. John Yau, *A Thing Among Things: The Art of Jasper Johns* (New York: Distributed Art Publishers, 2008), 9.

42. Yau, *The United States of Jasper Johns*, 6.

43. John Yau, *Corpse and Mirror* (New York: Holt, Rinehart, and Winston, 1983), 11.

44. Ibid., 16.

45. Ibid., 20.

46. For his reading of Johns's cross-hatchings, see Yau, *A Thing Among Things*, 96.

47. John Yau, *Corpse and Mirror*, 14.

48. John Cage, *A Year from Monday; New Lectures and Writings* (Middletown, CT: Wesleyan University Press, 1967), 75.

49. Wang, "Undercover Asian," 146. Wang offers a persuasive argument against accounts of Yau's early work as showing "no evidence of his ethnicity and subject position."

50. Wang, "Undercover Asian," 146–47.

51. Yu, "Form and Identity," 448.

52. Ibid., 450.

53. John Yau, *Corpse and Mirror*, 53.

54. Ibid., 35.

55. Ibid.

56. He points out that Johns made prominent use of the symbol in a silkscreen in *Reality and Paradoxes* in 1973, a year before the completion of *Corpse and Mirror*. Rosenthal, *Jasper Johns*, 26.

57. Critics have also recently turned their attention, along similar lines, to the "Genghis Chan" poems. See Yunte Huang, *Transpacific Displacement: Ethnography, Translation, and Intertextual Travel in Twentieth-Century American Literature* (Berkeley: University of California Press, 2002), 135–37; Sianne Ngai, *Ugly Feelings* (Cambridge, MA: Harvard University Press, 2005), 89–125; Timothy Yu, "Form and Identity," 454–55; Xiaojing Zhou, "Postmodern and Subversive Parody: John Yau's 'Genghis Chan: Private Eye' Series," *College Literature* 31, no. 1 (2004): 73–102.

58. Palumbo-Liu, *Asian/American*, 8.

59. Ibid., 72; see also Hye Seung Chung, *Hollywood Asian: Philip Ahn and the Politics of Cross-Ethnic Performance* (Philadelphia: Temple University Press, 2006), 64.

60. Mitchell, *Iconology*, 1, and *Picture Theory*, 67.

61. Mitchell, *Iconology*, 1, and *Picture Theory*, 69.

62. John Yau, *Borrowed Love Poems* (New York: Penguin, 2002), 60.

63. Walt Whitman, *Leaves of Grass: A Textual Variorum of the Printed Poems* (New York: New York University Press, 1980), vol. 1, 125.

64. The action attributed to Lorre in Yau's title, *recording*, operates then in at least two registers. On one hand, it implies a sound recording, as if Lorre were taking Whitman's emphasis on song as an occasion to offer up his own interpretation. On the other hand, recording implies a copy, which in turn implies fidelity to the original. The former entails difference, variance, and subjectivity, whereas the latter involves repetition, conformity, and objectivity.

65. John Yau, *Borrowed Love Poems*, 60.

66. Ibid.

67. Here is a partial catalog of the references in the poem: 1. "Narcoleptic Swill" refers to Lorre's role in *Tales of Terror* (1962) and a scene in which a besotted Lorre becomes sleepy because of alcohol. 2. "Me signaled pasty or patsy" perhaps refers to *The Patsy* (1964), a farce starring Jerry Lewis, which was Lorre's final film. This connects it to "I was a Poet in the House of Frankenstein," which ends with Karloff's film *Targets* (1968). 3. The lines "Custom labyrinths made to order, purveyor of mid-sized jungles / a gravedigger" refers to *Mr. Moto Takes a Chance* (1938), in which Lorre as Mr. Moto keeps tabs on an insurgent jungle tribe in Cambodia. He poses as an archaeologist, and another character refers to him disparagingly as a "gravedigger." Labyrinthine tunnels play a role in the plot. 4. "Contraband penetrating ring" and "Me criminal puss" obliquely refer to *Mr. Moto in Danger Island* (1939), in which Moto infiltrates a group of diamond smugglers by posing as a criminal.

68. John Yau, *Borrowed Love Poems*, 60.

69. Catherine Gallagher, "Undoing," in *Time and the Literary*, ed. Karen Newman, Jay Clayton, and Marianne Hirsch (New York: Routledge, 2002), 11–29.

70. Gallagher, "Undoing," 18. Gallagher actually differentiates between *Back to the Future*, which tries to force a kind of narrative tidiness, and this more chaotic form. I do not disagree with her characterization of the film itself, but I would suggest that, despite this attempt to produce a neat narrative closure, the conventions of the time travel/undoing plot dangerously open potential challenges to these more orderly narrative structures, namely by inviting an endless sequence of sequels, in which what is undone becomes so repeatedly and promiscuously undone that earlier moments of closure are rendered transient and irrelevant. *Back to the Future*'s film franchise bears testimony to this dynamic as do the sequels to *The Terminator* series, which Gallagher also cites. *The Terminator*, in fact, has been recently adapted into a television series in which sending people and terminators back in time becomes increasingly commonplace, more so than in the films, allowing for exponentially more chaotic possibilities of undoing.

71. For more commentary on Yau's Lorre poems, see Yu, "Form and Identity," 455–59. Yu focuses on the earlier Lorre poems in *Forbidden Entries*. The differences between these poems and the later versions that appear in *Borrowed Love Poems* are in degree and not in kind. The later poems, I would suggest, are more about Lorre's iconicity and more interested in archiving fragments of Lorre's roles, whereas the earlier prose poems are more interested in Lorre as a provisional subject that reflects on his life and career.

72. John Yau, *Borrowed Love Poems*, 60.

73. Ibid., 55.

74. Ibid.

75. Ibid., 57.

76. For commentary, see Marjorie Perloff, "Watchman, Spy, and Dead Man: Jasper Johns, Frank O'Hara, John Cage and the 'Aesthetic of Indifference," *Modernism/Modernity* 8, no. 2 (2001): 197–221.

77. Yau, *A Thing Among Things*, 82.

78. Jasper Johns, *Writings, Sketchbooks, Notes, Interviews*, ed. Kirk Varnedoe (New York: Museum of Modern Art, 1997), 59–60.

79. Yiman Wang, "The Art of Screen Passing: Ana May Wong's Yellow Yellowface Performance in the Art Deco Era," *Camera Obscura* 20, no. 60 (2005): 168. See also Mark Winokur, *American Laughter: Immigrants, Ethnicity, and the 1930s Hollywood Film Comedy* (New York: St. Martin's Press, 1996), 202.

80. John Yau, *My Symptoms* (Santa Rosa, CA: Black Sparrow Press, 1998), 170 (my ellipses).

81. Ibid., 169.

82. Ibid.

83. Ibid.

84. Ibid., 171.

Coda

1. With rare exceptions, she tends to downplay race in favor of universal humanism. See Yoko Ono, "Feeling the Space," *New York Times*, August 24, 1973, Op-Ed page. Reacting to a musician who tells her that he likes to work with "foreigners . . . specially the Oriental people," she thinks, "I was going to snap back and say, 'Well, I like to work with foreigners, too,' but then the whole thing suddenly hit me as being so funny, and I just said something to thank him for liking to work with foreigners. It's hard to remember about your slanted eyes and your skin in the melting pot of a recording session, but I suppose that is the first thing that hits them when they try to communicate. 'That Jap. You never know what she's thinking.' Next time you meet a 'foreigner,' remember it's only like a window with a little different shape to it and the person who's sitting inside is you."

2. Leslie Bow, *Betrayal and Other Acts of Subversion: Feminism, Sexual Politics, Asian American Women's Literature* (Princeton, NJ: Princeton University Press, 2001), 5.

3. Ibid.

4. Jerry Hopkins, *Yoko Ono* (New York: Macmillan, 1986), 88.

5. See "1980 *Playboy* Interview with John Lennon and Yoko Ono," http://www.john-lennon.com/playboyinterviewwithjohnlennonandyokoono.htm. "It's not like I'm some wondrous, mystic prince from the rock-'n'-roll world dabbling in strange music with this exotic, Oriental dragon lady, which was the picture projected by the press before." The interview has been reprinted as a book, but it underwent heavy editing. See David Sheff, *All We Are Saying: The Last Major Interview with John Lennon and Yoko Ono* (New York: St. Martin's Press, 2000).

6. Permissions to reprint the David Levine caricature were prohibitively expensive, but the image is readily found online as this book goes to press.

7. Ono, "Feeling the Space," Op-ed page, *The New York Times*, August 24, 1973, 33.

8. Bow, *Betrayal and Other Acts of Subversion*, 4.

9. See Lye, *America's Asia*, 2 and Palumbo-Liu, *Asian/America*, 398.

10. The frequently told story of their meeting in a London art gallery where Ono's work was exhibited serves as a kind of ur-narrative of their romance, which begins with Lennon's appreciation of Ono's avant-garde aesthetics. Lennon in fact encountered the artist's work before the artist herself.

11. Bow, *Betrayal and Other Acts of Subversion*, 4.

12. See Linda Kintz, "Performing Virtual Whiteness: The Psychic Fantasy of Globalization," *Comparative Literature* 53, no. 4 (2001): 338. Kintz glosses Teresa Bren-

nan, *History After Lacan* (New York: Routledge, 1993), 11–13. Specifically, Kintz discusses how Brennan historicizes Lacan's claims.

13. Peter Occhiogrosso, "Yoko Ono: The Reviled Force that Changed John Lennon," *Chicago Tribune*, December 10, 1980, B1.

14. Ibid.

15. Ibid., B4.

16. Betty Rollin, "Top Pop Merger: Lennon/Ono Inc.," *Look*, March 18, 1969, 40.

17. Rollin's memories of Ono at Sarah Lawrence are recounted in Jerry Hopkins's unauthorized biography of Ono. See Hopkins, *Yoko Ono*, 15: "Yoko 'sort of fell into the artsy group and epitomized the unclassifiable,' Rollin says."

"'She was thought of as quite ethereal. Some people thought of her as a little Oriental stereotype, because she was so quiet, almost geishalike,' Rollin says today. 'They minced around her. A respectful distance existed. She didn't have many friends. She seemed very shy. Ultimately, I felt sorry for her.'"

18. Rollin, "Top Pop Merger," 38.

19. Ibid., 40.

20. "Letters to the Editor," *Look*, April 29, 1969, 16.

21. Rollin, "Top Pop Merger," 40.

22. Ibid., 41.

23. "Art or Hokum?," *The Post-Standard*, September 27, 1971, editorial section. Of course, this prevalent attitude was not universal. Ono's work had many admirers and defenders, including, first and foremost, John Lennon.

24. Lye, *America's Asia*, 56.

25. Ibid., 55.

26. David Palumbo-Liu, *Asian/American*, 7.

27. Fredric Jameson, "Globalization and Political Strategy," *New Left Review* 4 (2000): 50.

28. Victor Bascara, *Model-Minority Imperialism* (Minneapolis: University of Minnesota Press, 2006), 13.

29. R. Radhakrishnan, "Globalization, Desire, and the Politics of Representation," *Comparative Literature* 53, no. 4 (2001): 318–19.

30. For an account of anti-Asian sentiment in American liberalism, particularly in labor movements, see Lye, *America's Asia*, 57–58, 141–42.

31. Sara Bongiorni, *A Year Without "Made in China": One Family's True Life Adventure in the Global Economy* (Hoboken, NJ: John Wiley and Sons, 2007), 197.

32. Ibid., 130–31.

33. Ibid., 16.

34. Ibid., 16–17.

35. Ibid., 6.

36. Ibid.

37. Ono's, "*Ceiling Painting (YES Painting),*" consists of a ladder that the viewer must climb in order to view (with a magnifying glass) a canvas with the word "YES" in small letters affixed to the ceiling. The story goes that Lennon strolled through the exhibit before it opened—he encountered the work before the artist herself—and was impressed with the optimism of the piece, which he felt was a refreshing contrast to the usual negative pessimism that he lamented in the avant-garde art of the time. See "1980 *Playboy* Interview."

38. Tom Zito, "Peace, Love, Art and Yoko," *The Washington Post*, October 9, 1971, C1.

39. Shin Yu Pai, *Works on Paper* (Lake Worth, FL: Convivio Bookworks, 2007).

40. One of the pieces she mentions is the piece that John Lennon was admiring when he met Yoko Ono. The viewer is supposed to take the hammer and drive in a nail, but Ono purportedly wouldn't let Lennon do it because the show hadn't yet opened. "1980 *Playboy* Interview."

41. Alexandra Munroe and Jon Hendricks, eds., *Yes Yoko Ono* (New York: Harry N. Abrams, 2000), 104.

42. Shin Yu Pai, *Equivalence* (Albuquerque: La Alameda Press, 2003), 58.

43. See http://news.bbc.co.uk/1/hi/england/2541761.stm

44. Pai, *Equivalence*, 57.

45. I thank Shin Yu Pai for sharing this information with me in personal correspondence (June 3, 2008).

46. Pai, *Equivalence*, 61.

BIBLIOGRAPHY

Adams, Megan. "Mei-mei Berssenbrugge and the Uses of Scientific Language," *HOW(ever)* 1, no. 3 (1984), http://scc.Rutgers.edu/however/print_archive/alerts0284.html

Ahmed, Sara. *Queer Phenomenology: Orientations, Objects, Others.* Durham, NC: Duke University Press, 2006.

Alcoff, Linda Martín. *Visible Identities: Race, Gender, and the Self.* New York: Oxford University Press, 2006.

———. "Who's Afraid of Identity Politics?" In *Reclaiming Identity: Realist Theory and the Predicament of Postmodernism,* edited by Paul Moya and Michael Hames-Garcia, 312–44. Berkeley: University of California Press, 2000.

Altieri, Charles. "Images of Form vs. Images of Content in Contemporary Asian-American Poetry." *Qui Parle* 9, no. 1 (1995): 71–91.

———. "Intimacy and Experiment in Mei-Mei Berssenbrugge's *Empathy.*" In *We Who Love to Be Astonished: Experimental Women's Writing and Performance Poetics,* edited by Laura Hinton and Cynthia Hogue, 54–68. Tuscaloosa: University of Alabama Press, 2002.

———. *Postmodernisms Now: Essays on Contemporaneity in the Arts.* University Park: Pennsylvania State University Press, 1998.

Appadurai, Arjun, ed. *The Social Life of Things: Commodities in Cultural Perspective.* New York: Cambridge University Press, 1986.

Bascara, Victor. *Model-Minority Imperialism.* Minneapolis: University of Minnesota Press, 2006.

Baudrillard, Jean. *The System of Objects.* Translated by James Benedict. London: Verso, 1996. Originally published as *Systèm des Objets* (Paris: Gallimard, 1968).

Benjamin, Walter. "The Task of the Translator." In *Illuminations,* translated by Harry Zohn, edited by Hannah Arendt, 69–82. New York: Schocken Books, 1969.

Berssenbrugge, Mei-mei. "Blurring the Borders between Formal and Social Aesthetics: An Interview with Mei-mei Berssenbrugge." Interview by Xiaojing Zhou, *MELUS* 27, no. 1 (2002): 199–212.

———. *The Heat Bird.* Providence, RI: Burning Deck, 1983.

———. *Hiddenness*. New York: Library Fellows of the Whitney Museum, 1987.
———. *Nest*. Berkeley, CA: Kelsey St. Press, 2003.
———. *Summits Move with the Tide*. New York: Greenfield Review Press, 1974.
———. "Three Conversations with Mei-mei Berssenbrugge," interview by Laura Hinton, *Jacket* 27 (April 2005), http://jacketmagazine.com/27/hint-bers.html
Berssenbrugge, Mei-mei, and Kiki Smith. *Endocrinology*. Bay Shore, NY: Universal Limited Art Editions, 1997.
———. *Endocrinology*. Berkeley, CA: Kelsey Street Press, 1997.
Bongiorni, Sara. *A Year Without "Made in China": One Family's True Life Adventure in the Global Economy*. Hoboken, NJ: John Wiley and Sons, 2007.
Bow, Leslie. *Betrayal and Other Acts of Subversion: Feminism, Sexual Politics, Asian American Women's Literature*. Princeton, NJ: Princeton University Press, 2001.
Brennan, Teresa. *History after Lacan*. New York: Routledge, 1993.
Brooks, Peter. *Body Work: Objects of Desire in Modern Narrative*. Cambridge, MA: Harvard University Press, 1993.
Brown, Bill. "How to Do Things with Things (A Toy Story)." *Critical Inquiry* 24, no. 4 (1998): 935–64.
———. "Reification, Reanimation, and the American Uncanny." *Critical Inquiry* 32, no. 2 (2006): 175–207.
———. "The Secret Life of Things (Virginia Woolf and the Matter of Modernism)." *Modernism/modernity* 6, no. 2 (1999): 1–28.
———. *A Sense of Things: The Object Matter of American Literature*. Chicago: University of Chicago Press, 2003.
———. "Thing Theory." *Critical Inquiry* 28, no. 1 (2001): 1–22.
Bürger, Peter. *Theory of the Avant-Garde*. Translated by Michael Shaw. Theory and History of Literature, Volume 4. Minneapolis: University of Minnesota Press, 1984. Originally published as *Theorie der Avantgarde* (Frankfurt: Suhrkamp Verlag, 1974).
Bush, Christopher. "The Ethnicity of Things in America's Lacquered Age." *Representations* 99 (2007): 74–98.
Butler, Judith. *Bodies that Matter: On the Discursive Limits of "Sex."* New York: Routledge, 1993.
———. *Gender Trouble: Feminism and the Subversion of Identity*. New York: Routledge, 1990.
———. "Sexual Ideology and Phenomenological Description: A Feminist Critique of Merleau-Ponty's *Phenomenology of Perception*." In *The Thinking Muse: Feminism and Modern French Philosophy*, edited by Jennifer Allen and Iris Marion Young, 85–100. Bloomington: Indiana University Press, 1989.
Cage, John. *A Year from Monday; New Lectures and Writings*. Middletown, CT: Wesleyan University Press, 1967.

Cartwright, Lisa. *Screening the Body: Tracing Medicine's Visual Culture*. Minneapolis: University of Minnesota Press, 1995.

Césaire, Aimé. *Discourse on Colonialism*. Translated by Joan Pinkham. New York: Monthly Review Press, 1972.

Cha, Theresa Hak Kyung. *DICTEE*. New York: Tanam Press, 1982.

———. *Earth* (1976). The Theresa Hak Kyung Cha Memorial Collection, Berkeley Art Museum.

———. "Paths." M.F.A. thesis, University of California, Berkeley, 1978. The Theresa Hak Kyung Cha Memorial Collection, Berkeley Art Museum.

Chang, Juliana. "Reading Asian American Poetry." *MELUS* 21, no. 1 (1996): 81–98.

———, ed. *Quiet Fire: A Historical Anthology of Asian American Poetry, 1892–1970*. New York: Asian American Writers' Workshop, 1996.

Chen, Fu-Jen. "Body and Female Subjectivity in Cathy Song's *Picture Bride*." *Women's Studies* 33 (2004): 577–612.

Chen, Tina. *Double Agency: Acts of Impersonation in Asian American Literature and Culture*. Stanford, CA: Stanford University Press, 2005.

Cheng, Anne Anlin. *The Melancholy of Race: Psychoanalysis, Assimilation, and Hidden Grief*. New York: Oxford University Press, 2000.

———. "Passing, Natural Selection, and Love's Failure: Ethics of Survival from Chang-rae Lee to Jacques Lacan." *American Literary History* 17, no. 3 (2005): 553–74.

Cheung, King-Kok. *Articulate Silences: Hisaye Yamamoto, Maxine Hong Kingston, Joy Kogawa*. Ithaca, NY: Cornell University Press, 1993.

Chiu, Jeannie. "Identities in Process: The Experimental Poetry of Mei-mei Berssenbrugge and Myung Mi Kim." In *Asian North American Identities: Beyond the Hyphen*, edited by Eleanor Ty and Donald C. Goellnicht, 84–101. Bloomington: Indiana University Press, 2004.

Chu, Patricia P. *Assimilating Asians: Gendered Strategies of Authorship in Asian America*. Durham, NC: Duke University Press, 2000.

Chuh, Kandice. *Imagine Otherwise: On Asian Americanist Critique*. Durham, NC: Duke University Press, 2003.

Chung, Hye Seung. *Hollywood Asian: Philip Ahn and the Politics of Cross-Ethnic Performance*. Philadelphia: Temple University Press, 2006.

Curtin, Maureen F. "Materializing Invisibility as X-Ray Technology: Skin Matters in Ralph Ellison's *Invisible Man*." *LIT: Literature Interpretation Theory* 9 (1999): 281–311.

Davidson, Michael. "*Ekphrasis* and the Postmodern Painter Poem." *Journal of Aesthetics and Art Criticism* 42, no. 1 (1983): 69–79.

De Man, Paul. *Aesthetic Ideology*. Edited by Andrzej Warminski. Minneapolis: University of Minnesota Press, 1996.

———. "'Conclusions' Walter Benjamin's 'The Task of the Translator' Messenger Lecture, Cornell University, March 4, 1983." *Yale French Studies* 69 (1985): 25–46.
Drucker, Johanna. *The Century of Artists' Books*. New York: Granary Books, 2004.
———. *The Visible Word: Experimental Typography and Modern Art, 1909–1923*. Chicago: University of Chicago Press, 1994.
Du Bois, W. E. B. *The Souls of Black Folk*. 1903; New York: Penguin, 1989.
Dworkin, Craig. *Reading the Illegible*. Evanston, IL: Northwestern University Press, 2003.
Dyer, Richard. *White*. New York: Routledge, 1996.
Ebert, Roger. "*The Ninth Gate*." *Chicago Sun-Times*, March 10, 2000. http://rogerebert.suntimes.com
Eng, David L. "The End(s) of Race." *PMLA* 123, no. 5 (2008): 1479–93.
Evans, Jessica, and Stuart Hall. "What Is Visual Culture?" In *Visual Culture: The Reader*, edited by Jessica Evans and Stuart Hall, 1–20. Los Angeles: Sage, 1999.
Fanon, Frantz. *Black Skin, White Masks*. Translated by Charles Lam Markman. New York: Grove Press, 1967. Originally published as *Peau Noire, Masques Blancs* (Paris: Editions Du Seuil, 1952).
Feng, Peter X. *Identities in Motion: Asian American Film and Video*. Durham, NC: Duke University Press, 2002.
Fernández-Cid, Miguel. "Words on Images." In *Richard Tuttle: Field of Stars: A Book on the Books*, 5–12. Galicia: Centro Galego de Arte Contemporánea, 2002.
Foster, Hal. "Obscene, Abject, Traumatic." *October* 78 (1996): 107–24.
———. *The Return of the Real: The Avant-Garde at the End of the Century*. Cambridge, MA: MIT Press, 1996.
Foucault, Michel. *The Order of Things: An Archeology of the Human Sciences*. New York: Vintage, 1973. Originally published as *Les Mots et les choses: Une archéologie des sciences humaines* (Paris: Gallimard, 1966).
Fraser, Nancy. "Rethinking Recognition." *New Left Review* 3 (2000): 107–20.
Fried, Michael. *Absorption and Theatricality: Painting and Beholder in the Age of Diderot*. Berkeley: University of California Press, 1980.
———. "Almayer's Face: On 'Impressionism' in Conrad, Crane, and Norris." *Critical Inquiry* 17, no. 1 (1990): 198.
———. "Art and Objecthood." In *Art and Objecthood: Essays and Reviews*. Chicago: University of Chicago Press, 1998.
———. *Realism, Writing, Disfiguration: On Thomas Eakins and Stephen Crane*. Chicago: University of Chicago Press, 1987.
Friedman, Susan Stanford. *Penelope's Web: Gender, Modernity, H. D.'s Fiction*. New York: Cambridge University Press, 1990.
Fujita-Sato, Gayle. "'Third World' as Place and Paradigm in Cathy Song's *Picture Bride*." *MELUS* 15, no. 1 (1988): 49–72.

Gallagher, Catherine. "Undoing." In *Time and the Literary*, edited by Karen Newman, Jay Clayton, and Marianne Hirsch, 11–29. New York: Routledge, 2002.

Goldberg, Julia. "The Two Women Who Broke Up the Beatles." *McCall's*, July 1971, 72–73.

Gombrich, Ernst Hans. "*Icones Symbolicae*: Philosophies of Symbolism and Their Bearing on Art." In *Symbolic Images: Studies in the Art of the Renaissance*, edited by E. H. Gombrich, 123–99. London: Phaidon, 1972.

Grossman, Allen. "The Poetics of Union: An Inquiry toward the Relationship of Art and Policy." In *The American Renaissance Reconsidered*, edited by Walter Benn Michaels and Donald E. Pease, 183–208. Baltimore, MD: Johns Hopkins University Press, 1985.

Hagstrum, Jean H. *The Sister Arts: The Tradition of Literary Pictorialism and English Poetry from Dryden to Gray*. Chicago: University of Chicago, 1958.

Haraway, Donna. "Situated Knowledges: The Science Question in Feminism and the Privilege of Partial Perspective." *Feminist Studies* 14, no. 3 (1988): 575–99.

Hayot, Eric. *Chinese Dreams: Pound, Brecht, Tel quel*. Ann Arbor: University of Michigan Press, 2004.

Heffernan, James. *Museum of Words: The Poetics of Ekphrasis from Homer to Ashbery*. Chicago: University of Chicago Press, 1993.

Hollander, John. *The Gazer's Spirit: Poems Speaking to Silent Works of Art*. Chicago: University of Chicago Press, 1995.

Hopkins, Jerry. *Yoko Ono*. New York: Macmillan, 1986.

Huang, Yunte. *Transpacific Displacement: Ethnography, Translation, and Intertextual Travel in Twentieth-Century American Literature*. Berkeley: University of California Press, 2002.

Jameson, Fredric. "Globalization and Political Strategy." *New Left Review* 4 (2000): 49–68.

———. "Hans Haacke and the Cultural Logic of Postmodernism." In *Hans Haacke: Unfinished Business*, edited by Brian Wallis, 38–50. Cambridge, MA: MIT Press, 1986–87.

———. *The Political Unconscious*. Ithaca, NY: Cornell University Press, 1987.

———. *Postmodernism: or, The Cultural Logic of Late Capitalism*. Durham, NC: Duke University Press, 1991.

Jeon, Joseph J. "Speaking in Tongues: Myung Ki Kim's Stylized Mouths." *Studies in the Literary Imagination* 37, no. 1 (2004): 125–48.

Johns, Jasper. *Writings, Sketchbooks, Notes, Interviews*. Edited by Kirk Varnedoe. New York: Museum of Modern Art, 1997.

Johnson, Barbara. *Persons and Things*. Cambridge, MA: Harvard University Press, 2008.

Kang, Laura Hyun Yi. *Compositional Subjects: Enfiguring Asian/American Women*. Durham, NC: Duke University Press, 2002.

Keller, Lynn. *Thinking Poetry: Readings in Contemporary Women's Exploratory Poetics*. Iowa City: University of Iowa Press, 2010.

Kim, Claire Jean. "The Racial Triangulation of Asian Americans." *Politics and Society* 27, no. 1 (1999): 105–38.

Kim, Elaine H. "'Poised on the In-between': A Korean American's Reflections on Theresa Hak Kyung Cha's *Dictée*." In *Writing Self, Writing Nation: A Collection of Essays on* Dictée *by Theresa Hak Kyung Cha*, edited by Elaine H. Kim, 3–30. Berkeley, CA: Third Woman Press, 1994.

Kim, Myung Mi. *The Bounty*. Minneapolis, MN: Chax Press, 1996.

———. *Commons*. Berkeley: University of California Press, 2002.

———. *Dura*. Los Angeles: Sun and Moon Press, 1998.

———. Interview with James Kyung-jin Lee. In *Words Matter: Conversations with Asian American Writers*, edited by King-Kok Cheung, 92–104. Honolulu: University of Hawai'i Press, 2000.

———. *River Antes*. Seattle, WA: Atticus/Finch, 2006.

———. *Under Flag*. Berkeley, CA: Kelsey St. Press, 1991.

Kim, Sue J. "Theresa Hak Kyung Cha and the Politics of Form." *Journal of Asian American Studies* 8, no. 2 (2005): 143–69.

Kim-Renaud, Young-Key. Introduction to *The Korean Alphabet: Its History and Structure*. Honolulu: University of Hawai'i Press, 1997.

Kintz, Linda. "Performing Virtual Whiteness: The Psychic Fantasy of Globalization." *Comparative Literature* 53, no. 4 (2001): 333–53.

Klein, Edward F. "Romanization of Korean: Do Armchair Linguists Have the Answer?" *Korea Journal* 22, no. 8 (1982): 16–23.

Kloepfer, Deborah Kelly. "Fishing the Murex up: Sense and Resonance in H. D.'s 'Palimpsest.'" *Contemporary Literature* 27, no. 4 (1986): 553–73.

Koshy, Susan. "Morphing Race into Ethnicity: Asian Americans and Critical Transformations of Whiteness." *boundary 2* 28, no. 1 (2001): 153–94.

Krieger, Murray. *Ekphrasis: The Illusion of the Natural Sign*. Baltimore, MD: Johns Hopkins University Press, 1992.

Kristeva, Julia. *About Chinese Women*. Translated by Anita Barrows. New York: Urizen Books, 1977. Originally published as *Des Chinoises* (Paris: Éditions des Femmes, 1974).

———. *Powers of Horror: An Essay on Abjection*. Translated by Leon S. Roudiez. New York: Columbia University Press, 1982. Originally published as *Pouvoirs de l'horreur* (Paris: Éditions du Seuil, 1980).

Lee, Chang-rae. *Native Speaker*. New York: Riverhead Books, 1995.

Lee, Hyun Bok. "Romanization of Korean: In Defence of the MOE System." *Korea Journal* 22, no. 8 (1982): 61–70.

Lee, Sang Oak. "The Second Best Compromise: The National Academy of Sciences' Proposal on Romanization of Korean." *Korea Journal* 22, no. 8 (1982): 5–15.

Levinas, Emmanuel. *Totality and Infinity: An Essay in Exteriority*. Translated by Alphonso Lingis. Pittsburgh, PA: Duquesne University Press, 1961.

Lewallen, Constance M., ed. *The Dream of the Audience: Theresa Hak Kyung Cha (1951–1982)*. Berkeley: University of California Press, 2001.

Lim, Shirley. Review of *Picture Bride*. *MELUS* 10, no. 3 (1983): 95–99.

Ling, Jingi. *Narrating Nationalisms: Ideology and Form in Asian American Literature*. New York: Oxford University Press, 1995.

Lippard, Lucy R. *Six Years: The Dematerialization of the Art Object from 1966 to 1972*. Berkeley: University of California Press, 1973.

Lippi-Green, Rosina. *English with an Accent: Language, Ideology, and Discrimination in the United States*. London: Routledge, 1997.

Liu, Warren. "Making Common the Commons: Myung Mi Kim's Ideal Subject." In *American Poets of the 21st Century*, edited by Claudia Rankin and Lisa Sewell, 252–66. Middletown, CT: Wesleyan University Press, 2007.

Lowe, Lisa. *Critical Terrains: French and British Orientalisms*. Ithaca, NY: Cornell University Press, 1991.

———. *Immigrant Acts: On Asian American Cultural Politics*. Durham, NC: Duke University Press, 1996.

———. "Unfaithful to the Original: The Subject of *Dictée*." In *Writing Self, Writing Nation: Essays on Theresa Hak Kyung Cha's* Dictée, edited by Elaine H. Kim and Norma Alarcón, 35–69. Berkeley, CA: Third Woman Press, 1994.

Lukács, Georg. *History and Class Consciousnes; Studies in Marxist Dialectics*. Transated by Rodney Livingstone. Cambridge, MA: MIT Press, 1970. Originally published as *Geschichte und Klassenbewusstsein* (Berlin: Malik-Verlag, 1923).

Lye, Colleen. *America's Asia: Racial Form and American Literature, 1893–1945*. Princeton, NJ: Princeton University Press, 2005.

———. "Form and History in Asian American Literary Studies." *American Literary History* 20, no. 3 (2008): 548–55.

———. "Introduction: In Conversation with Asian American Studies." *Representations* 99 (2007): 1–12.

———. "Racial Form." *Representations* 104 (2008): 92–101.

Macann, Christopher. *Four Phenomenological Philosophers: Husserl, Heidegger, Sartre, Merleau-Ponty*. New York: Routledge, 1993.

Mao, Douglas. *Solid Objects: Modernism and the Test of Production*. Princeton, NJ: Princeton University Press, 1998.

Melville, Herman. *Moby Dick*. New York: Norton, 1967.

Merleau-Ponty, Maurice. *Phenomenology of Perception*. Translated by Colin Smith. New York: The Humanities Press, 1962. Originally published as *Phénoménologie de la Perception* (Paris: Gallimard, 1945).

Meyer, James. *Minimalism: Art and Polemics in the Sixties*. New Haven, CT: Yale University Press, 2001.

Michales, Walter Benn. *The Shape of the Signifier: 1967 to the End of History*. Princeton, NJ: Princeton University Press, 2004.

Miller, Tyrus. "Avant-garde and Theory: A Misunderstood Relation." *Poetics Today* 20, no. 4 (1999): 549–79.

Mitchell, W. J. T., ed. *Against Theory: Literary Studies and the New Pragmatism*. Chicago: University of Chicago Press, 1985.

———. *Iconology: Image, Text, Ideology*. Chicago: University of Chicago Press, 1986.

———. *Picture Theory: Essays on Verbal and Visual Representation*. Chicago: University of Chicago Press, 1994.

Morrison, Toni. *Playing in the Dark: Whiteness and the Literary Imagination*. Cambridge, MA: Harvard University Press, 1992

Mullen, Harryette. "Poetry and Identity." In *Telling It Slant: Avant-Garde Poetics in the 1990s*, edited by Mark Wallace and Steven Marks, 27–40. Tuscaloosa: University of Alabama Press, 2002.

Nakamura, Lisa. *Digitizing Race: Visual Cultures of the Internet*. Minneapolis: University of Minnesota Press, 2007.

Ngai, Sianne. "The Cuteness of the Avant-Garde." *Critical Inquiry* 31 (2005): 811–47.

———. *Ugly Feelings*. Cambridge, MA: Harvard University Press, 2005.

Nguyen, Viet Thanh. *Race and Resistance: Literature and Politics in Asian America*. New York: Oxford University Press, 2002.

Occhiogrosso, Peter. "Yoko Ono: The Reviled Force that Changed John Lennon." *Chicago Tribune*, December 10, 1980, B1, B4.

O'Keeffe, Georgia. *Georgia O'Keeffe*. New York: Viking Press, 1976.

Omi, Michael, and Howard Winant. *Racial Formation in the United States: From the 1960s to the 1990s*. 2nd ed. New York: Routledge, 1994.

Ono, Yoko. "Feeling the Space." *New York Times*, August 24, 1973, Opinions and Editorials.

Orton, Fred. *Figuring Jasper Johns*. Cambridge, MA: Harvard University Press, 1994.

Otter, Samuel. *Melville's Anatomies*. Berkeley: University of California Press, 1999.

Pai, Shin Yu. *Equivalence*. Albuquerque, NM: La Alameda Press, 2003.

———. *Works on Paper*. Lake Worth, FL: Convivio Bookworks, 2007.

Palumbo-Liu, David. *Asian/American: Historical Crossings of a Racial Frontier.* Stanford, CA: Stanford University Press, 1999.

———. "Universalisms and Minority Culture." *Differences: A Journal of Feminist Cultural Studies* 7, no. 1 (1995): 188–208.

Park, Ed. "Sound Bitten: *Commons* by Myung Mi Kim." *Village Voice* 47, no. 18 (May 7, 2002), 121.

Park, Josephine Nock-Hee. *Apparitions of Asia: Modernist Form and Asian American Poetics.* New York: Oxford University Press, 2008.

———. "'Composed of Many Lengths of Bone': Myung Mi Kim's Reimagination of Image and Epic." In *Transnational Asian American Literature: Sites and Transits*, edited by Shirley Geok-lin Lim, John Blair Gamber, Stephen Hong Sohn, and Gina Valentino, 235–56. Philadelphia: Temple University Press, 2006.

———. "'What of the Partition': Dictée's Boundaries and the American Epic." *Contemporary Literature* 46 (2005): 213–42.

Perloff, Marjorie. *Poetic License: Essays on Modernist and Postmodernist Lyric.* Evanston, IL: Northwestern University Press, 1990.

———. "Watchman, Spy, and Dead Man: Jasper Johns, Frank O'Hara, John Cage and the 'Aesthetic of Indifference.'" *Modernism/Modernity* 8, no. 2 (2001): 197–221.

Phelan, Peggy. *Unmarked: The Politics of Performance.* New York: Routledge, 1993.

Radhakrishnan, R. "Globalization, Desire, and the Politics of Representation." *Comparative Literature* 53, no. 4 (2001): 315–32.

Roediger, David R. *The Wages of Whiteness: Race and the Making of the American Working Class.* New York: Verso, 1991.

Rollin, Betty. "Top Pop Merger: Lennon/Ono Inc." *Look*, March 18, 1969, 36–42.

Rosenthal, Mark. *Japer Johns: Work Since 1974.* Philadelphia: Thames and Hudson, 1989.

Rowe, John Carlos. "Culture, US Imperialism, and Globalization." *American Literary History* 16, no. 4 (2004): 575–95.

Scott, Grant. *The Sculpted Word: Keats, Ekphrasis, and the Visual Arts.* Hanover, NH: University Press of New England, 1994.

Sheff, David. *All We Are Saying: The Last Major Interview with John Lennon and Yoko Ono.* New York: St. Martin's Press, 2000.

Silverman, Hugh J. "The Text of the Speaking Subject: From Merleau-Ponty to Kristeva." In *Merleau-Ponty Vivant*, edited by M. C. Dillon, 183–94. Albany: State University of New York Press, 1991.

Simpson, Megan. *Poetic Epistemologies: Gender and Knowing in Women's Language-Oriented Writing.* Albany: State University of New York Press, 2000.

Smith, Kiki. "In Her Own Words: Interview with David Frankel." In *Kiki Smith*, edited by Helaine Posner, 31–44. Boston: Bulfinch, 1998.

Song, Cathy. *Picture Bride*. New Haven, CT: Yale University Press, 1983.

Spivak, Gayatri Chakravorty. "French Feminism in an International Frame." In *In Other Worlds: Essays in Cultural Politics*, 134–53. New York: Routledge, 1987.

Steiner, Wendy. *The Colors of Rhetoric: Problems in the Relation between Modern Literature and Painting*. Chicago: University of Chicago Press, 1982.

———. *Pictures of Romance: Form against Context in Painting and Literature*. Chicago: University of Chicago Press, 1988.

Stewart, Garret. "*Cinécriture*: Modernism's Flicker Effect." *New Literary History* 24 (1998): 731.

Stoller, Silvia. "Reflections on Feminist Merleau-Ponty Skepticism." *Hypatia* 15, no. 1 (2000): 175–82.

Sullivan, Shannon. "Domination and Dialogue in Merleau-Ponty's *Phenomenology of Perception*." *Hypatia* 12, no. 1 (1997): 1–19.

———. "Feminism and Phenomenology: A Reply to Silvia Stoller." *Hypatia* 15, no. 1 (2000): 183–88.

Sumida, Stephen H. "Pictures of Art and Life." *Contact II* 7 (1986): 52–55.

Takada, Mayumi. "Annihilating Possibilities: Witnessing and Testimony through Cinematic Love in Theresa Hak Kyung Cha's *DICTEE*." *Literature Interpretation Theory* 17 (2006): 23–48.

Tejaswini, Niranjana. *Sitting Translation: History, Post-structuralism, and the Colonial Context*. Berkeley: University of California Press, 1992.

Trinh, T. Minh-Ha. "White Spring." In *The Dream of the Audience: Theresa Hak Kyung Cha (1951–1982)*, edited by Constance M. Lewallen, 33–50. Berkeley: University of California Press, 2001.

Tuttle, Richard. *Perceived Obstacles*. Köln: Verlag der Buchhandlung Walther König, 2000.

Uba, George. "Coordinates of Asian American Poetry: A Survey of the History and a Guide to Teaching." In *A Resource Guide to Asian American Literature*, edited by Sau-ling Cynthia Wong and Stephen H. Sumida, 309–31. New York: Modern Language Association, 2001.

———. "The Representation of Asian American Poetry in *The Heath Anthology of American Literature*." In *Re-Visioning Asian America, Locating Diversity*, edited by Soo-Young Chin, James Moy, Wendy Ng, and Gary Okihiro, 185–93. Pullman: Washington State University Press, 1995.

———. "Versions of Identity in Post-Activist Asian American Poetry." In *Reading the Literatures of Asian America*, edited by Shirley Geok-lin Lim and Amy Ling, 33–48. Philadelphia: Temple University Press, 1992.

Vernet, Marc. "Blinking, Flickering, and Flashing of the Black-and-White Film."

In *Apparatus*, edited by Theresa Hak Kyung Cha, 357–69. New York: Tanam Press, 1980.

Voris, Linda. "A 'Sensitive Empiricism': Berssenbrugge's Phenomenological Investigations." In *American Women Poets in the 21st Century: Where Lyric Meets Language*, edited by Claudia Rankine and Juliana Spahr, 68–93. Middletown, CT: Wesleyan University Press, 2002.

Wald, Priscilla. "'Chaos Goes Uncourted': John Yau's Dis-orienting Poetics." In *Cohesion and Dissent in America*, edited by Joseph Alkana and Carol Colatrella, 133–58. Albany: State University of New York Press, 1994.

Wang, Dorothy J. "John Yau and the Politics of Ethnic Self-Identification." In *Asian American Literature in the International Context: Readings on Fiction, Poetry, and Performance*, edited by Rocío G. Davis and Sämi Ludwig, 135–56. Hamburg: LIT Verlag, 2002.

Wang, Yiman. "The Art of Screen Passing: Ana May Wong's Yellow Yellowface Performance in the Art Deco Era." *Camera Obscura* 20, no. 3 (2005): 159–91.

Whitman, Walt. *Leaves of Grass: A Textual Variorum of the Printed Poems*. New York: New York University Press, 1980.

Widiss, Benjamin. "Exchanging Pleasantries for History: Pleasantville's Escalating Appropriations." Paper presented at the International Narrative Conference, Burlington, VT, April 22–25, 2004.

Wiegman, Robyn. *American Anatomies: Theorizing Race and Gender*. Durham, NC: Duke University Press, 1995.

Winokur, Mark. *American Laughter: Immigrants, Ethnicity, and the 1930s Hollywood Film Comedy*. New York: St. Martin's Press, 1996.

Wittgenstein, Ludwig. *Remarks on Colour*. Edited by G.E.M. Anscombe. Translated by Linda L. McAlister and Margarete Schättle. Berkeley: University of California Press, 1977.

Wong, Sunn Shelley. "Sizing Up Asian American Poetry." In *A Resource Guide to Asian American Literature*, edited by Sau-ling Cynthia Wong and Stephen H. Sumida, 285–308. New York: Modern Language Association, 2001.

Yao, Steven G. *Foreign Accents: Chinese American Verse from Exclusion to Postethnicity*. New York: Oxford University Press, 2010.

———. *Translation and the Languages of Modernism: Gender, Politics, Language*. New York: Palgrave Macmillan, 2002.

Yau, John. *Borrowed Love Poems*. New York: Penguin, 2002.

———. *Corpse and Mirror*. New York: Holt, Rinehart, and Winston, 1983.

———. *My Symptoms*. Santa Rosa, CA: Black Sparrow Press, 1998.

———. *A Thing Among Things: The Art of Jasper Johns*. New York: Distributed Art Publishers, 2008.

———. *The United States of Jasper Johns*. Cambridge, MA: Zoland Books, 1996.

Young, Iris Marion. "Throwing Like a Girl: A Phenomenology of Feminine Body and Comportment, Motility, and Spatiality." In *The Thinking Muse: Feminism and Modern French Philosophy*, edited by Jeffner Allen and Iris Marion Young, 51–84. Bloomington: Indiana University Press, 1989.

Yu, Timothy. "Form and Identity in Language Poetry and Asian American Poetry." *Contemporary Literature* 41, no. 3 (2000): 422–61.

———. *Race and the Avant-Garde: Experimental and Asian American Poetry Since 1965*. Stanford, CA: Stanford University Press, 2009.

Zhou, Xiaojing. *The Ethics and Poetics of Alterity in Asian American Poetry*. Iowa City: University of Iowa Press, 2006.

———. "Postmodern and Subversive Parody: John Yau's 'Genghis Chan: Private Eye' Series." *College Literature* 31, no. 1 (2004): 73–102.

Zito, Tom. "Peace, Love, Art and Yoko." *The Washington Post*, October 9, 1971, C1.

INDEX

Page numbers in italics indicate photographs

CONTEMPORARY NORTH AMERICAN POETRY SERIES

Industrial Poetics: Demo Tracks for a Mobile Culture
By Joe Amato

What Are Poets For? An Anthropology of Contemporary Poetry and Poetics
By Gerald L. Bruns

Postliterary America: From Bagel Shop Jazz to Micropoetries
By Maria Damon

Purple Passages: Pound, Eliot, Zukofsky, Olson, Creeley, and the Ends of Patriarchal Poetry
By Rachel Blau DuPlessis

On Mount Vision: Forms of the Sacred in Contemporary American Poetry
By Norman Finkelstein

Jorie Graham: Essays on the Poetry
Edited by Thomas Gardner
University of Wisconsin Press, 2005

Gary Snyder and the Pacific Rim: Creating Countercultural Community
By Timothy Gray

Urban Pastoral: Natural Currents in the New York School
By Timothy Gray

Racial Things, Racial Forms: Objecthood in Avant-Garde Asian American Poetry
By Joseph Jonghyun Jeon

We Saw the Light: Conversations between the New American Cinema and Poetry
By Daniel Kane

History, Memory, and the Literary Left: Modern American Poetry, 1935–1968
By John Lowney

Paracritical Hinge: Essays, Talks, Notes, Interviews
By Nathaniel Mackey
University of Wisconsin Press, 2004

Behind the Lines: War Resistance Poetry on the American Homefront
By Philip Metres

Hold-Outs: The Los Angeles Poetry Renaissance, 1948–1992
By Bill Mohr

Frank O'Hara: The Poetics of Coterie
By Lytle Shaw

Renegade Poetics: Black Aesthetics and Formal Innovation in African American Poetry
By Evie Shockley

Radical Vernacular: Lorine Niedecker and the Poetics of Place
Edited by Elizabeth Willis